Soldiers On Wheels

(Drivers of the RASC, RCT, and RLC)

By
Brian (Harry) Clacy

This book is dedicated to the memory of
Holly Elouise Clacy
12th December 2001 – 20th November 2017

Corps Cap Badges

RASC　　　　RCT

RLC　　　　RACT

Contents

518303 Lieutenant Colonel Terry Byrne

479471 Lieutenant Colonel David Birrell

24212830 Corporal Richard Makinson

24267087 Warrant Officer Class 1 Chris Iddon

24484265 Warrant Officer Class 2 Ted Fost

24627424 Driver Tim Butterworth

525131 Lieutenant Colonel Cameron Macnish

24736118 Staff Sergeant Lee Hunt

24836475 Sergeant Richie Temple

24911149 Staff Sergeant Derek Robson

Ancestry of the British Army's transport formations

The Royal Waggoner's	1794 – 1795
The Royal Wagon Train	1799 – 1833
Land Transport Corps	1855 – 1857
The Military Train	1857 – 1869
Army Service Corps	1869 – 1881
Commissariat and Transport Corps	1881 – 1886
Army Service Corps	1889 – 1918
Royal Army Service Corps	1918 – 1965
Royal Corps of Transport	1965 – 1993
Royal Logistic Corps	1993 - to date

Acknowledgements

I'd like to take this opportunity to thank the following people for their invaluable help in the making of this book:

Terry Cavender is not only a retired Army Officer, Scribe, Author, and Gentleman of the Royal Corps of Transport, he is also one of the nicest men my wife Nicky and I have ever had the pleasure to meet. Terry has proof read, and improved, every part of my books as soon as I have completed each Chapter. I really don't know how to thank you Tel old son, I do know that if I offered you money, as a Yorkshireman I'm sure you would feel very insulted... so to avoid causing you any embarrassment, I won't bother going down that road mate. I'm sure a written thank you in this book will suffice. If I ever need any advice, on any subject, I will always come to you first my friend, your help on lots of problems I've experienced, has been priceless.

Ken Blake, like **Terry Cavender**, is a font of all knowledge about the Transport Corps' of the British Army and the soldiers who have served within its ranks. Ken was my first point of call when I needed some photographs of the Cap Badges used on the cover of this book. He also sent me a photo of a Royal Australian Corps of Transport (RACT) Cap Badge that I've used on page 14. Thank's Ken, you're a star mate, a frigging beer drinking monster.

Ric Spurr is an ex 63 (Parachute) Squadron Airborne soldier who also became a team member of the Silver Stars RCT Freefall Parachute Team. **Ric** interpreted and explained to me, in very simply Crap Hat language, about **Tim Butterworth's** complicated ramblings on what a fucking 'Dummy Pull' jump means. During his interview for this book, Tim waffled on and on and on and on and on about doing 'Dummy Pull' free-fall parachuting whilst he was in his Basic Training at Colerne. The author never understood a word of what he was talking about and had to telephone **Ric Spurr** for a less complicated interpretation. Fuck me Tim, you must have landed on your head a few times old son! Thanks **Ric**.

I must also thank **Ritchie Temple** for his elaborate, amusing and detailed information about the Assiniboia den of iniquity in Medicine Hat, commonly referred to as the Sin Bin by many British Soldiers who have 'Soldiered' in Canada. Dirty boys. Richie also patiently did a second interview with me on Skype after my wife Nicky Clacy had accidentally deleted our first interview from my Dictaphone, before I'd had a chance to write up the notes. **Ritchie Temple** also helped me get my new mobile phone back from a Bielefeld taxi-driver, who was 30 kms away by the time I'd realised it had fallen out of my pocket in his cab. It really was an eventful 10 Regt reunion in June 2018.

Lennie Bantleman provided the author with some of the information (*that Ted simply couldn't recall*) about Ted Fost's comrades in 30 Sqn at the Junior Leaders Regiment in Colerne. Thanks Len.

Eric Hartley BA MA (Hons) MA of **ELK Marketing & Planning Ltd** which is based in Beverley East Yorkshire, have produced yet another superb book cover using **Ken Blake's** photographs of the Corps cap badges. Eric also did some great work on the origional map that Lieutenant/Captain Bob Birrell RCT used during his time as a Company Commander fighting during the War in Dhofar. All of the hand-written notes were penned by Bob himself whilst in his location at Sarfait.

I'd also like to thank **Melanie Jones** who works behind the bar in the Golden Tulip Hotel in Bielefeld. I met **Melanie** before going to the 10 Regt RCT reunion at Catterick Barracks on 9th June 2018 and whilst pulling me a large Warsteiner Beir she told me, "Bielefeld is a really boring place now the RCT soldiers have gone." Thanks **Mel**, you have no idea what that will mean to so many RCT soldiers who read my books. It was a real pleasure to meet you.

And lastly, I want to thank every Trog/Trogg who has taken the time to tell me their stories so I could write them into the history of our Corps, including Gus South, whose chapter will be included in the very next book.

Thank you all for your time and support.

Brian (Harry) Clacy

Foreword

By Lieutenant Colonel (Retired) T C Byrne MBE
The RCT in transmission – 'Out with the old' and 'In with the new'…. again.

In 1965 the Royal Army Service Corps (RASC) was disbanded and the Royal Corps of Transport (RCT) took its place in the Order of Battle (ORBAT) of the British Army. Nothing much changed regarding the Driver Trade, but for other trades in the RASC, the changes were more dramatic, and careers were affected.

For the next 28 years, the RCT established an army-wide reputation for transport excellence which included the creation of the Master Driver appointment; this position led to a fully accountable Ministry of Defence (MOD) operated Driving Licence Authority (DLA). The advent of fully mechanised Infantry Battalions and more self-propelled Royal Artillery (RA) guns, necessitated a requirement for more Driver Training, enhanced Motor Transport (MT) Management, and a greater attention to Traffic Accident Reduction.

In 1970, the RCT took the lead in providing armoured transport support for the troops serving in Northern Ireland. Up to that point the Infantry had provided their own drivers from within their Battalion MT Section's. When the RCT took over responsibility for the 'Pigs' and Saracen's, some were found to be in a shocking state and were barely serviceable. The Infantry drivers simply hadn't been given sufficient training in the Driver Role, and the First, Last, and Halt Parades were rarely observed. When the RCT Drivers took over responsibility for all of the transport in the Province, those Infantry drivers that had been relieved of their MT duties were then able to bolster the badly depleted ranks of the Infantry Sections on 'Footsies.'

Few soldiers, other than the Support Services (which includes MT), know the meaning of the phrase, 'Nothing is more certain than change.' In the RCT the Bedford RL 3 Ton truck became the Bedford 4 Ton MK, the AEC Mk 1 'Old Knockers' became the AEC Mk 3 Militant (that came with powered steering and synchromesh gears). The Corps was overjoyed at the arrival of the Alvis Stalwart, finally a truck that could swim. Definition of the word Stalwart – a loyal, reliable, and hard-working supporter of or participant in an organisation or team. The 'Stolly' had arrived in the RCT and was much loved by those RCT Drivers who put her through her paces.

The Stolly was a leap into the future, but the Corps remained frustrated that it couldn't find the perfect Army motorcycle. The RCT went through stages of using the BSA 350 (B40) Triumph before moving onto the Can-Am and Armstrong. The changes for the RCT went on and on. Replenishment Parks (RP's) became Divisional Supply Areas (DSA's), Distribution Points (DP's) continued, but Immediate Replenishment Groups (IRG) were invented to deliver supplies direct to A2 Echelons and beyond.

The humble Jerrycan was 'reduced in the ranks' to the ignominious job of emergency reserve fuel, (only 2 Jerrycans per truck) as Bulk Fuel took over. Pipelines, Bulk Fuel Installations (BFI), Truck Tanker Fuel (TTF), and Unit Bulk Refuelling Equipment (UBRE) became the order of the day. RCT Operators using the equipment had to be educated in ensuring that contamination of woodlands, hedgerows, roads, waterways, flora and fauna did not occur. For the greater part, the Corps managed to achieve that.

Other changes were of a more personal nature. No more need for 13 studs on a boot sole as 'Boots Ammunition' were replaced with the Dunlop Moulded Sole (DMS) boot, but soldiers still needed anklets or puttees, (Remember that only Bishops and Farmers wear gaiters). With the arrival of the Boots Combat High the ankle supporting puttee was finally made redundant. The old-fashioned 38 Pattern webbing was replaced by the more modern 58 Pattern webbing; with that came the realisation of how much more equipment a soldier could carry, and that factor would be included on the requirements of the new Combat Fitness Test (CFT). The military world is forever changing.

Those of us who were lucky enough to have served in the RASC and RCT were sceptical about the arrival of the Royal Logistic Corps (RLC) in 1993. Naturally, each preceding Corps had nothing but distain for the 'New Lot.' The trades we have in our new Corps reflects the close relationship we have with our 'Forming Corps,' Trog's/Trogg's (Royal Corps of Transport) Blanket Stackers (Royal Army Ordnance Corps) Chunkys (Royal Pioneer Corps) Slop Jockey's/Water Scorchers (Army Catering Corps) are all included in the new RLC cap-badge. The clever process of including parts of the forming Corps previous cap-badges is commendable and a credit to our senior Officers at that time. The 'new' RLC cap- badge comprises elements of the RCT star, the RAOC cannons and cannon balls, the RPC axes and the ACC moto 'We Sustain.'

Our Corps had always worked through the Stores Depot and Re-Supply system with our colleagues in the RAOC, labour for the Depots, Site Defences were provided by the RPC and of course, last but not least, the Chefs were never far away providing the much needed 'Grub.'

What has never changed, however, is the calibre of our soldiers. They still follow the 'Brewster' example - when that brave soldier from the Royal Wagon Train (another of our predecessors) who on the 18th of June 1815, delivered the much-needed Powder and Shot to the 3rd Guards at Hougoumont Farm, during the Battle of Waterloo, and by doing so, saved the day.

Today's 'Loggies' of course would do just the same, and are doing it, differently of course, but with the same determination and courage. They would organise a Combat Logistic Patrol (CLP), the most effective combat supply delivery system ever invented, which can only be provided by RLC experts with a wide range of skills. Front-line soldiers don't care where their ammo, fuel, food, water, spares, medical supplies and everything else comes from, they just want it to arrive on time and at the right place.

It's a good thing for them that, just like our predecessors, the members of the RLC, like their predecessors, can, and do, deliver.

T C Byrne MBE
Lt Col (Retd)
Late RASC, RCT, and RLC

Introduction

This is the fourth book I've written about the lives and personal careers of soldiers who have served in the Royal Army Service Corps, the Royal Corps of Transport, and the Royal Logistic Corps.

My first three books were entitled 'Harry was a Crap Hat', 'Rickshaws Camels and Taxis', and 'Most Roads Led to 10 Regt'.

All of these books have been a labour of love for me to create because I have met some of the most amazing soldiers the British Army has had the honour to serve within its ranks. Unfortunately, there are a lot of other truck driving soldiers in the world that I'm not going to get the chance to interview, simply because there will never be enough time. On each of the RASC, RCT and RLC Facebook sites, we are constantly getting notifications about losing yet another Trog/Trogg because of either some sort of cancer, or that bloody dreaded heart disease. British Army Drivers have always fought and died hard, but they never go out with a whimper.

I'm not going to put British Army Truck Drivers up on a special pedestal, because the majority of you don't bloody deserve to be there, but I do have to say that whenever I've met yet another Corps member for yet another interview, it has been like meeting up with my own brother David and his family. Every one of you Trog's/Trogg's are like my brother, you've made me laugh out loud until my sides ache about similar experiences we've been through, and you've also made me cry my heart out over some of the more tragic episodes in our lives. However, not all of the episodes we talked about during the interviews were included in each chapter, mainly because the Trog's/Trogg's involved didn't wish certain details to be put down on paper, for a variety of reasons.

This book contains details about some of the most extraordinary incidents that have happened to some more extraordinary soldiers who have served in the logistics element of the British Army. In previous books I've written about Championship winning RASC and RCT boxers who have won just about anything and everything there was to win in a Forces boxing ring, both as individuals as well as in a team, I've included personal stories about RCT soldiers who met the criteria to serve in the SAS, Airborne Forces, and Commando units, and how they gave blood sweat and tears to attain these special qualifications. The other books also tell the tales of soldiers who rose through the ranks to ultimately become a WO1 Regimental Sergeant Major (RSM) or were eventually commissioned into the Corps'. I've written about what it was like to serve as a Tank Transporter Driver, an Air Despatcher, a Petrol Tanker Driver, a Drill Sergeant at Buller Barracks, on a Landing Ship Logistics (LSL), as an APC Driver in Northern Ireland and everything else in-between, which includes tours in Iraq, Bosnia, Canada, Cyprus, Belize and Afghanistan. And don't get me started on the soldiers who went through the ranks to become Commissioned Officers and have been awarded gallantry medals and MBE's.

'Soldiers On Wheels' is another book that tells of other RASC, RCT and RLC military careers and what each soldier/officer had to go through to achieve what they did. This includes a Corps soldier who served as an undercover Operative with 14 Intelligence (The Det) in Northern Ireland, an RCT officer who dodged mortar shells and bullets in a relatively unknown war in Dhofar, a Radio Operator who drove a Saracen Ambulance during Operation Motorman in Northern Ireland in 1972, a Staff Sergeant who served out in Afghanistan as an Airborne soldier, but didn't actually get his wings up until he came back to the UK after completing his tour. The book also includes a chapter about a well known Australian Officer who transferred from the Royal Australian Corps of Transport RACT and into our own RCT, in which he served in Iraq, Afghanistan, Northern Ireland, Bosnia and with a British Military Army Training Team in Sierra Leone in West Africa.

This book also tells of three men who eventually became Lt Col's in the Corps, one of which, started his career as a Junior Private at the Junior Soldiers Training Battalion RASC at Taunton in 1962. Surely not I hear you cry, those are the sort of things that can only be included in an Andy Mcnab or Chris Ryan novel, not the sort of things that boring army drivers would have the guts or drive (pardon the pun) to achieve.

Well, as in all of my other books, the incredible facts about drivers of the British Army are here for all and sundry to read in, 'Soldiers On Wheels'.

Brian (Harry) Clacy

Lieutenant Colonel T C Byrne MBE
(late RASC, RCT and RLC - 1962 to 2002)

Lt Col Terry Byrne MBE

If you ever have the good fortune to be speaking to anyone who has served in the Royal Army Service Corps (RASC), Royal Corps of Transport (RCT) or Royal Logistic Corps (RLC) it's guaranteed that the conversation will, at some stage, include a mention of Terry Byrne. This charming and charismatic Soldier, and Officer, has served in a combination of all three Transport Corps for forty years, and is known to all and sundry.

Terry's parents, Larry and Anne Byrne, lived in Williamstown which is about 40 miles west of Dublin's fair city. After the Second World War, Terry's dad worked on local farms where he earned a meagre wage with which to provide for his wife and eight children. Life was tough for everyone living in the gloom and austerity of the post-World War Two era, and probably more so for Terry Byrne.

During the Second World War, Southern Ireland had remained impartial to the UK's fight against Nazi Germany, as they had when the armies of the German Empire desecrated Belgium during World War One. Regardless of their country's policy though, over 200,000 citizens from Eire joined the British Army during the 1914 - 1918 War and took up the cudgels. Francis Byrne, Terry's uncle, did the same at the outbreak of World War Two and he travelled to Liverpool where he joined the Lancashire Regiment, his enlistment would eventually take him to the Hell Hole of the Death Railway in Burma. Private Francis Byrne made the ultimate sacrifice when he died as a Far East Prisoner of War (FEPOW) in 1944. Terry's Aunt, Patti Byrne also did her bit when she joined the Royal Navy and his dad Larry Byrne joined the RAF at the end of the war. The Byrne's had done more than their bit for the British war effort. They must have had the same principles as the Irish poet Francis Ledwidge who was killed at the Third Battle of Ypres in 1917. Lance Corporal (Lcpl) Francis Ledwidge is well known for this heartfelt and honest statement, "I joined the British Army because she stood between Ireland and an enemy common to our civilization, and I would not have her say she defended us while we did nothing at home but pass resolutions."

Larry Byrne was eventually allotted a placement in the RAF's Air Sea Rescue organisation when he was posted to RAF Porthcawl in Wales (*Porthcawl was eventually renamed Stormy Down in 1940*). Larry's previous experiences of sailing off the coast of Dublin probably swayed the RAF recruiters to grab him for 46 Air Sea Rescue Squadron, which was commanded by Flight Lieutenant Doug Lucas RAF. RAF Porthcawl in South Wales was opened on the 1st of June 1939 and was mainly used as an RAF Air Gunnery and Bomber Training establishment. The increased RAF air traffic flying over the Bristol Channel and North Atlantic Ocean highlighted the need for a coastal Air Sea Rescue unit to be based near Porthcawl; this is where Larry served his time in uniform until he had completed his Service.

When Larry returned home to Eire after the war, he found life was tough for everyone in the post-war era. Jobs were few and far between and those that were available weren't exactly rich pickings, and things hadn't improved much by the late 1950's and early 1960's. Anne Byrne gave her eldest son, Terry, some great advice, "You've got to get away from Southern Ireland son, you need to go somewhere where you can earn yourself a decent living." But where could he go? On the back page of a Hotspur comic he'd been reading, Terry had spotted an advert about joining up in the British Army. After entering his personal details on the form, he cut it out of the comic and sent it off to the highlighted address.

Subsequently, on a cold and damp September morning in 1962, Terry said goodbye to his family and headed off to Belfast in Northern Ireland. His journey involved a 30-minute walk into the town of Kells, followed by a bus trip into the City of Dublin where he caught the train north to Belfast. In today's modern world youngsters probably won't understand that this was a difficult and anxious journey for a 14-year-old Irish lad, especially one who had rarely been outside of the village where he lived and, in those days, wasn't in possession of a mobile phone. When he arrived at Belfast Central Railway Station, Terry asked a Porter for directions to the Army Information Office in Clifton Street, which turned out to be only a 20-minute walk away. Terry booked in on arrival at the Recruiting Centre and over the next two days he did a lot of written, practical, and medical examinations, "Turn to your right and cough"! The twenty or so potential recruits came from places like Cork, Kerry, and Galway in Southern Ireland as well as various towns and villages from all over Northern Ireland. Terry found it difficult understanding the varied regional accents. During their two-day assessments these young potential recruits had the 'pleasure' of an overnight stay in the Belfast YMCA hostel.

At the end of day two, the lads who had passed the written, physical, and medical tests, were taken to Belfast docks where they were then shepherded onto a ferry by an accompanying Guards Colour Sergeant. Terry, naively, thought that the accompanying NCO didn't look coloured at all, "His skin looked just the same as the rest of us." The thought of travelling on a ferry to Liverpool in England excited Terry, but by the time the ship had docked, and he'd got his feet back on dry land, he was very pleased that he hadn't signed up to serve in the Royal Navy.

On arrival at Lime Street Station in Liverpool, the huge and very smart Colour Sergeant peered down at the bewildered youngsters from beneath the slashed peak of his pristine cap, "Right you lot! Gather round and listen in!" He then barked out a series of travel instructions, "You are all now going to be given your final destinations, your railway tickets, and a packed lunch for the journey. When you do arrive at your journey's end, you **'will'** report to the person on the platform wearing a military uniform, whoever that may be, that soldier **'will'** have arranged the necessary transport to convey you to your relevant camp. Any questions? No! Right! My job of looking after you lot is now over, from this point onwards, you are all on your own."

The potential recruits went off to different platforms in groups of three or four and began their journeys onto the Junior Soldiers Training Battalions at Troon, Chepstow, Rhyl, and Oswestry. After they had all dwindled away, Terry was the only one left standing in front of the Guards Colour Sergeant, (Terry had by now worked out that the Colour Sergeant wasn't from deepest Africa). The formidable Colour Sergeant shouted out some last-minute instructions that have stuck in Terry's head throughout his entire army career, "Byrne! You'll be travelling down to Taunton on your own! Change at Crewe and Bristol! Good luck lad!" Fear and panic started to set in for Terry, "I'd never heard of any of these places and I also didn't have a clue where any of them were." When he found the right platform and train, Terry sat in a window seat so that he could observe the station names as the train pulled up at each platform. Crewe came up quite soon after leaving Lime Street Station and after scurrying off the train, Terry was directed by the Rail staff to the platform he needed for the Bristol train.

It was a long trip from Crewe down to Bristol, and after a couple of hours, panic again started to gnaw its way into Terry's stomach as they still hadn't reached Bristol. He started to think that maybe he'd got on the wrong train? After 3 ½ hours the train pulled into Bristol Parkway and a relieved Terry very quickly jumped off the train, he was extremely relieved that he'd finally arrived at his penultimate destination. All he had to do now was get on a train to Taunton and he could stop worrying. After the train had pulled out of the station Terry looked around and soon noticed the whole place was like a ghost town. There wasn't a soul about, and certainly no-one wearing an army uniform.

Terry eventually spotted a man in a railway uniform and approached him, asking him when the next train for Taunton would be arriving. The railway man had some unwelcome news for Terry, telling him in a very strong west-country accent, "Taunton. You've got to be joking m'dear, the Taunton train don't leave from 'ere. You should've got off at Bristol Temple Meads a bit further up the line. Still, not to worry, there'll be another train along in about two hours or so." When he eventually arrived at Taunton Station, Terry approached a very smart, but clearly cheesed off 'Army man', who'd been stood around waiting on the platform for a further two hours, just because some Irish twit didn't know his Parkway from his Temple Meads.

Back in 1962, Norton Manor Camp, just outside Taunton in Somerset, was the home of Junior Leaders Battalion, Royal Army Service Corps, (Jnr Ldrs Bn RASC) where Lt Col I (Ivor) R Renwick RASC was the Commanding Officer and WO1 (RSM) J (Jack)

Dibden RASC was the Regimental Sergeant Major. So far, Terry was suitably impressed with the British Army and its transport organisation. The fact that Ivor and Jack had kindly given him individual treatment and made sure he was dealt with on a 'one to one' basis, was fantastic. Terry had had his own personal escort in an Austin Champ vehicle come to pick up him alone from the railway station. It wasn't until that night that Terry suddenly realised that because of his unique travel arrangements from Belfast, he'd arrived 24 hours earlier than the rest of his intake. Terry had struggled with the accents of the other lads in Belfast, but now he had to try and understand the different regional English accents and that infernal 'Army Speak.'

The Orderly Screw (Corporal) instructed his 2i/c (Second in Command) who was usually a Lance Jack (Lance Corporal) to get the 'Duty Clutch' (Duty Driver) to, "Take this sprog (Recruit) to the QM's (Quartermaster's Stores) and issue him some bedding (*Terry explains that bedding in Ireland was straw from a barn and was mainly used in rabbit hutches*), also, issue him with some Diggers (*Knife Fork and Spoon*) and make sure that he signs for it all on a 1033." An Army Form G 1033 was the 'Issue and Receipt' voucher that was used at the Quartermasters Department to list military equipment on loan to a soldier. The soldier had to sign the form to agree that he had received the equipment and that it was all in good order. The Corporal then continued, "When you've done that, take him to his billet (Barrack Block) in Connaught Platoon, Room 1, and then take him over to the Cookhouse and make sure he gets some Nosh (Food)."

Terry thought to himself, 'What are they talking about?' The only part of the instructions that he understood was "Room 1." It was all a complete mystery for a couple of weeks until he started picking up and understanding the military jargon (Terminology). The 'Duty Clutch' made Terry carry his bedding over to Connaught block before taking him to the Cookhouse. Terry thought the Cookhouse was a wonderful place because the

'Nosh' was hot, plentiful, nourishing, and excellent. When Terry went back to his large dormitory style room in Connaught Platoon, he started to feel that his bed-space was a very lonely place that night, but in a way, he was glad he was on his own, because that night he sobbed himself to sleep.

The following morning Terry was taken to the Cookhouse where he enjoyed a huge British Army breakfast, after which he hung around in Connaught Platoon, waiting for the rest of his Platoon intake to arrive on camp. When his comrades did eventually appear, he discovered that they were all young lads from Scotland, Liverpool, Birmingham, Newcastle, Norfolk, Somerset and Wales. Nobody could really understand what the JNCO's were saying but Terry was one step ahead of the other sprogs, he could at least tell them what a Bed-space, Bedding, Nosh, Diggers, Duty Clutch, and what the QM's was all about. Terry had hit the ground running at the Junior Leaders Battalion RASC at Norton Manor Camp.

Once the 'Sprogs' had been issued with their complete allocation of uniforms and equipment, they had to be 'shorn' by the camp barber, (that's a barber that worked on camp, not a limp wristed hairdresser), so they all looked like refugees from a German concentration camp. The next day the recruits started doing the mundane everyday things that every soldier has to do, simply because their Troop Sergeant said, "Because I bloody well told you to do it! Now bloody well get on with it!" Any extra shouting was down to the fact that the Sergeant wanted it done better and quicker than the recruit had done it previously.

The recruits were given instructions by some very bossy Junior NCO's on how their lockers should be laid out every day for an inspection. Their socks had to be folded and then rolled up, so they looked like the socks were smiling at you (don't ask). How to blacken their issued 'brown' canvas plimsoles with one tin of Kiwi black boot polish (don't ask), and how to shape their new berets using two sinks, one full of very hot and the other full of very cold water (don't ask), and how to get rid of the nipples on a new pair of ammunition boots, using a lit candle and a hot spoon (again, don't ask). Recruits had to do that to their boots before bulling them so that they shone like the sun on a hot summers day. Terry remembers the Training NCO's shouting at the recruits, "For God's sake stop bloody asking why and just bloody well get on with it!"

Young trainees were also instructed to write a letter home to their parents explaining that they were having an excellent time and that everything in the Army was wonderful. Terry opened his document/writing case, (which he still has in his car today), to take out a writing pad and an unused envelope so that he could write home to his family. When he undid the writing case, a sealed letter, addressed to Terry, dropped out onto the linoleum floor. The envelope contained a Birthday card from his family back in Southern Ireland; his mum had surreptitiously placed the envelope in the writing case before Terry had left the house. He'd opened it on exactly the right day - it was his first day in the Battalion and he was just 15 years old. A Training NCO issued the recruits with some brown wrapping paper and string so that they could bundle up their civilian clothes and send them home. They wouldn't need them again because wherever they went from that time onwards they would always be wearing uniform. Terry tried to imagine the excitement and exhilaration amongst his siblings when his parcel was delivered by the Postman. He then wondered about their disappointment after they'd ripped it open, only to find that all it contained was the civilian clothes that he'd been wearing when he'd left home.

After their first week in training, the new recruits had to start attending the weekly Pay Parade. They had to march up to a table which was covered with an Army blanket, behind which sat, exuding an air of majesty, their Platoon Officer, a Pay Corporal and their Platoon Sergeant. Recruits had to march up to the table, halt smartly and, after having their pay book filled in by the Corporal, were then presented with £2 by the Platoon Officer. After saying, "Pay and Pay Book correct, Sir!" the Junior Soldier saluted the Officer and did a right turn before moving on to their Platoon Sergeant. The Sergeant then informed the Junior Soldier that he owed money for his "Recently issued, Stable Belt, Tracksuit, Boot Polish, Blanco Paste, and Platoon Funds." After handing over his recently acquired, and hard-earned, £2, the Platoon Sergeant returned a miserly 10 shillings and 6 pence in change. This continued for the next 6 weeks until the soldier had paid off his outstanding debts for the itemised incidentals. Terry never received a definitive explanation about precisely what the Platoon Funds were for, but he surmised it was to pay for the additional tins of yellow wax that the Junior Soldiers used to polish the room and corridor linoleum floors.

Church Parades were considered by most recruits to be a break from the turmoil and challenges of their military training. Sunday was deemed to be a sedentary day, reserved for singing hymns, playing sports, and praying, rather than doing runs, marching, adventure training, Nuclear Biological and Chemical Warfare and Weapon Training etc. Sunday's were an easy day in fact. Recruits were automatically absorbed into the Church of England team without any complaints, but Terry had been raised as a Catholic and educated in Kells by the 'Christian Brothers.' His educators were a somewhat harsh religious order who he describes as a 'Legal Bunch of Thugs.' (Thankfully the Brotherhood has now all but been disbanded). Terry was the only soldier on the camp who stated quite categorically that he was a Roman Catholic (RC) and he needed to attend a Roman Catholic Church. All other Vicars, Rabbi's, Padrés, Buddha's, etc, and their worshippers, were sinners and Terry didn't want to risk burning in hell for involving himself with any of that lot.

As there wasn't an RC Church on Norton Manor Camp, the WVS (Women's Voluntary Service 1938 - 1966) Lady, a certain Mrs

Fanny Blazier, who used to wander around the camp carrying a blind poodle – (don't ask) was summoned by the Padré and told to, "Take this stroppy little git to Mass in Taunton will you." After doing what he had to do at the RC church service in Taunton, Terry was kindly invited to join the congregation for cups of tea and cream cakes in the RC church's communal room. You certainly didn't get that sort of indulgence with the Church of England lot on camp.

The following Sunday a Bedford RL lorry had to be provided to take Terry and another ten recently inspired Catholic Junior Leaders to prayers at the RC Church in Taunton. When the Priest had concluded his service, the RASC Junior Leaders were cordially invited to join in the 'post-service party' and enjoy some tea and sticky buns. The accompanying RASC Corporal, who knew precisely why the recent converts were there, politely declined the Priests' invitation because, "I'm afraid the lads just don't have the time, Father, we really must be getting back to camp." In due course, an empty room was found in Norton Manor Camp which was then conveniently turned into a rather nice RC Church, where unfortunately tea and cakes were not provided.

Terry fell foul of the Regimental Provost Staff (RP Staff) when he got ready for his very first bout of leave, after three months of intense military training, he'd 'Passed Off' the square and was now looking forward to seeing his family again, albeit only for about a week or so. Soldiers travelling on public transport in the early 1960's wore uniform, so before leaving the camp, Terry and his comrades were paraded and inspected to make sure they were smart enough to proceed on leave. After the Platoon Sergeant had scrutinised every aspect of their uniform and given them the 'Go Ahead', each Junior Leader then reported to the Sqn Clerk who issued them with Rail Warrants and Travel Documents. Terry stood to attention in front of the eagle-eyed Corporal Clerk, dressed in his immaculately pressed BD (Battle-Dress) uniform and wearing a pair of highly bulled Ammo-Boots.

The Corporal Clerk looked Terry up and down and then noticed an instruction on Terry's travel documents, it read, **'Warrants will not be issued to any soldier travelling to Southern Ireland if they are wearing uniform.'** Now, if you remember correctly, Terry had been instructed to send his civvies back home to his parents in Williamstown not long after he'd arrived in Norton Manor Camp. Everything he now had available to wear was all in various shades of Khaki and that screamed out to the public at large, 'THIS YOUNG MAN IS A BRITISH SOLDIER!' The ever-helpful Mrs Fanny Blazier was summoned once again and told to, "Take this twit into Taunton and buy him some civilian clothes, will you?" Terry explained, "It was probably just as well, because I'd filled out a bit with all that physical training and excellent army nosh, so my old clothes probably wouldn't have fitted me anyway."

During the process of his 2½ years of hard graft at Norton Manor Camp, Terry had reached the exalted rank of Junior Sergeant and when he eventually 'Passed Out' (*Graduated*) from the Battalion, he marched away with his Army Education Certificates which would allow him to be promoted to a Senior Non Commissioned Officer (SNCO) rank in the Regular Army. In addition, he'd passed his driving tests on the Austin Champ, the Bedford RL 3 Ton Truck and he also held a motorcycle licence to ride a BSA 500cc (M20) Motorcycle. With all those qualifications and licences, Terry was undoubtedly going places and the first place was going to be, 12 Company RASC at Pinewood Camp, Liebenau, West Germany.

Terry's Troop Staff Sergeant (Tp SSgt) in A Troop, 12 Company RASC, (A Tp, 12 Coy RASC) was the indomitable SSgt Harry Blackburn RASC, who was a professional Mechanical Transport (MT) soldier who had boxed as a heavyweight for the RASC. He was also the very best SNCO needed to teach these 'young pups' about everything they needed to know to become excellent RASC Drivers. Harry was a long serving and old-style RASC soldier who was annoyed at the arrival of these young 'upstarts' from the

Junior Leaders Battalion. He knew that they'd gained enough military qualifications at Taunton for them to gain promotion all the way up to the rank of Warrant Officer.

Harry Blackburn, however, was like a lot of the other RASC SSgt's at that time, some of whom could barely read and write and would more than likely never achieve the definitive goal of wearing the WO2 Warrant Officer's crown, on the right forearm of their uniforms. The British Army was still going through massive post World War Two changes at that time. The old-school soldiers, who had given so much during their time in the Army, were now being replaced by a more educated, enthusiastic, and energetic type of soldier. Along with the old RASC vehicles, the 'Old Sweats' were being phased out at the same time.

After doing their own trials, the Drivers in 12 Coy RASC would eventually be issued with a new type of vehicle that could operate over the most extreme of field conditions, not only that, but it could also swim! The Mark 1, Truck, High Mobility Load Carrier HMLC, 6x6, 5 Ton, Alvis/Stalwart, would ultimately, and popularly, become known as the 'Stolly'. The 'Stolly' had a variant of the same Chassis built into the Saracen Armoured Personnel Carrier used by the British Army in Northern Ireland, the Saladin Armoured Car used in the Aden and Dhofar campaigns, the Salander (*used by Artillery Units*) and the Alvis Salamander MK 6 Crash Tender (Fire Engine) used on RAF airfields.

The 'Stolly had a Rolls Royce B81, 8 Cylinder, Water Cooled, 6.5L petrol engine, and on a full tank of petrol it could travel 400 miles at a top speed of 39 Mph, or at 6 Knots when operating on water. It had a 5-speed gear box and could carry 38 fully equipped troops, or 5 Tons of stores. Stalwarts were driven by a Driver, who sat in the central seat of the cab with a crew passenger seated on the left side of him; the only access into the driving compartment was through two hatches on the roof of the vehicle cab. The British Army bought the 'Stolly' into operation to take over from the unsuccessfully trialled FV 431 Tracked Load Carrier which was designed to operate just behind Infantry, Tank and Artillery units deployed into the field. The 'Stolly', and its RASC/RCT Drivers, were going to take on the responsibility of close logistic support and would be getting up close, and personal, with all of the Teeth Arms (*front-line fighting troops – not those serving in the Royal Army Dental Corps*)!

The Alvis Company in the UK sent its Engineer/Representatives out to 12 Coy RASC to teach them how to operate this new style vehicle, the Engr/Rep also told Terry and his mates to let rip with the vehicle and give the 'Stolly' as hard a time as they could. They wanted to make sure the vehicle was 'Squaddie Proof.' The Drivers also had to make notes of any inadequacies they found with the vehicles and make any recommendations where they felt that the Alvis Company could make improvements on the overall driving experience for Army Drivers. SSgt Harry Blackburn, Terry Byrne, and his mates in A Tp were chosen to conduct some of the trials, they 'Splash Dumped' the Stolly's into the River Weser at full speed and threw them all over the place on some extreme terrain on the local training area. In doing so, they came up with many modifications (*over 100 in total*) that might be of benefit: (*Incidentally, if you put 'Stolly jump' into a You Tube search engine, you'll be able to see some of the hair-raising things that Terry and his mates performed in their Mk 1 Stalwarts.*) Their ideas included:

1. There was a gap in the instrument panel near the choke lever, that gap allowed an annoying light to shine straight into the Drivers eyes whilst driving at night, or during a night move into location under black-out conditions, it had an adverse effect on the Drivers night vision and this observation resulted in the dashboard being redesigned.

2. Whilst doing the Royal Engineer Amphibious and Watermanship Course on the River Weser, it was noted that a drop-down splash board underneath the windscreen would improve the drivers vision whilst driving on the water.

3. Spring-loaded mirror arms on the sides of the 'Stolly' would prevent damaging the vehicles mirrors whilst driving in a heavily wooded area, this would also prevent the Driver from having to get out of the vehicle to pull the mirror arm in, and out, every time the vehicle entered or left a wooded location.

4. The trial teams all put in a strong recommendation for a cab heater to be installed into the Mk 2 Stolly's because they were, "Bloody freezing" during the water trials, and thought 'God alone knows what it'll be like during any winter Exercises'.

The trials went extremely well and the Drivers from 12 Coy RASC had a ball bouncing around in this new wonder vehicle, both in and out of the water. Terry must have impressed SSgt Harry Blackburn because in less than 12 months he was marched in front of the OC and promoted to Lance Corporal. During this phase of his army career (1965 – 1968), Terry deployed on Field Exercises in the South of France with 12 Coy RASC, and then to Libya with 12 Squadron RCT (12 Sqn RCT), (the RASC had been officially disbanded and the RCT formed, on the 15th of July 1965).

12 Sqn RCT went out to Libya to provide Transport Support on a Brigade Level Exercise, Terry was based on Al Temimi Airfield, about 60 miles West of Tobruk. On the Exercise itself, a newly promoted Lance Corporal (LCpl) Terry Byrne RCT, was responsible for supplying the Tanks and Royal Artillery Guns with their fuel requirements which he did using Jerry cans on the back of a Bedford RL 3 Ton truck. This was in the days before Unit Bulk Refuelling Equipment (UBRE) came into vogue. Terry explains, "We Brits were the last modern-day Army to realise the need for

a bulk re-fuelling system in the field and we continued using Jerry cans for too many years. The RCT had to co-operate and comply with the Infantry and Tank Regiment's tactical requirements when we went up to resupply them, they wanted us to do our job silently, so that their locations wouldn't be compromised by the enemy. The introduction of UBRE jeopardized that operating system because the generator pump equipment on the back of our four Tonners, was very noisy and wasn't tactically savvy. The system changed slightly in that the RCT deployed just behind the tank hides where the armoured vehicles lined up and refuelled from a UBRE, before deploying into their unit hides.

Within 18 months of returning to Liebenau, Terry was promoted to full Corporal, which was, for a 20 years old soldier in the RCT, quite an achievement. In 1967 the Sqn sent Terry to 6 Trg Bn in Yeovil to complete his six-week B1 Trade Training Course, which consisted of six weeks of crawling about underneath Army vehicles and learning how to run a Servicing Bay, which was right up there on Terry's dream-sheet.

The B1 Course was held in Lufton Camp, which co-incidentally was where the Women's Royal Army Corps (WRAC) accommodation was located. The men's accommodation was positioned in Houndstone Camp, Yeovil on the other side of a road, surrounded by tall security fences. Male soldiers were only allowed admission into Lufton Camp for the duration of their Course lessons and if they were signed into the camp by a female soldier during the evenings (*WRAC soldiers were only allowed to sign in one male soldier each*), all male soldiers were strictly forbidden from entering the female accommodation at any time. If a soldier was lucky enough to get an evening invite into the NAAFI Club by a Women's Royal Army Corps (WRAC) soldier, he had to be accompanied by that young lady at all times and escorted back to the guardroom to be signed back out again by 2200 hours, and not a minute later.

Terry didn't have a WRAC girlfriend whilst on his B1 Course, so there was no way he could get into the NAAFI Bar for a few quiet beers in the evening. This is where a petit 19-year-old WRAC Clerk called Private Eunice Dower comes into the picture. Eunice had a WRAC friend called Sue who asked Eunice, "Can I book a soldier into camp using your name, he's a mate of my boyfriend and he only wants to get into the NAAFI Bar for a few quiet beers." Eunice originally came from Abercynon in South Wales and regardless of her diminutive stature; she could be a formidable person when annoyed. As a special favour to Sue, Eunice signed Cpl Terry Byrne RCT (*Sue's boyfriends' mate*) into the camp and then watched him saunter off into the NAAFI bar. Like all good RCT soldiers, he was chasing down the scent of proper ale. By 2200 hours Terry hadn't returned to the guardroom so Eunice could account for him and sign him back out of Lufton Camp. A slightly miffed Private Eunice Dower WRAC boldly marched into the NAAFI Bar and started shouting, "Corporal Byrne! Corporal Byrne! Come on Corporal Byrne, you should've been out of here by now, get yourself down to the Guardroom immediately, you need to be signed out of the camp! NOW!" This incident set a precedent for Eunice for the next 50 years, because Terry and Eunice were married in her home town in South Wales on 15th June 1968, and she's been hollering at him ever since!

Since Eunice and Terry got married she has successfully, and consistently, been running around like a headless chicken to support Terry throughout his military career. After they were married, the happy couple honeymooned in Southern Ireland and went to visit his family. Unfortunately, Eunice had to leave the WRAC when they returned to Lufton Camp because female soldiers simply weren't allowed to be married if they wanted to continue with their Army careers. After the honeymoon holiday, Terry went back to 12 Sqn RCT in Liebenau and applied for a Married Quarter. Unfortunately, in the 1960's, Married Quarters weren't as freely available as they are today, and so they were informed that they'd have to wait. Eunice went back home to Wales and lived with her mum (*Elizabeth*) and dad (*Trevor*) until a Married Quarter became available, Eunice's' dad Trevor Dower was a miner by trade.

Corporal Terry Byrne talking with a Swiss Soldier on Nijmegen marches.

Whilst they waited for notification of being allocated a Married Quarter in Liebenau, Terry applied to go on the International Four Day Marches at Nijmegen in Holland, Terry eventually went on to do these marches on five other occasions. These marches are held every year to commemorate the Allied Airborne landings during 'OPERATION MARKET GARDEN' in September 1944. They can be attempted individually or as a team and are made available to Civilians and Servicemen from all Corps and Regiments from nearly every country around the World. The commemoration honour is primarily not a race or competition, it is merely a tribute to those soldiers who fought in Holland towards the end of the Second World War, but most soldiers don't treat it as such. For four days, everyone taking part (*most military teams were in squads of 10 Servicemen/Servicewomen*) had to march around a designated route of 25 Miles a day. British service personnel carried 25lb of webbing on the march and in 1968, when Terry did it; they also carried a personal weapon with them. The best and fittest soldiers that Terry ever saw on his marches in Holland were a Swiss contingent of Alpine Soldiers who completed the 25 miles a day faster than any other group.

Terry wasn't the sort of soldier to let the grass grow under his feet, and the British Army was always trying to keep up with him. In 1965 he was a Junior Sergeant in the Jnr Ldrs Bn RASC at Norton Manor Camp in Taunton, and less than five years later he was promoted to the rank of Sergeant before being posted as an MT Instructor to the MT Wing of the Army School of Mechanical Transport (ASMT) at Bordon in Hampshire. Fortunately, there was a surplus of Married Quarters in the Bordon Garrison and Eunice was able to join Terry there for the first time since they'd been married. It wouldn't be long before the British Army temporarily separated them again though, because of his posting to Bordon, Terry found himself attracted to yet another great love of his life.

Terry was besotted with the 'Stolly' when he was posted to 12 Sqn RCT, but when he met up with a young Swedish beauty called the Volvo BV (Bandvagn) 202, he couldn't decide which one he loved more. The BV 202 was an all-terrain, rubber tracked, military truck that was in use with the Swedish Army at the time, its low ground pressure was less than that of an average adult male skier, this resulted in it being able to operate on the deepest and softest of snow conditions. The front and rear cars were connected by a unique articulated, hydraulic steering unit operated by a proper steering wheel, unlike other tracked vehicles which used tillers to steer the vehicle. All four tracks were driven as with any normal 4x4 wheeled vehicle. Like the 'Stolly', the vehicle could also swim (at about 3 mph) and it was already being used by Allied Command Europe (ACE) Mobile Force United Kingdom Land Forces (UKLF) that deployed on Exercise to Norway in defence of NATO's Northern Flank. The problem was that the Infantry and Royal Marine (RM) Commando's who were using the vehicles, were inadvertently abusing and wrecking them because they simply didn't know how to drive a BV 202 properly. The initial issue of BV's were transported out to Norway on RCT Landing Ships Logistic (LSL's) by the deploying British Infantry and RM Commando units, and when they were brought back to the UK for storage during the Summer months, Combined Vehicle Depot staff (CVD) discovered that most of the gear-boxes and clutches were either totally wrecked or completely burnt out.

To solve the problem of the poor driving techniques, the School of Mechanical Transport in Bordon sent Sgt Terry Byrne RCT, and Sgt Jim Taylor Royal Artillery (RA) out to Sweden for 14 weeks. Terry and Jim met up with the training staff at the Swedish Army School of Transport in Stockholm where they deployed on an Exercise with them and other Swedish Army units. The extreme temperatures out on the Exercise area in Lapland were a nut-freezing -30°C. The Swedish Exercise was very similar to the Troop Commanders Courses that they ran back in Bordon. During the Exercise, Terry and Jim learned how to maintain the BV 202's and how to drive this unique vehicle properly, both on the snow and in the freezing water.

On their return to Bordon, the two Sgt's set about writing a Training Programme and Instruction Manuals so that they could pass on the invaluable information that they'd learned from the Swedish Army Instructors, to the British Infantry's Unit Instructors. In future, any Battalion of Infantry that was deploying out to Norway would send their best instructors to the Army School of Mechanical Transport in Bordon to learn from Sgt Terry Byrne RCT and Sgt Jim Taylor RA, about how to properly drive and maintain the BV 202 in a harsh winter environment.

These Infantry instructors could then go back to their own garrisons and pass on that knowledge to their own Battalion MT drivers who, hopefully, wouldn't wreck any more vehicles. The resolute and tough little BV 202 eventually progressed onto the BV 206 and Terry explains that it, "Proper won its spurs during the Falklands War in 1982".

Two and a half years later Terry was posted back to Taunton (*where the unit was now called the Junior Leaders Regiment RCT (Jnr Ldrs Regt RCT)*) as the Sergeant Instructor of Senior Troop, it was a job he really enjoyed because he was passing on all his knowledge and experience about the importance of proper MT work to future young RCT Drivers. In 1974 Terry was promoted yet again and as a consequence was posted to Duisburg, West Germany as Tp SSgt of A Tp, 11 Sqn RCT in 4 Armoured Division Transport Regiment RCT (4 Armd Div Tpt Regt RCT). The posting meant he would be in charge of a Tp of Drivers who drove the old AEC Mk1 Militant's, affectionately known by all RCT Drivers as, 'Knockers.'

Once he was established in Duisburg, Terry applied for, and cruised through, his Master Driver Course which went hand-in-hand with being promoted to Warrant Officer Class 2. A very proud moment for Terry was when, as Master Driver, he was put in charge of the Drivers and Vehicles representing the Regiment and the work of the RCT in 4th Division, on the Queen's Silver Jubilee Parade in Sennelager on Saturday 7/7/77. Terry's beloved 'Stolly' was now starting to bow out of the British Army in all its finery, they were going to be inspected by Her Majesty the Queen on such a great occasion. A vacancy for the MD job in Duisburg came available and Terry simply moved on from A Tp and did the job initially as a SSgt, when 4 ADTR was ordered to move to another garrison in West Germany, the entire Regiment was transported, lock, stock, and barrel, 130 miles north-east from Duisburg to Minden where they remained 4 Armoured Division Transport Regiment RCT (4 Armd Div Tpt Regt RCT). Terry was eventually promoted to WO2 and became the MD of Minden Garrison and 4th Division. His next posting was going to be vital if he was to become a WO 1 Regimental Sergeant Major. He needed to gain the experience of running his own Sqn as a Squadron Sergeant Major (WO2 SSM), and he was destined to get bucket-loads of that experience at 26 Sqn RCT in Northern Ireland.

26 Sqn was permanently based in Lisburn, Northern Ireland and in a strange way, the unit was a very specialised, and diverse RCT unit. On a daily basis, the Sqn's Dvrs were operating a mixture of Staff Cars, Cement Mixer Trucks, Coaches, General Transport Trucks, Library Vans, 'Sneaky Beaky' cars as well as Armoured Personnel Carriers (APC's). The Sqns' Dvrs chauffeured VIP's like Lieutenant General Sir Timothy Creasey, who at that time was the General Officer Commanding Northern Ireland (GOC NI), and Prime Minister, Margaret Thatcher, when she occasionally visited the Province. In hand with those duties, 26 Sqn Staff Car Dvrs had to be trained in Close Protection duties, Anti-ambush Drills, Special Car Transfers. All of those pre-requisites resulted in the Staff Car Dvr selection process being very closely monitored.

In the words of Terry Byrne, "Those soldiers selected for Staff Car Driving duties had to be a bit special. They needed to be a bit wary and they also had to be good, experienced, and mature soldiers whose personal admin was above reproach. My Dvrs and NCO's in 26 Sqn had a completely different attitude when compared to the RCT lads carrying out the consistent Roulement tours (Operation Banner) all over Northern Ireland. We were there all the time and were constantly aware of the security implications for us as soldiers, as well as for our families. The Roulement Sqn's were only in theatre for 4 – 6 months and did their tours without worrying about their families having to live permanently in a dangerous and all enclosing hostile environment. Once the Roulement tours were over, those lads went back to BAOR or other parts of the UK where they had the luxury of 'switching off' every time they went back to their MQ's or barrack blocks."

Terry did 2½ years as the SSM of 26 Sqn RCT and during that time, he served with two OC's, Major's Paul Holtam and Martin Cubitt and they often oversaw the re-supply convoys to British Army outposts like XMG (Crossmaglen) and Forkhill on the border between North and Southern Ireland. Accompanying Infantry and RE escorts would reconnoitre and clear the roads, culverts, and possible ambush points on the route before the logistic convoys set off, and in some places the Infantry were actually dug into ditches at the side of the roads. During these operations the RCT, RE and Infantry soldiers would closely work together around the clock. Each RCT vehicle had to be double-manned during those Logistic Patrols. Terry Byrne feels strongly that, "The war in Northern Ireland, and believe you me it was a war, was all about the Junior NCO's, Pte's and Dvrs. The Officers and we Senior NCO's were there merely as admin staff, and nothing more."

When Terry was eventually promoted to Warrant Officer Class 1, he wanted his next promotion to come along with a Regimental Sergeant Majors' slot. Unfortunately though, he had to accept that the RCT system would post him to wherever they wanted him to go, and he'd have to do whichever job the Corps gave him. "The fact that I wanted to be an RSM was irrelevant to RCT Manning and Records. I was allocated a Master Driver job in Cyprus, and that was what I had to do, and to the best of my abilities. It was a command job in a geographically isolated location and so before taking up the post; I took a week of personal leave and visited the Army School of Mechanical Transport (ASMT) at Normandy Barracks, Leconfield in East Yorkshire. The ASMT had only recently been opened and because I'd done all of my previous training at Bordon in Hampshire, I wanted to learn about the school's structure and what sort of courses they were running. During my fact-finding visit to

Leconfield I gained some valuable and useful information which included important contacts and support networks. Added to that, I made sure I obtained some Royal Society for the Prevention of Accidents (ROSPA) contact telephone numbers so that I could run safety campaigns in Cyprus, and from where I could gather plenty of relevant reading material and posters."

Cyprus was a pretty good posting for all soldiers, whatever their job was, and so it was for Terry and Eunice, but within two years Terry's Commanding Officer, Lt Col Richard Arlidge RCT, was encouraging him to apply for a commission in the RCT. Over the previous few years Terry had attuned himself to the fact that he'd like to apply for a commission and finish his Army career as an Officer, but he also felt he wasn't ready for that step because he'd never held the position of Regimental Sergeant Major. Although Lt Col Arlidge was disappointed that Terry didn't apply for his commission whilst in Cyprus, he understood his desire to fill an RSM's appointment before doing so, and anyway, time was still on Terry's side because in the promotion stakes, he was still ahead of the game.

Terry explains that his next posting was, "The best job I've ever had in my life." Although he was already a WO1, his next job was going to put him in the exalted position of RSM at 4 Armoured Division Transport Regiment (4 ADTR) which was based in Minden, West Germany. 4 ADTR's RSM, WO1 Mick (Voodoo) Davis RCT (later Captain) would coincidentally be heading out to Cyprus to take over the position of Garrison Sergeant Major (GSM) in Dhekelia. Mick explained on the handover/takeover that 54 Sqn RCT was going to leave Minden and move to Lübbeke as an independent Engineer Support and Ambulance Sqn, and that 12 Sqn RCT (*Terry's old unit*) was coming in to replace them. It fell on Terry shoulders to organise and orchestrate a mini-Jubilee parade which would involve five Sqn's on parade at the same time. He would also have to plan and coordinate a massive Drive-past in front of the CO and his many honoured guests. To help the CO envisage the overall plan of the parade, Terry, with the assistance of his five SSM's, built a huge model of the Parade Ground in St Georges Barracks, and using building blocks and toy vehicles he demonstrated exactly how the parade was going to proceed. On the day itself, the paraded proceeded without a single hiccup, apart from it being the coldest day on record in Minden. *Authors note: RSM's are very important and powerful men, but not even they can do anything about the weather.*

During his 2-year tenure as RSM at 4 ADTR, Terry was still mulling over the idea of taking a commission. He didn't know how long the process would take and even if he did apply, there was no guarantee that he would be accepted. "No matter how good you think you are, it's never a given that you'll be accepted and granted a commission in the British Army." says Terry, "The system decides whether or not you are good enough for a Short Service Commission (SSC)." Terry applied, and was selected for an SSC, whereupon he did the abridged knife and fork course at Buller Barracks, Aldershot with Colonel John D MacDonald (*Col J D MacDonald was one of Terry's previous OC's and was later promoted to Major General and became the Corps Commander*). On his first day after completing the Course, Terry was still a WO1, the next day he was commissioned as a 2ND Lieutenant, and on day three, the chrysalis blossomed into a fully-fledged 518303 Captain T C Byrne RCT. Once he was commissioned, Captain Terry Byrne was then posted to 3 Armoured Field Ambulance (3 AFA) in Sennelager, West Germany (*probably the worst lager in the world*) as the unit's Motor Transport Officer (MTO).

There was an unwritten word of advice for all RCT Officers who'd just been granted an SSC. It was said that, "No-one in their right mind would volunteer to be posted into a Field Ambulance as an MTO." Terry hadn't been privy to that bit of gossip though, and so, unwittingly, he took over from Captain D J (Dave) Owen RCT, the outgoing MTO. Dave introduced Terry to the Field Ambulances' CO and during their brief interview the CO stated,

"I've only got 6 months left here at 3 AFA Captain Byrne, so go out there and don't change anything because Captain David Owen has got everything just right. You can make a name for yourself when the next CO takes over." Terry accepted the directive and went around Sennelager learning about the soldiers under his command, which sometimes included the medics, and he educated himself on how to be a good commissioned officer.

There was also a lot to learn about his new job, which included, Dressing Station tent formations, the size of area needed to set everything up in a wood or building, conducting a reconnaissance for a Field Ambulance and Exchange Points (XP's), as well as the Access and Exit points needed for both wheeled and tracked ambulances. A lot of this stuff Terry had already done in the RCT but there were variations when dealing with a tented unit like the Medics. Once in location, Terry would be responsible for the movement and deployment of all his vehicles and the security of the location, which included dealing with the guard duties. Medics have a passive role in the field and so if the unit were given any, "We need to go and beat someone up" jobs, they were done solely by the RCT Drivers. To be fair to the Medics, Terry was very impressed with their tactical awareness, "They were brilliant at setting up their metal-poled Dressing Station in complete silence, both at night and during the day. The unit trucks had to be methodically loaded so that the first things needed on deployment, were the last things loaded on the trucks before leaving their barracks. From the start of the Exercise, (Startex) to having the Dressing Station up and running could take about 24 hours, but in a real war scenario the Medics could be doing tailboard treatments as soon as the vehicles arrived in location. As much as he enjoyed his time at 3 AFA, Terry would refer any future RLC SSC Officers to the opening comments at the start of the previous paragraph.

The remaining postings in Terry's career were, in the main, Quartermaster positions. Some readers, incorrectly, will probably turn over the following pages assuming that they will be filled with piffle and bilge about stock rotation, NBC suits and shelving units. General Erwin Rommel, (The Desert Fox), was famously quoted as saying that "All battles are either won or lost by the Quartermaster before the shooting even starts." In essence, Rommel was absolutely right, because if an Army doesn't have enough fuel, rations, weapons, ammunition or the right clothing and equipment, then it will struggle to overcome an enemy that is better prepared. The Battle of Stalingrad during WW2 is a perfect example, many Wehrmacht soldiers simply froze to death for the want of some decent winter clothing.

Major Terry Byrne RCT was promoted during his time as the QM of 2 Inf Div Tpt Regt RCT (2nd Infantry Division Transport Regiment) in Catterick, North Yorkshire. During his tenure in the post Terry had to deploy with 2 Div on 'Exercise Lionheart.' He had to arrange for the Territorial Army Dvrs of 216 Sqn RCT to fly out to Brussels in Belgium where they would pick up their pre-stocked vehicles from a Combined Vehicle Depot (CVD). Terry was the first person from his unit to deploy to Belgium so that he could check everything was in order before signing for the entire fleet of vehicles, their tool-kits, tow bars, convoy flags, and in fact, the whole kit and caboodle. When 216 Sqn's soldiers arrived at the airport in Brussels they were all bussed to the CVD where they signed for their individual trucks and after loading up their personal kit, they headed off to Sennelager in convoy. The Sqn laagered up in Sennelager for a few days before driving to their Exercise locations prior to the War Games starting; they would then have to do the whole move again when they returned back to the UK on Endex (End of Exercise).

Terry is very passionate about **'his'** Corps and its capabilities, "During massive NATO Exercises like 'Lionheart' and 'Spearpoint', the Infantry and Armoured Regiments simply played at their war roles, but we in the RCT did everything for real. Complete Armies were setting up camp in BAOR and they all needed fuel, rations, spares, medical evacuation (Simulated and 'No-Duff' cases) even though it was 'just' an Exercise." He further explained about his own 'Exercise' experiences, "I had to organise getting the whole of 2 Div Tpt Regt RCT, which included TA soldiers from Tynemouth, into Theatre by whatever means were available. Drivers were then dispatched to the correct Ammunition Depot to pick up the right Ammunition (*albeit simulated loads*). Arrangements also had to be made for the TTF Drivers to fill up with sufficient fuel from the Army Fuel Depot in Warendorf, so they could get all of the loaded trucks to the reinforcement area in Sennelager. And all this was before the bloody Exercise had even started."

The reader should understand that Terry's involvement in the Exercise was only a small part in comparison to what the rest of the Corps was doing at the same time. Air-trooping of soldiers, stores and vehicles in RAF C130's was overseen by RCT Air Movements Clerks, and the use of Landing Ship Logistics (LSL's) Maritime vessels from 17 Port and Maritime Regt RCT, the Tank Transporters that were used to get the Tankies and Cavalry units to their starting points, all added up to a massive and complex logistic operation.

In 1991 Terry was given the 'heads up' that he was going to be awarded an MBE (Member of the Most Excellent Order of the British Empire), even though recipients aren't given a certificate explaining the reasons why they have been bestowed with the decoration. Terry knew it was for all the hard work he'd done in both Northern Ireland and Catterick Garrison. The Commanding Officer, Lt Col O T 'Ozzy' Hall RCT, was the one who informed Terry about the MBE award. He'd dragged him up to his house telling him, "I think we need to have a little drink Terry." Terry received a letter from Buckingham Palace explaining that he needed to keep quiet about the award until the New Year's Honours list was released. Eunice and their two children, Karen and Chris, went up to Buckingham Palace and witnessed Major

Terry Byrne become Major Terry Byrne MBE. Terry was overwhelmed by the medal presentation but even today he still says, "These things don't come up with the rations you know, but I have to pay credit to all those soldiers and civilians who worked so very hard with me which enabled me to be granted the award." A return posting to Duisburg and 3 ADTR as the RQM followed.

Over the next few years, the British Army did a draw-down of its Armed Forces based in the British Army of the Rhine (BAOR) and Terry was very much involved in the transition. He relocated 3 Div RCT back to the UK and closed down Glamorgan barracks in Duisburg, he also shut down 38 Sqn RCT in Mulheim, 68 Sqn RCT in Rheindahlen and three Mobile Civilian Transport Groups (MCTG's), some of which became part of the new BAOR units. This concluded with the disbandment of 2 Group RCT and the closure of Caernarvon Barracks in Dusseldorf. Terry then moved to Sennelager to Command 607 MCTG/72 Transport Sqn RCT before finally returning to the UK as the RQM of DST Leconfield in Yorkshire.

A recommendation that Major Terry Byrne MBE was to be appointed as the QM at DST Leconfield was rumoured to have come from the Corps Commander himself, Maj Gen Martin White, was once Terry's CO when he was the RSM at 4 ADTR. To fill a Lt Col appointment as a Major was always going to be a challenge, but with a very big job to do maybe all that was needed was big boots, a big mouth, and the ability not to take any crap. Terry fitted that bill perfectly. (*Terry's words, not the authors*) There were many challenges that needed addressing when Terry took over as DST's QM. The introduction of EU Driving Licenses and new testing requirements, which included theory testing, was having a serious impact on capacity and delayed getting soldiers through their driving qualifications. A whole new approach was needed and the DST Command Team, including Terry, set to with wide ranging changes to crack the problem. The solutions to the problems included an increased throughput, more instructors and vehicles, contract driving, satellite testing stations, new accommodation blocks and new dining facilities. The QM Team, under Terry's management, worked daily miracles throughout this very challenging time and Terry feels that they all should feel very proud of what they achieved.

Terry's last couple of weeks at DST Leconfield involved him handing over all of the Quartermaster accounts and his very large budget to the incoming QM, the late Lt Col D J (Dave) Winkle RLC who had previously served with Terry in 26 Sqn. For 2 years Terry had been living in the Officers' Mess at Leconfield and he travelled home to Winterton-on-sea most weekends. Eunice drove up to Leconfield to help Terry pack up all his gear and then transported it all down to his new posting in Colchester. Before leaving the camp they both walked over to say goodbye to the Commandant, Brigadier M J (Tom) Blythe L/RCT. As they walked into his office Terry noticed that the Brigadier was pouring some champagne into three glass flutes. The Commandant had been informed through official channels that Terry had been selected for promotion to Lieutenant Colonel. So, he congratulated Terry and Eunice and they drank a toast in bubbly, Terry apparently remarked at the time, "About bloody time!"

The new job at Colchester was going to be one of the biggest challenges Terry had ever taken on, as the OC Logistic Support Unit (LSU). He was also part of the project team assigned to rebuild and run the Garrisons' Workplaces and Single Accommodation for the next 35 years. The Garrison needed to be completely rebuilt and the detailed plans even went down to what sort of bicycle sheds were going to be installed outside each building. The whole project went out to tender and Terry was working from 0600 hours till 2200 hours every single night. He had to run his unit and deal with five different contractors who all wanted answers to the same questions. He attended meeting

after meeting after which he went back to his office and disseminated those answers to all the contractors, even if they hadn't asked the question Mc Alpine was the contractor who won the bid, "They were brilliant to work with," says Terry, "They also had a couple of 'knob-heads' working for them, but you get that in all walks of life I suppose. I had to do the job properly though, because it was important for the soldiers who were going to move into the place. I had to get it right for them." Terry hung his boots up after leaving Colchester because the project had taken its toll, "I was over the moon to be leaving the Army, I simply didn't want to do anymore."

But he did, and still does more. Terry adopted a run-down and poorly equipped Marine Cadet Unit in his local village. They only had 10 cadets in the unit who had very little equipment and were poorly run. By the time Terry had finished obtaining uniforms, webbing, mess tins, ponchos and also writing their training programmes for them, their nominal roll had increased to 60 regularly attending cadets.

Today, Terry is the President of the RASC and RCT Association, Norfolk and Norwich Branch and is their Standard Bearer. He also serves on the Association Committee of Management and is the President of the Master Drivers Association. Terry has asked the author to tell you the reader, "If you know Terry Byrne and are ever in Winterton-on-Sea, then call in at the 'Fisherman's Return Pub' and tell the bar staff to put the bill on the 'Colonels' tab. You will have to answer a couple of security questions before you get your pint though.

479471 Lieutenant Colonel David Robertson Birrell
RCT and RLC 1965 – 1997

David Robertson Birrell was a Post War baby who was born in Dunfermline Scotland on the 20th of December 1946. He's always been called 'Bob' by his family and friends, but to this day he has no recollection of when everyone started calling him 'Bob', it's simply been that way for as long as he can remember. Soldiering has been a part of his family history in pretty much the same fashion, it's always been that way and there's obviously something in the Birrell DNA that makes them compatible to a military lifestyle.

During the First World War, Bob's uncle, on his mother's side of the family, was under-age when he enthusiastically enlisted into the British Army. David James Dickson was described in the local newspaper as being an:

'Enthusiastic Boy Scout who was enamoured of a soldier's life. When the war broke out he was engaged as a volunteer messenger with troops stationed at Leven, in Fifeshire. But he wanted to do more than that, and by making a misrepresentation of his age, which he claimed was seventeen, he enlisted into the Royal Scots, although his actual age was only 14½. The officials were deceived owing to his more than ordinary height for a boy of his years.

After a lapse of fifteen months, his father informed the authorities about his real age and David was returned to his family in Scotland. In civil life again, David manifested great restlessness. Three weeks had only elapsed when he disappeared, and the young patriot had been in France two months serving with the Gordon Highlanders before his parents were able to trace him. His father wrote to the Commanding Officer, pointing out the boys age and expressing the hope that if retained he would not be put into the firing line. The letter unfortunately reached the Commanding Officer (CO) two days after the lad was killed and in a letter to the father the CO expressed regret that the letter had been received just too late, otherwise his wishes would most certainly have been complied with.'

The newspaper clipping stated that David was 16 years old when he died, but Bob was assured that he was actually only 15 ½ years old.

Bob's father Danny was a policeman before the outbreak of World War Two and when called to arms he enlisted into the Royal Military Police (RMP). Before he retired from the army in 1968, Danny had risen through the ranks from Lance Corporal (LCpl) all the way up to Lieutenant Colonel (Lt Col). During the war, Lt Col Danny Birrell RMP had served in India, Palestine and had also taken part in the invasion of Sicily in 1943. During the Sicily campaign he was badly injured during an intense German mortar barrage, the attack culminating with him being hospitalised for many months. After the war Danny, returned to Scotland and eventually Bob came along in 1946.

At the age of 11, Bob was packed off to the Dollar Academy Boarding School near Stirling. He states, somewhat sardonically, "I wasn't very bright at school, but I was bloody good at rugby. Sport really was the only thing I was any good at." His father, still serving in the RMPs, was eventually posted to HQ Scottish Command in Edinburgh and as a result Bob changed from being a Boarder at the Dollar Academy to being a 'Day Boy' at the Edinburgh Academy. "I really enjoyed my time at Boarding school and I have to say, it taught me to be self-sufficient. My father suggested that I become an accountant when I graduated from school, but because I was hopeless at maths and couldn't add a column of numbers together to save my life, that put the kibosh on a career in accountancy I'm afraid.

Bob Birrell (schoolboy)

Whilst I was still only 15 years old, I became aware of the fact that the army Subalterns in my father's unit always seemed to be having a good time wherever they were, each of them also drove a nice car and had a pretty girl on their arm. I thought to myself, 'Yeah, that all looks pretty good to me!' I decided there and then that I wanted to be an officer in the British Army."

When Bob was medically examined by a doctor, it was discovered that his eyesight was good enough for him to be commissioned into the British Army but was below the required standard for a placement on the Royal Military Academy Course at Sandhurst (RMAS). This resulted in Bob being commissioned much earlier than he expected because he had to go through the Officer Training Course at Mons Officer Cadet School in Aldershot. The Mons system was for young men who wanted to qualify for a Short Service Commission (SSC) rather than attending the longer Sandhurst route.

At the age of 18 ½, Bob was commissioned on a 3-year SSC contract, after which he could extend his military career with an offered Regular Army Commission, subject to being deemed good enough once he'd completed his 3-year SSC, which is exactly what he did. When interviewed for this book, Bob flippantly stated that the Mons commissioning Course was harder than going through Sandhurst (there was a 30 – 40 % failure rate on the Mons Course), but having said that, he also believes that the Dollar Academy was a lot harder than the Mons Program. "It was hard work at Mons but not any harder than life was at Boarding School, in fact, my time as a boarder at the Dollar Academy was a brilliant introduction to what a life in the army was going to be like." Getting up early, cold showers, making sure his room and bed were squared away each morning before going down for breakfast, having to iron his own school uniform and polishing his shoes was a great training regime for a career in the British Army.

The Royal Army Service Corps (RASC) was still in existence when Bob reported to Mons, but he knew that in 1965 the Corps would soon be changing-over from the RASC to the RCT. By the time his SSC Course had finished, Bob was commissioned as a 2nd Lieutenant and he then needed to find a Corps that would welcome him into their family. Cars, trucks, and engines were of great interest to Bob whilst he was growing up and continued to be so after passing his Commissioning Course at Mons. He therefore applied to Join the RCT and reported to Buller Barracks in Aldershot to be given an in-depth interview by an RASC/RCT Lt Col to see if he was suitable and that he was wanted in the Corps. Unsurprisingly, the Corps accepted him.

The Course that Bob had just completed at Mons OCS was never meant to be easy and the syllabus was Infantry orientated (which would eventually come in very useful when he went out to fight in the war in Dhofar). There was no 'Special to Arm' training done at Mons OCS. Royal Armoured Corps (RAC), RCT, Royal Army Ordnance Corps (RAOC) and other Corps' training was all subsequent, and it was all carried out on the Junior Officers Course (JOC) at each relevant Corps' Depot. Every officer who completed the Mons officer Course left as a qualified Infantry Platoon Commander. Bob states that his main purpose in life after been granted the Queens Commission, was to look after the men he was charged to command. He told the author, "I've worked with a lot of officers whose main interest in life was their own careers and furthering their personal ambitions, most possibly at the expense of the men they were there to look after. I've always taken a very dim view of that sort of attitude and it's served me very well because soldiers aren't stupid. They're well aware of what's going on around them and if they know you are doing the best by them, then whenever I was in the shit, which I inevitably was, they'd always come and pull me out of it."

Bob's first posting was to 5 Squadron, 8 Regiment RCT, in Munster, West Germany and he thought that his Commanding Officer, Lt Col Roy Royle RCT, didn't rate him very highly. Roy seemed a very stern officer, "I tried to do well by him but thought - I'm not really succeeding - because he always seemed to be unimpressed by me." First impressions, though, can often be misconstrued. Bob became aware of that nearly 40 years later in 2001, not long after his father had died. Whilst sorting out some

2nd Lt Bob Birrell A troop 8 Regt RCT.

of his father's private papers, Bob found a personal letter that Lt Col Royle RCT had written to his dad a few months after he'd arrived in 8 Regt. Bob gave a copy of the beautifully hand-written letter to the Author so it could be included in his Chapter. The letter was simply dated Sunday evening (18th Feb) and it read;

Dear Danny,

May I say what tremendous pleasure it gave me to receive your very kind letter. How nice of you to have written it.

During Bob's last few days here, I was on the point of writing to you when he told me that you would be leaving Salisbury very soon! Even now I must send this to your old office. I hope they redirect it properly.

Bob was just the sort of young officer any Commanding Officer would give a lot to have in his Regiment.

I watched him develop with a very genuine interest. He must have been one of the youngest subalterns in the British Army when he arrived! He grew up quite quickly and in quite a short time was making his presence felt with his (slightly) senior fellows. As you know he qualified at the PT School and, later, at the rugged Outward-Bound School.

He was one young man I <u>never</u> had to worry about at weekends etc. He has the happy knack of living life to the full and always doing something creditable. In fact, he ran so many activities in the Regiment – Motorsport, Canoeing, Motorcycling – and took part in so many others, that at one time I wondered whether he was overdoing it! However, he seemed to thrive on it!

All this you probably know, but one aspect of his life here may not have been disclosed in detail! Of course, all the young men try to find partners for our dances or other social occasions. About half fail altogether and the others find British nurses and teachers. (A dowdy lot in the main, I regret to say!) I shall not forget for a long time the slightly triumphant look on Bob's face when he first introduced Jackie to Yvonne and me at a Mess dance. To say she was a sensation was putting it mildly. Certainly, the prettiest girl for miles around, she was accomplished and spoke perfect English. <u>And</u> he continued to squire her for the rest of his time here in a somewhat masterful way which warned off many a would-be intruder!! I'm afraid I didn't do as well at eighteen!!

Well enough. Suffice to say that I've enjoyed all the association with your talented and sensible son.

I know both Maurice Wood, his CO and John Greenwood, OC 26 Squadron. I've written to them both at length about Bob and they've replied promising to keep an eye on his career.

Please let us have your address as, indeed, we'd love to see you again and we well might try to get up so that I can show Yvonne something of Scotland.

My very best of good wishes in your new and exciting career. It sounds just too good to be true.

Yours sincerely

Roy Royle

Notes on the content of the above letter sent to the author by Bob Birrell:

1. The Jacquie that Lt Col Roy Royle RCT was referring to was a spectacularly beautiful German girl who was a teacher in the local primary school – she was Bob's constant girlfriend for about a year but when he was posted to Northern Ireland they inevitably drifted apart. That was at a time before Mobile Phones, Facebook and E-Mails existed.

2. Lt Col Maurice Wood RCT was Commander Transport at Headquarters Northern Ireland in Lisburn and Maj John Greenwood RCT was the OC of an independent 26 Sqn RCT when Bob was posted there.

3. Bob's father had just retired from the Army and had become Head of the Road Accident Research Unit, based in Scotland.

4. Bob's reaction on finding this letter amongst his dad's personal papers was one of astonishment. "I thought 'Bloody Hell', Roy Royle obviously did rate me as a young officer and clearly thought I was a good chap, but he wasn't going to tell me that though."

RCT Troop Commanders are only as good as their Senior and Junior NCO's (as well as their Drivers). Bob thought that he was very lucky to have two of the very best SNCO's in the Corps. His Troop Staffie was SSgt Alan Maskell and Sgt Eddie Donovan was his Troop Admin Sgt. They were both very experienced RCT SNCO's and for two years they expertly guided him through the awkward, and problematic early phases of his army career as a 2nd Lt. Bob states, "I learned an awful lot from them."

In the early months of 1968, Bob was posted from 8 Regt in Munster to 26 Sqn RCT in Lisburn, Northern Ireland. It was during that time that he was promoted to full Lieutenant which he sarcastically describes as, "The other pip came up with the rations I suppose." Bob had always been interested in racing cars, trucks, and engines; whilst in Northern Ireland he built and part-shared his first racing car and picked up the skills needed to drive a car at high speed. Bob states, "To be honest, those sorts of skills don't appear overnight you know. Amongst other things, you have to learn how to safely enter and exit the corners of a race track at the fastest possible speeds on the edge, and all the time trying to keep the car on the track without rolling or spinning the damned thing."

Bob's first experiences of novice racing was whilst driving his very own beaten up 1.0 Litre Austin Healey Sprite whilst on his Junior Officers Course at Buller Barracks in Aldershot. He drove to the track in the Austin Healey, raced in it, and then after the competition, in the very same knackered car, drove back to camp. "I picked up the skills needed as I went along. Experience helps out a lot, but in the end each driver must have a certain amount of natural talent to begin with I suppose."

Bob was sitting in the Ante-room of the Officers' Mess one weekend and was feeling particularly bored. He was reading a racing magazine when a notice caught his eye about a race event taking place down in Dover that weekend. Bob and the Austin

Healey immediately headed straight off to the small novice race meeting at Lydenn Hill near Dover. He explained, "In the end, I didn't do too well in the race but everyone has to start somewhere I suppose." Apparently, it was easier to race in those days because amateur race-drivers didn't need all of those expensive extras like, fire-proof suits, helmets, first aid equipment, fire extinguishers, trailers, or support vehicles and staff. Bob couldn't have afforded all of that kit anyway and ultimately he sold his beaten-up Austin-Healy for only £120.

In 1968 Bob was posted out to the Far East where he served in 3 Sqn RCT, which was part of 28th Commonwealth Infantry Brigade in Terendak Camp, Malacca in Malaysia. 3 Sqn RCT moved from Terendak Camp to Singapore, a couple of months after Bob had arrived in the Sqn. Whilst serving in the Far East, Bob persuaded a wealthy American (*who owned an air-conditioning firm*) to buy a brand-new Formula Ford racing car and also sponsor him every time he raced the car. The state -of-the -art racing car alone cost Bob's sponsor £1200, and in 1969 that was a lot of money; his sponsor also paid for everything else to do with Bob's racing commitments.

Bob's first three months of racing was a great success and in 12 weeks he'd already won back over half of the money that his sponsor had paid out. It was a great time for Bob because he was constantly indulging in the two great loves of his life, soldiering and racing motor cars. The British Army didn't give him any encouragement or financial help at all, and so when he became a more senior officer in the RCT, Bob gave as much help, reassurance, inspiration, and reinforcement to anyone he served with to do different things within the Corps. Bob had to take leave every time he attended a Race Meeting, and at times, as a consequence, it was a struggle to meet all of his military and racing commitments.

On return from the Far East, Bob was posted to 29 Regt RCT at South Cerney and whilst there, he travelled all over the world. One of his many trips with the Regiment involved Bob deploying out to Gambia in West Africa with the Overseas Deployment Squadron. The following story is famous with a lot of RCT officers and SNCO's who served in the Corps in the late 1960's, and right up to the early 1990's. The following account was compiled by Bob Birrell and Terry Cavender, who were both working at the Defence School of Transport (DST) Leconfield as Retired Officers (RO's) at the time. Bob was RO2 BAMA Secretary and Terry was SO2 Media Ops. The finished article was included in copies of the RLC Monthly Magazine, 'The Sustainer,' and the magazine editor paid out the princely sum of £150 for permission to publish the article.

'Crocodile Dunfermline'
(A.K.A. Lieutenant Colonel (Retd) Bob Birrell)

Visitors to the Officers' Mess Bar at South Cerney Army Base may well have heard of the atrocity committed by a madman who many years ago bred and released vicious crocodiles into the Ashton Keynes Water Park, thus introducing an extra element of surprise and danger. I have had the tale related to me at least twice. I was that madman, perhaps since the revelation won't now affect my chances of becoming a General, the time has come to reveal the real story.

It was all a very long time ago. I was the token Subaltern in the Overseas Deployment Squadron and spent most of my time in barracks, lobbying for detachments and exercises in remote places. I was pretty successful at it, there were a lot of the much despised 'married pads' whose wives would not allow them out to play (at least that was my take on the situation). Anyway, in due course I found myself on a Military Exercise in The Gambia, a country whose existence I'd not been hitherto aware. I won't bore you with the military aspects, but after play had ended we were all invited to the palatial residence of the local Billionaire (something to do with peanuts I was told). Of much greater significance was his extremely attractive daughter! We enjoyed the evening together and I vaguely remember her showing me their pond full of crocodiles. Not having total control of my senses by this time, (apparently) I'd made some vacuous remark about always having wanted to own a crocodile.

'Fast Forward' to the next morning, nursing a medium hangover when there was a knock on the hotel room door. It was a servant boy from the previous evening, carrying a large box. "Missy has sent you this," he said. Now, dear reader, there are no prizes for guessing the contents of the box, the problem was – what would I do with it? Not thinking sufficiently quickly, I had the lad tip the contents of the box into the hotel bathtub.

Fortuitously we were due to fly back to the UK the following day, I say 'fortuitously' because the hotel management failed to share my sense of fun and enthusiasm at my new adventure. I had, by that stage, warmed to the idea of owning a crocodile in Gloucestershire. Most of the boring Officers had equally boring Labrador dogs, that inevitably accompanied them to the office each day. "Now," I thought, "Could I train a crocodile to lie still under my desk?" I was getting ahead of myself. How was I going to get the croc back to RAF Lyneham? No problem, my trusty Sergeant had just the thing. His vital supplies of typewriters, paperwork, forms and a million and one other boring things were contained in a fibre-glass Thomas Bin. I won't bore you with the details of the negotiations, but after a fair amount of plying him with drink, a still reluctant Sergeant agreed to surrender his precious container in exchange for the sandbag I'd found as a replacement.

There was a minor hitch in that I had no idea how to introduce the croc into the Thomas Bin without my losing a few fingers. Fortunately, my lady-friend was able to send her man across to 'do the business.' I should add here that the croc, (by now named

'Abercrombie') was still very young and was only about two feet long. I had at that stage, still to learn how much more growing 'Abercrombie' had left to do.

To cut more drama from the tale, 'Abercrombie,' snug in his new fibre-glass accommodation, was duly loaded onto the allocated Hercules C130 Transport Aircraft. That in itself was not entirely uneventful. For some long-forgotten reason, I'd also acquired 5 African parakeets which were also loaded onto the 'Herc.' Sadly, my pride and joy in the form of an African Grey parrot, was apprehended by the RAF Hercules pilot, and after a fairly senior row, I had to concede and donated the bird to a rather startled taxi driver at the airport. In effect, the African Grey was 'grounded.'

I can't imagine that it was a regular occurrence to take 5 parakeets and a live crocodile through customs at RAF Lyneham, but we did all make it. The long-suffering Sergeant didn't though. He was made to empty his suspicious looking sandbag onto the inspection counter and had its contents minutely inspected. It was quite some time before he emerged and the atmosphere on the home run was, well – 'frosty' hardly begins to describe it!

Good old 'Abercrombie' lived quite happily (I think) in the Officers' Mess bath at South Cerney. Over the next few days, I made a point of trying to learn more about the care and maintenance of a 'croc'. My most urgent need was to find out just how much larger he would become. It was with mounting anxiety that I was told that he was, "probably a long-nosed African crocodile and that he should grow no longer than 12 feet!" I was also told that his water should be changed twice per day and be kept at a constant 60 degrees. I'm not sure exactly what the Zoo thought about my protestations about how difficult that would be with the bath.

'Abercrombie,' by this time, was getting a touch irritable (as were some of the Officers living in the Mess – deprived of the only bath with a shower-head)! Actually, the shower-head was an essential tool in the perilous act of water changing. The procedure was to aim the shower-head, set at the maximum temperature, directly at the croc, who would then scuttle to the other end of the bath. That gave me about 2 seconds to snatch the plug out and drain the water. Once empty, the procedure was repeated, this time replacing the plug. All of that called for lightning fast reactions and a superb hand/eye co-ordination. Naturally, 'Abercrombie' had all of those attributes and could certainly move quickly. There was also the continued problem of feeding 'Abercrombie.' The Zoo had told me that croc's liked well-rotted fish, up to a month old, so my stock with my fellow Officers' mess members was not improving.

All of this was further complicated by my impending deployment on the Adventure Training Camp taking place at Penhale in Cornwall. I had just 36 hours to locate a willing 'Croc Minder' which proved to be remarkably difficult. The RQM (Regimental Quartermaster), was particularly fond of scotch, so after a 'softening up' session in the bar and a gift of his favourite bottle, he somehow agreed to be the minder. He did seem to be a little less confident after I'd given him a demonstration of the water changing procedure. Notwithstanding, I set off to join the Regiment in Penhale.

I'd been in Penhale for about 24 hours when I was summoned by the Adjutant, a really great guy called Captain Charles A Colvin RCT (later Lt Col). Charles was concerned for the state of mind of the Quartermaster. He showed me a rather bizarre signal claiming that I was responsible for a rapidly growing crocodile which was threatening to outgrow its bath habitat. Clearly the old boy had suffered some sort of mental breakdown and Charles wanted to know how the Quartermaster was behaving when I'd last seen him.

I could only explain (as best I could) how I'd grown bored with the Field Officer's Labrador dogs and that as soon as 'Abercrombie' was trained he would make an interesting addition to Regimental life. The Adjutant was, as I said, a great chap who (much) later became a good friend – but on that occasion he failed to share my vision. Inevitably I found myself explaining everything to the aforementioned officer. Some 20 years later he told me that he'd had the utmost difficulty keeping a straight face during our rather one-sided dialogue. To cut a long story short, he gave me full marks for 'showing form' – and 3 days to get rid of 'Abercrombie' if I wished to continue in the Regiment.

I am assuming that you, gentle reader, have almost certainly not had to dispose of a crocodile in Gloucestershire. The local Cirencester pet shop was particularly unhelpful, claiming to deal in nothing more aggressive than rabbits. I considered using a thunder-flash grenade, but soon discarded that idea on the grounds of the cost of a new bath. I even tried the Citizens Advice Bureau in Swindon, who listened patiently to my tale – and then put the 'phone down on me.

After this passage of time, I can't remember how, after hundreds of 'phone calls, I found my saviour – a self-proclaimed 'Crocodologist' from Evesham. I explained to him that he would need to collect 'Abercrombie,' which included removing him from the bath. To my unbounded relief, he did appear and duly removed the croc and took him away to a better life, leaving us with the only problem – the purchase price for 'Abercrombie.' We started off haggling at £300, but (very quickly) agreed on £5, (actually I would have happily paid him)!

So that ends the real story of the South Cerney croc. The story of the parakeets and their diet of cheese & onion crisps in the Officers' Mess Bar is another tale for another day. So – 'On, On – Crocodile Dunfermline!'

In a parody of the phrase used in the song, 'Deck of Cards', the author would like to post the following words, "and friends, the story is true, he knows, for Bob was that soldier and officer."

Bob's thirst for soldiering hadn't been quenched by his time served at 29 Regt RCT, in fact, it had just whetted his appetite for a more active and dangerous lifestyle in uniform. The Aden Campaign had finished some years earlier and whilst at 26 Sqn RCT, he'd witnessed some of the early riots, shootings and violence in Northern Ireland. Bob had learned that the British Army was looking for volunteers to serve in a clandestine and dangerous area of operations. He applied for an interview with a 2 Star General (The General Officer Commanding (GOC) at Headquarters South West District - down at Wilton) to see if they thought he was made of the right stuff to take part in an unknown 'Shooting War' in the Middle East.

The General warned Bob that if he was put forward for the assignment, and he did deploy to where he was needed, "No matter how well you do out there Lt Birrell, you'll probably miss out on the chance to attend the Staff Course and you'll never go on to become a General." Bob was adamant though, "I think that is a plus for me General," he said, "because I definitely don't want to become a Staff Officer." The General wished Bob every success in whatever he undertook and told him, "I think you should leave my office then Lieutenant Birrell and go off on your adventure to Dhofar." The General had obviously reached the conclusion that Bob was made of the right stuff to take part in a war in the Middle East.

Bob was then posted over to Northern Ireland on attachment to the Duke of Edinburgh's Royal Regiment (DERR) for 6 months because he needed to up his Infantry skills before being sent anywhere else in the world. The Posting Order came to him through PB8 Posting's Branch who were orchestrating Bob's application to go to Oman/Dhofar. On arrival at Ballykinler, Bob assumed that because he was an RCT officer, the DERR's were more than likely to make him their Motor Transport Officer (MTO) during his attachment, but he couldn't have been further from the truth.

He was appointed as OC Recce Platoon (*Authors note: This is considered to be a plum job within all Infantry Regiments and Bob was somewhat surprised at the* appointment) and during his attachment he spent most of his time based and working out of the RUC Station at Newton Hamilton in South Armagh, "It wasn't a particularly nice or friendly place," Bob sardonically told the Author. "I was guided through this very sharp learning curve by a very confident and excellent Fijian Colour Sergeant, whose name I'm afraid escapes me now. We took out plenty of four-man patrols during which I learned how to navigate across country at night. I absorbed a lot military knowledge from the DERR's, particularly about how to operate furtively as an Infantryman." Unfortunately, Bob feels that for security reasons a lot of the operational activities that he undertook with the DERR Recce Platoon, should be left out of this book. However, his time spent with the DERR Recce Platoon was a full-on time and it was an essential training tool that really sharpened his Infantry skills in readiness for his time in the Dhofar war. After his attachment with the DERR's, who Bob describes as, "A bloody excellent Infantry Regiment," it was arranged for him to go on the next available Arab language Course at the Royal Army Education Corps Depot (RAEC) at Beaconsfield in West London.

Bob joined other students who, like him, were all looking for some kind of adventure not available to mainstream officers of the British Army at that time. They all did a 3-month Arab Language Course at the end of which, they had to be able to speak in fluent Arabic because where they were going on loan service, none of the soldiers they would be commanding could speak a word of English. The Curriculum was extremely testing and at the end of each day every student was given yet another

20 Arabic words written on pieces of white card to take away with them. The English equivalent words were written on the reverse side of each of the cards. Those 20 words would be the work regime for the following days' drudgery and they had to study them during their own leisure time, not that they got a lot of that. Sounds easy when you say it like that, but they were also working a 6-day week which meant that there would be about 120 Arabic words to learn every week. The students took the hand-written cards down to the local pub and practiced their homework over a few pints of beer. They would show a written Arab word to someone who then had to pronounce it correctly and state the English translation.

Captain Bob Birrell RCT, a Company Commander in the Desert Regt in Dhofar. This photograph was taken shortly after a failed Adoo attack using an 82 mm mortar.

After successfully graduating from the Arab language course at Beaconsfield, Bob eventually checked in at Heathrow airport and caught a flight out to Muscat in Oman. When he arrived there, Bob stepped out of the aircraft and felt like he'd just opened the door to a blast furnace, the heat outside the aircraft being very dry, intense and oppressive. He was greeted at 'Arrivals' by another British Army loan officer who took him to Brigade HQ, where the Brigadier briefed Bob on what he would be doing next. "Right, you are going to be in the Desert Regiment which is based down near the Dhofar/Yemen border. You'll spend one day here getting kitted out and at first light tomorrow, you'll be flown 600 miles down to Dhofar. At some stage or other you'll transfer into a Shorts Skyvan aircraft at Salalah airfield before being flown on to your location at Capstan Fire Support Base in an Augusta Bell 205 helicopter. There is a high probability that you will be under fire when you arrive at your location at Sarfait. Any questions? No, right, let's crack on then!"

Bob Birrell pointed out to the author during his interviews for this book, that between the years of 1963 and 1976, the British Army surreptitiously provided trained British Army officers to the Sultan of Oman to help quell the Omani Civil war. The 'Dhofar Rebellion' was eventually quashed by a combination of Omani, Iranian, Saudi Arabian, Jordanian, Pakistani, UAE, Egyptian, and British officers and soldiers. The majority of those forces were led by Officers from all branches of the British Armed Forces, but in particular Royal Marine and trained British Infantry officer's. Any necessary air cover was provided by Omani Strikemaster jets.

Captain Errol Harries RCT and Bob Birrell were the only two RCT officers to actually command Infantry Company's during the shooting war in Dhofar. When Errol had completed his contract with the Sultan of Oman, he returned to the British Army and took command of 1 Sqn RCT, based in Colchester, Essex. Within a couple of years though, Errol left the British Army after signing yet another contract with the Sultan of Oman and continued fighting in the Dhofar War for a number of years. After commanding 1 Sqn RCT, the British Army wanted him to attend

Captain Bob Birrell trying out one of the Sultan of Oman's Saladins for size.

Staff College so he could progress further up the rank structure, but after fighting in a proper shooting war, the logical assumption is that everything must have paled by comparison for Major Errol Harries RCT. *(Authors note: Let's face it, nothing can possibly compare to the adrenaline rush of having enemy soldiers trying to kill you day after day)*. Bob describes Errol as being, "a lovely chap who unfortunately died a couple of years ago, on the 30th of August 2016".

Bob's location (see the map overleaf) during the Dhofar Rebellion was on the border with Yemen which was a few hundred miles north of where the Aden Campaign was lost by the British. *(Authors note: To be fair, the British Army were fighting against a Yemen terrorist organisation that was being supported by both Communist China and the Soviet Union)*. The British-led Company sized outposts were all that stood between the attacking communist organisations in Yemen and the rich oilfields in Oman. If the oilfields fell into Soviet hands, then certainly other Organisation of the Petroleum Exporting Countries (OPEC) would surely fall the same way. It was an extension of President Eisenhower's Communist Domino Effect.

Until the British quietly gave a helping a hand, the Sultans' Forces were poorly equipped with World War Two small-arms and its soldiers didn't have many professional military leaders. The Sultan of Oman, who had himself been trained at RMA Sandhurst, desperately needed help to defeat an organised fight against a powerful, and communist backed regime. Bob and the other outposts were less than 500 miles away from Aden, which fell under the Communist/Terrorist pressure in 1964. The Sultan's hired officers and men were fighting against an enemy force that were simply referred to as the Adoo, an Arabic word meaning enemy or foe. The Adoo were trying to force the Sultan's Army back so they could have control of the **Hormuz Straight**. Fourteen oil tankers (which is an estimated 17 million barrels of crude oil), pass through the Strait of Hormuz every single day (which represents 35% 0f the world's oil shipments) through a gap which is less than 30 miles wide. This makes the Strait of Hormuz a very strategic location in relation to the world's seaborne oil shipments.

One hour after arriving at Salalah airfield, Bob was jumping off a helicopter at his new location in Sarfait and trying to avoid getting killed by incoming mortar rounds. Bob's initial thought was, "Bloody hell! Someone's trying to kill me!" He met his Company Commander who was standing in for the guy Bob was replacing. Bob was to be the Company 2i/c until his Company Commander finished his tour, after which Bob would assume Command and Control of the entire Company himself. Bob would be entirely isolated at Sarfait, the nearest 'friendlies' being some 3-5 Kms away. The journey was only a few minutes flying time by helicopter from Sarfait, but choppers were a very expensive, rare, and precious commodity. Helicopters were only to be used when no other option was available, and even then, only for such items as ammunition and water re-supply missions or emergency casualty evacuation (CASEVAC). *Authors Note: For further reading on this subject read* **In the Service of the Sultan**: *A first Hand Account of the Dhofar Insurgency by Ian Gardiner. Pen and Sword Books Ltd 2006.*

Bob's Sub-divisions at Sarfait consisted of two platoons of Infantry (*approximately 120 Arab soldiers*) and a Section of Mortar Men, spread out over an area the size of several football pitches and located on the top of a jebel (*A Middle Eastern mountain or hill*). Bob explained that, "The only other British voices I heard from when I arrived at Sarfait, until I left two years later, were those of British Officers using the Brigade Network. I loved every minute of my time out there because I was in action every day and doing what soldiers should be doing. We were fighting and helping the Sultan to win a war." Two days after arriving in Dhofar, Bob had a wake-up call into the realities of his new surroundings. Major Johnny Braddel-Smith, a British loan officer from the Royal Marine Commandos who was commanding a Company in the Northern Frontier Regiment, was killed in action that day. It brought it home to Bob that this was a proper war in which even British trained elite forces were being killed.

For the next 6 months, Lt Bob Birrell RCT lived in a small but solidly built rock shelter that any self-respecting British tramp wouldn't want to be seen dead in. There were defensive sangars built on the Sarfait position, made out of oak timbers, corrugated iron sheets, and topped off with plenty of large rock boulders. Bob's sangar received a direct hit from an enemy mortar shell one day and he was concussed, the explosion had the same effect on him as being hit on the nose from a decent right cross punch. The Sangers were spread over a square acre and Bob's was right at the front so that he could observe the Dhofar/Yemen Border.

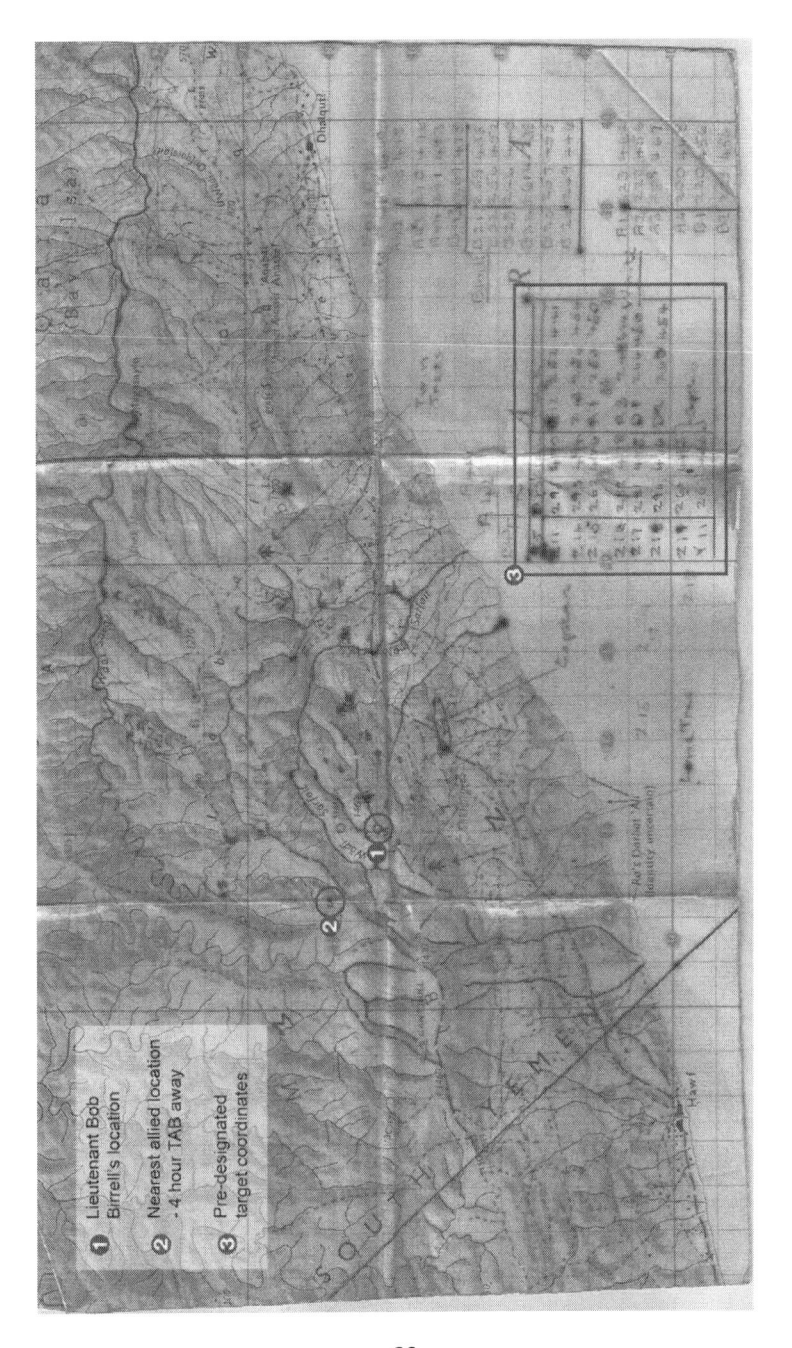

① Lieutenant Bob Birrell's location
② Nearest allied location - 4 hour TAB away
③ Pre-designated target coordinates

Every day the Adoo either shot or mortared his position in the hope of killing him and his soldiers. In retaliation, Bob gave fire-missions to his own mortars and directed the Sultans Strikemaster jets onto targets for rocket and bombing missions to break up the enemy attacks on his own location.

Bob's location was attacked by the Adoo virtually every day, using a mixture of weapons:

1. The 122mm Katyusha (*Russian for 'Little Kate'*), Multiple Rocket Launchers that were used against the attacking German Forces during their OPERATION BARBAROSSA campaign in WWII. The Soviet Union were supplying the Russian designed and produced *(from the late 1930's onwards)*, wholly inaccurate mobile missile launchers, to the Yemen Forces for use against the Sultans Armed Forces, (Captain Bob Birrell RCT being just one of them). During WWII the German army hated these weapons because of the widespread damage they caused, and the unmistakable howling sound when launched. The Germans called them 'Stalin's Organs.' (*Check it out on You Tube*).

2. The DShK 12.7 X 108mm HMG (Heavy Machine-Gun), had a maximum firing range of 2500 metres and could pump out its ammunition at 600 Rounds Per Minute (RPM). (*Again, Check it out on You Tube*).

3. The 82mm Russian made Mortars. Incidentally, the British Mortar uses 81mm ammunition which meant that the Yemen Forces could use our captured rounds in their mortars because of the 1mm extra circumference gap, but we couldn't use their captured mortar rounds in ours, because they simply wouldn't fit into the tubes. Not that we would have used any captured weaponry anyway simply because they would more than likely have been booby-trapped. During another incident, Bob went out and surveyed the

Sarfait location after it had been mortared yet again, to make sure there weren't any unexploded and dangerous ordnance left lying on the ground and found the fin of an exploded British 81mm Mortar Round. Bob states, "That was clear evidence that our enemies were using imported ammunition from Aden that had been left behind by the British when they left there in 1967."

When not defending his own location; Bob spent the rest of his time inspecting and organising the locations defences, requesting resupply and CASEVAC missions, commanding and controlling Infantry patrols, setting up and commanding night-ambushes. Bob had to arm Claymore Mines for the ambushes himself, the Dhofar soldiers were so uneducated, they'd probably have aimed them towards their own positions rather than set them against the enemy. Bob had to oversee even the basic duties because nothing could be left to the soldiers in his location, "In a British Infantry Company a Platoon Commander could rely on a Sgt to call in a fire mission or to command a mortar crew and give its crew a set of fire-control orders, but the men we had with us couldn't even read, write or count in their own language. The majority of them had never been to any type of school."

Life in the field during the Dhofar War was incredibly busy, harsh, and stressful if you compared it to a Platoon Commanders job in an average British Army unit. Whilst commanding his location at Sarfait, Bob had to be a master of all military trades:

1. Mortar Fire Controller.
2. Artillery Fire Controller.
3. Forward Air Controller (FAC) for the Strikemaster jets.
4. Quartermaster.
5. Tactical disposition of his soldiers and weapons where they were needed most.

Bob was assigned his own orderly who brought him a cup of tea every morning in his Sangar. Bob spent a lot of his conscious hours in his Sangar being shot at whilst listening in on the Brigade Network for any information about possible surprise attacks on his own location. When he wasn't out patrolling, recceing, or setting up ambushes against the enemy, he and his own troops all survived on Omani Rations, usually consisting of tinned Lamb or Goat meat. On the rare occasions that they did receive fresh rations, it wasn't a particularly pleasant experience for Bob. If the pressure on his location was somewhat decreased because enemy action was reduced, then locations were sent live goats or lambs by helicopter so that they could be slaughtered by having their throats cut whilst facing Mecca. Bob said, "It was a horrible experience watching those poor creatures slowly die as the blood drained from their bodies." He added, "The meat also produced a very chewy curry."

Having said all of that, Bob overwhelmingly enjoyed most of his Dhofar War experiences, so much so, that he stayed on for another contract, eventually completing 2 years in Dhofar. In 1975 the BBC Foreign News Reporter, Jon Snow, was sent to Bob's location to do a televised news report on the war in Oman. Sarfait was reputedly under attack every single day of the year and it was thought that he could get some great action film footage. Unfortunately, the day that Jon Snow and his BBC camera crew turned up, nothing happened for the first time in over 2 years. Captain Bob Birrell RCT came to the rescue for the BBC, even though Jon Snow and his film crew hadn't a clue what was going on around them, Bob started giving his mortar crews some fire orders to beat back an attack, an attack that wasn't actually happening. Jon Snow gave a very melodramatic piece to camera whilst Sarfait wasn't actually being attacked and Bob's outgoing mortars exploded on a nearby ridgeline. The news report caused more of a fuss at the Foreign Office in London because the British military involvement in the Dhofar War was supposed to be kept hidden under wraps.

The Sultan of Oman presented £250 to each of the loan soldiers serving in his Army. The money could be used to buy an air-ticket back to the UK so that they could take some well-deserved leave. Bob put the money towards buying a Honda 400cc motorbike whilst he was on leave in the UK, he thought that might be a lot more fun. Whilst he was drinking in a pub in Chelsea, a 'friend' said if Bob took the bike down to Hurn Airport in Bournemouth, he'd get it flown out to Oman for him. It was all arranged on little notes and, "I'm sure we can," and "If you can," promises, and the ever reliable, "Can't see why not," assurances. Believe it or not, reader, the motorbike turned up at Salalah Airfield a couple of days before Bob was due to leave Dhofar. Bob's insane plan was to ride his new motorbike up into Turkey, through Greece, Italy, Switzerland, Germany and on into the UK. He explained, "I obviously wouldn't attempt anything like that today, but back then I was young and stupid. I'd also had people trying to kill me during the previous 2 years and so I had a sense of proportion about the trip."

Captain Bob Birrell RCT loaded his motorbike onto an Iranian Air Force C 130 Hercules aircraft In Dhofar, and they both flew off to Tehran military Airport. The Iranian Air Force personnel at Salalah assured Bob that they would inform their counterparts in Tehran that he was travelling on one of their aircraft with a motorbike, but unhappily for Bob, they didn't. Captain Bob Birrell RCT was placed under arrest when he landed in Tehran Military Airport and was locked up in the Guardroom because no-one knew who he was, or why he had 'stowed away' on one of their military aircraft. Bob smooth-talked his way out of jail and went around to the civilian side of the airport in the hope of getting onto a civilian flight, going anywhere out of Iran. Regrettably, as he didn't have an entry visa for the country he had recently, and illegally invaded, he was now right up shit-creek and didn't have a paddle to help him get out again.

What he did have though, was a 400cc Honda motorbike. After distracting his military escort, he got on the motorbike and hightailed it straight out of Tehran. After 2 days hard riding Bob eventually arrived at an Iran/Turkey border crossing point which was completely backed up with traffic. He rode the bike to the front of the queue where a military guard pointed his loaded SMG at Bob's chest and ordered him to, "Go no further!" A quickwitted Bob pointed to an Iranian officer who was standing 30 feet away but still on the Iranian side of the border crossing, "He told me I could go through." The guard ordered Bob to remain where he was whilst he went and had a word with his boss. As the guard was speaking to his officer and had his back towards Bob, Bob reacted instinctively, "I buggered off into Turkey and didn't stop until I was at least 100 miles over the other side of the border."

Bob had been working with a Brigade of Iranian soldiers when he was in Dhofar and he knew how piss-poor their shooting skills were, so he wasn't worried because had they shot at him, "It would have been sheer luck if they'd hit me with any rounds as I roared over the border crossing point, but had I had given myself up to the soldiers at the customs post, I'd probably have still been stuck out there today."

Travelling through East Turkey was pretty wild according to Bob, "The kids would often throw stones at me to try and knock me off the bike. It wasn't until I armed myself with a big stick which I used as a lance, and charged towards them, that they started giving me a bit more respect. Once I'd got past Ankara everything started to get a bit more civilised. After I'd passed Istanbul and got over the Bosphorus Mountains, it was all plain sailing after that." Bob made it a rule never to pass a petrol station without filling up his petrol tank. He didn't know how far a full tank of petrol would actually take him. At one particular petrol station the electricity was out and so he waited for 24 hours until the power was restored before filling up again and resuming his journey. Bob didn't have a GPS system in those days, but his natural guidance system got him back to the same pub where he'd bought the motorbike whilst back in the UK on leave. He stayed at his club in London before travelling up to Scotland to visit his parents for a week. It had taken him a month to travel all the way back to the UK from Iran and he took 2 months leave after getting back on home ground.

Before he came back into the warm embrace of the RCT system, Bob received a letter from the OC of 60 Sqn RCT in Catterick whilst he was still out in Dhofar. It was some time before his Contract had finished with the Sultan of Oman and someone had popped the envelope into the Army mail system, unbelievably, the communique had made its way out to Bob in Oman. The letter was from his new OC at 60 Sqn RCT which was based in Catterick Garrison, Yorkshire. The OC told Bob that he needed him for an important Exercise in BAOR and politely asked him, "Would you mind awfully, cancelling your end of Contract leave and come to Germany with the Sqn for this rather important military Exercise?" Bob wrote a short letter to his new OC that put him unequivocally in the picture, "Sir, I do realise you have an 'important' Exercise in BAOR coming up at about the same time I should be joining 60 Sqn RCT, but I am currently under fire from some enemy soldiers who want to kill me. PS: No, I won't be cancelling my leave." It was Bob's polite way of saying, "No, you can piss off!"

When Bob eventually arrived in Catterick Garrison, 60 Sqn RCT was being commanded by a different OC who was, "A bloody good bloke actually." The Major offered Bob the chance to return to Dhofar and re-take command of his own Company there. Bob told the OC that being offered the chance of becoming 2I/C of a peace-time Sqn wasn't exactly tempting. The OC then pulled out the big guns after inviting Bob round to his Married Quarter for dinner, "Ok Bob, what if I offered you the chance to help me run the Sqn as my 2I/C and let's see how we get on, shall we?" The two of them then proceeded to get pissed together and never looked back. Bob told the author, "I definitely made the right decision in staying with the RCT. In 60 Sqn I was responsible for planning all of the Sqn's training and running the Exercises. I have to say that the guys in 60 Sqn were really good soldiers. We did a six-month tour of Belfast in 1977 and two emergency tours covering the tanker driver's strike in 1978."

After leaving 60 Sqn, Bob then took a Grade 3 Staff job at the Ministry of Defence (MOD) in London where he was a Project Officer making films for Officer Recruiting. "It was really good fun and got me out of the office which was the main thing for me. I do remember one particular recruiting film was centred around the Women's Royal Army Corps (WRAC) training college at Camberley in Surrey. Three months after the film was released the MOD shut the college down and all of the potential WRAC officers started going to Sandhurst instead, which resulted in the film becoming utterly useless". The senior officer who was the Director of the WRAC had an input into what was to be included in the film, and those working on the film eventually came up with what they called a 'Treatment', which were suggested seams that made up the entire film.

Bob was involved in hooking up with certain events and Exercises that were going to happen anyway and got the bits and pieces they needed for a film. For instance, if some film footage of tanks were needed, he would hook up with an Armoured Exercise that was going to happen in BAOR and get the shots that were required. Likewise, he might go down to Larkhill for any Royal Artillery shots (*Authors note - pardon the pun*) that were needed. At one stage every arm of the Army sent one of their officers to be filmed doing their job, so that if any particular Corps or Regiment needed a film making, the MOD would have some background shots to put into the film. It usually took 2-3 days of filming to complete each Regiment's sequence.

Taking command of a Sqn or Company of men is a great leap that every officer aspires to achieve, and Bob felt that way when, in the early 1980's, he attained the position of OC 8 Sqn RCT, which was just a small part of 27 Regiment RCT in Aldershot. He already knew some of the men in his new Sqn, WO2 Ken Pemberthy RCT was to be his Squadron Sergeant Major (SSM) and right-hand man. The two of them had already played rugby together for many years in the RCT. SSgt Steve Bentley RCT (later WO 2) was to be his Chief Clerk (CC) who would run the Squadron Orderly Room, Bob describes Steve as being a very intelligent man. Within a short time of taking over the Sqn, Bob had to take the unit over to Nicosia in Cyprus on a United Nations (UN) tour. "Some of the earlier tours entangled a lot of units into a lot of shot and shell in Cyprus, there was none of that when 8 Sqn deployed though. We had a great tour."

After the UN tour was completed, Bob returned to Aldershot with 8 Sqn and to his surprise, he was summoned to the Regiment's Commanding Officer and immediately committed to a Field Exercise in Wales. The men were somewhat disgruntled, they hadn't seen their families for 6 months and now they were going off to Wales on a Field Exercise. To placate his men, Bob promised them a guaranteed two weeks block-leave when Endex was called after the Welsh Exercise. As is the life of a soldier at times, things never quite turn out the way you expect them to, and in 1982 the Argentinian Forces invaded the Falkland Islands before the lads of 8 Sqn could begin their two weeks block leave. 8 Sqn RCT was heavily involved in the UK's massive ammunition outload in preparation for the Falklands War.

Two of the biggest jobs the Sqn had to deal with were the collection of virtually all the ammunition from Central Ammunition Depot (CAD) Longtown in Cumbria, and CAD Kineton near Birmingham. After loading up their Foden Flat-Bed Trucks with live-ammunition, the 8 Sqn Drivers had to drive to Portsmouth or Marchwood Ports where their cargo would be transferred onto the relevant ships that would then convey the bullets and bombs down to the South Atlantic. For several weeks, Bob and his subordinate officers directed 8 Sqn's Drivers and NCO's on the massive operational out-load. "We sent the lads off to various depots to fill up with ammunition. They then took the loads all the way down to Portsmouth or some other UK port to unload, and then returned to Aldershot for 8 hours sleep and we plugged in another 2 RCT Drivers who then did another loop of the circuit. We carried on like that for several weeks until the ships were loaded with everything that both 3 Commando, and 5 Infantry Brigade needed to oust the Argentine Forces from the Falkland Islands. Everyone involved worked incredibly hard on the outload and it was an extremely rewarding time."

During his time Commanding 8 Sqn RCT, Bob took them over to Denmark on Exercise Amber Express and over to BAOR on many ACE Mobile Force (Logistics) (AMF (L)) Field Exercises, which was just as well really because of the poor state of the barracks that 8 Sqn soldiers had to live in, in their Aldershot Barracks. The flat roofed buildings had mould on most walls and no matter how much Bob complained about it, nothing was ever done. It was a big bone of contention for Bob, but not even the Brigadier could get anything done about the problem. Bob was due to be posted but was given a six-month extension in 8 Sqn RCT. He told his full Colonel Commander that he could leave him at the helm of 8 Sqn for ever as far as he was concerned.

In the intervening years Bob was posted to 2 Group RCT which was based in Dusseldorf, West Germany where he became involved in the preparation and planning of all the Reservist units deploying out to BAOR in the event of the Soviet Union attacking NATO. He also got married to Eileen during this period of time before being posted to Chertsey as a Military Vehicle Expert. "It was a Grade 3 Staff Officer Trials job at the Royal Armoured Research and Development Establishment (RARDE) at Chertsey.

"I loved that job because it wasn't just about shuffling bits of paper around my desk."

For two years Bob was involved in dealing with the administration of the new vehicles that were coming into use in the British Army, like the Challenger 2 Main Battle Tank which was doing a 24-hour test run on the 28th of January 1986. Bob had just got home from work when his wife Eileen told him the news that a Challenger had exploded, killing all seven crew that were on board at the time. Bob's initial thought was, 'Seven killed. There are only four crew members on a British Challenger Main Battle Tank, the Commander, Gunner, Loader/Operator and the Driver. What the heck were the other three soldiers doing in the tank?' He picked up his car keys and headed towards the front door because 'It' was obviously going to hit the fan and he'd need to be in work. It was a major incident and he'd have to be there to help make sense of what had caused the explosion and what had caused seven of his trials team to be killed. As he was passing the lounge door, he looked at the TV screen and saw the news flash about the Space Shuttle Challenger disaster!

Bob's next posting was as the Training Major at 151 Regiment (Volunteers) RCT in Croydon, "I've never worked as hard in my life" said Bob, "At 151 Regt RCT I was working 7 days a week. I had to do all the planning for each Exercise and then I'd have to oversee the Exercise and training through each weekend. I was told before I went to Croydon that I'd have to raise my game when working with Territorial Army (TA) soldiers because they'd expect a lot of you as a Regular Army officer." He was also advised that he would have to be right in everything he said and did, because Territorials expect you to live up to their expectations. Planning the unit's Annual Camp in BAOR was an extremely busy time for Bob, "What the TA lacked in experience they more than make up for with enthusiasm. They were very good at doing something that they knew how to do, like unloading a railhead. They're were not quite as well trained as

Regular soldiers but nonetheless, the soldiers at 151 Regiment RCT were impressive guys when you consider that they had their own civilian careers and lives to contend with as well".

Bob's next posting involved him working a lot with Service-personnel of the RAF. He took over as the 2IC of the Joint Services Air Trooping Centre (JSATC) at Leyton Buzzard. It was there that Bob was involved in the planning for the casualty evacuation (CASEVAC) programme for the First Gulf War. "The plans catered for a much higher casualty rate than we actually suffered, thankfully. I spent a week flying around the UK in a helicopter visiting virtually every airport in the country. I had to recce for the in-load of possible casualties and liaise with the local Area Health Authorities and Police Forces about what was likely to happen when the war eventually started. Bob was also involved in making the arrangements for the reception of British Families at Gatwick Airport, these expatriates had been captured by the Iraq army when they'd invaded Kuwait and Saddam Hussein had used them as human shields. The British Foreign Office eventually persuaded the Iraqi Government to release them and they were all air-lifted out of the area and returned back to the UK.

Bob made great friends with Lieutenant Colonel Ritson Harrison RCT who was the Commanding Officer of 29 Regiment RCT when he was posted back into his old unit as the 2I/C. Bob arrived as a Major but was eventually promoted to the rank of Lieutenant Colonel for the job at South Cerney, Lieutenant Colonel Ritson Harrison and Bob became very close friends during his posting to 29 Regt RCT and remain so today. The late Major John Gray RCT, who was an ex- tank Transporter operative, was also in the unit and they also became great friends during his time at 29 Regt, John sadly died in 2017 and Bob went to his friends' funeral at Tidworth Military Cemetery to pay his deepest respects to him.

In just under 12 months the MOD was looking to post Bob yet again and he was ultimately sent as Commander SO1 Transport and Movement Officer North East District at Imphal Barracks in York, where he remained in that post for the next five years. The MOD eventually raised its ugly head yet again and gave Bob a couple of options for another posting. His options were (Option 1) a post at MOD London or (Option 2) to sit behind a slightly different desk at Logistic Executive (Army) (LEA) which was located in Andover, Hampshire. Given these two rather unappetising choices, Bob decided to take his own third option and applied for a Retired Officer (RO) post at the Defence School of Transport (DST) in Leconfield. He was awarded the position and became the Secretary of the British Army Motoring Association/Army Motorcycling Association (BAMA/AMCA) for the next 15 years. Most of his time was spent out of the office arranging Land Rover and Motorbike cross country navigation competitions for the army. He travelled to different Training Areas to recce the land, meet the people involved and book a suitable time-frame for each competition. He then had to arrange for the admin people to run the show and convince unit Commanding Officers to let their soldiers participate.

During his time at Leconfield, Bob utilised his experience working on Officer Recruiting Films and made a film called 'Drive To Win.' The film laid out exactly what BAMA was offering RCT units in terms of training experience for their soldiers. When Bob showed the film to DST's Commandant, the Brigadier saw Bob sitting astride an army motorbike, outside DST Headquarters, explaining what BAMA could offer army units and their soldiers in terms of training value. When he'd finished his spiel, the camera cut to Bob doing an impressive wheelie on the motorbike up the road towards Hangar 1. The Commandant was heard to exclaim, "Good grief, Bob, I didn't know that you could do that sort of thing!" Bob had to inform the Brigadier that the camera crew had cut the filming and allowed SSgt Hodgkins RCT to get on the bike and do the wheelie.

Someone ultimately decided that Bob Birrell and the BAMA services were no longer required. It was believed that if a soldier had done any sort of navigation and cross-country driving then there was no point in repeating the training. At a meeting Bob gave his opinion of the officers' reasoning, "That is the biggest load of nonsense I've ever heard in my life," scowled Bob, he continued, "Have you ever heard of the expression Skill Fade?" He went on to give the following analogy that was simple enough for anyone to understand, "If an Infantryman is told to go on the ranges and fire 10 rounds at a Figure 11 target in the prone position, he might as well go and hand his rifle into the armoury and leave it there until war is declared. Let's face it, he knows how to load and fire the weapon and surely that is enough?" It made no difference though because Bob retired from his RO job 3 months later and during that time he worked closely with Terry Cavender, of whom Bob says "He made life very easy for me during those last few difficult months at Leconfield. I owe Terry Cavender an awful lot for everything he's done for me, more than the reader of this book will ever know. He covered my tracks beautifully whilst I was working at DST, Terry is a top man."

Bob continues to compete in his latest racing car around mainly European race-tracks, in fact, when the author tried to arrange another interview with him, Bob contacted him from Riga in Latvia and texted him on his mobile phone, stating, "Sorry Brian, but I'm doing some racing in Riga at the moment and I won't be driving back to the UK for a couple of days yet. Can I contact you next week when I get home? Kindest regard's, Bob."

Authors note: I now have to remind you dear reader that Bob Birrell was born in 1946 and is now 72 years old. He drove himself and his racing car, in a large van out to a racing tournament which was spread out over Belgium, Lithuania, Riga (Latvia), and Karlskoga in Sweden over a period of four weeks. He then drove himself and his racing-car back to Yorkshire in his van. Kind of makes me ashamed of myself when I whinge to my wife about being too old to go out for a 3-mile run these days.

Lt Col (Retd) Bob Birrell - Motorsport Experience

1968 - 69	**1 Litre F4 in Ireland**
	Self-constructed and driven car – 1 win
1970 - 71	**Driving fully sponsored FF1600 in Singapore/Malaysia Clubmans & International Grand Prix achieving:**
	6th place at Singapore Grand Prix 1971
	3rd place in Malaysian Grand Prix 1971
	5th place Penang Grand Prix 1971
1972- 74	**Driving self-prepared FF1600 in UK races**
1976 - 81	**Formula Super Vee**
	Driving in International Championships, UK & Europe
	Later as works Shannon driver
1982 - 83	**Driving F3 in UK, German, French & Italian Championships**
1984 - to date	**Historics - racing in UK, Europe, Macau, New Zealand, Australia in following cars:**
	Jaguar XK120, MGB, Lotus Elan, Brabham BT21B, Brabham BT6, Chevron B28 F5000, Elva BMW 7S, Lola Mk 2 & Lotus 20
1989 - to date	**Board Member of Historic Sports Car Club**
1997 - 2011	**CEO British Army Motoring Association (BAMA)**
	Running 18 events each year, as well as 20 Off Road Motorcycle Events – Trials & Enduro
1998 - 2007	**Member MSA Race Committee**
1998 - 2007	**Member MSA Historic Committee**
2003 - 2007	**Chairman MSA Historic Race Committee**
1996 - 2010	**Trackday Instructor Ferrari Owners Club**
2002 - to date	**ARDS Instructor rising to A Grade**
	Working mainly at Croft and Elvington
2014 - to date	**Trackday Instructor for Mission Motorsport**

Bob Birrell has raced around 97 different race-tracks around the world, which could possibly be a record for an amateur racing driver. He has also competed against some of the F1 greats like Ayrton Senna and Emerson Fittipaldi.

Bob Birrell's RCT racing car.

24212830 Corporal Richard Makinson
RCT 1970 – 1982

Lance Corporal Richard Makinson on a Range day near Oerlinghausen with 9 Sqn RCT.

The reasons why young men join and leave the British Army are numerous and varied. In Richard Makinson's case, the events were both tragic and sad, but ultimately, they were episodes in his life that he had no control over.

Richard was born in Camberley near Aldershot, Hampshire only nine months after his dad Louis, had returned from the Second World War. Sergeant Louis Makinson joined up in September of 1939 at the outbreak of WW2 and he continued serving with the Royal Corps of Signals until being discharged in 1957. He wasn't the first Makinson to join the armed forces either; during the First World War, Louis' father had served in the RAMC (Royal Army Medical Corps) as a Medic. But like most Servicemen returning from any war, Sgt Louis Makinson and his Medic dad rarely talked about what they had seen and done. Richard knew that his dad had served in Arnhem during WWII, but Louis never went into the details of what he'd seen and experienced.

The Makinson family all originated from County Durham. In August 1921 Richard's dad was born into the mining dynasty, but he and his brothers all wanted to get out of the mines and do something different with their lives, even if that meant joining up and going to war. One of Louis' brothers joined the Royal Navy in 1936 and another emigrated to Australia and never returned. Richard now has four generations of cousins living in Australia. Louis and his brothers all lived at home with their parents in a coalminer's terraced house in County Durham. These small cramped houses were in numbered streets that didn't have names. From the pit-head, each street was numbered upwards, the Makinson's living in house number 6 in street number 11. Up to the age of five, Richard had lived with his Grandfather in County Durham whilst Louis was serving out in Malaya. One day his mum, Mary, simply collected him and took him back down to Camberley so that they could all live like a proper family. Like most Service children, Richard wasn't in Aldershot Garrison for very long before his dad Louis received yet another posting. This time he was posted to the School of Signals which was based in Catterick Garrison at that time.

In 1954, Sgt Louis Makinson and his family were again posted, this time they all went from Catterick Garrison to Essen in West Germany where he was attached to 5 AGRA (Army Group Royal Artillery). Over the next three years, Richard and his siblings moved from Essen to Lüneburg and finally on to Oldenburg in Lower Saxony. It was on Lüneburg Heath that Field Marshal Bernard Montgomery officially accepted the surrender of Germany's Armed Forces on the 4th of May 1945. In his own indomitable way, 'Monty' told the Germans:

"You must understand three things; firstly, you must surrender to me unconditionally all the German forces in Holland, Friesen and the Frisian Islands and Heligoland and all the other Islands in Schleswig-Holstein and in Denmark. Secondly, when you have done that, I am prepared to discuss with you the implications of your surrender: how we will dispose of those surrendered troops, how we will occupy the surrendered territory, how we will deal with the civilians, and so forth. And my third point: if you do not agree to point 1, the surrender, then I will go on with the war and I will be delighted to do so. All your soldiers and civilians may be killed." After a brief discussion, the Senior German Officers rather sensibly and rapidly signed the Allied unconditional surrender document.

It was 9 years after WW2 had ended that Richard and his family moved into a married quarter, situated at the end of Tirpitz Strasse in Oldenburg. It was there that Richard witnessed just one result of FM (Field Marshal) Montgomery's declaration. At the end of the road where he lived the British Army had located a DP (Displaced Persons) Camp. There were DP Camps all over Germany, Austria and Italy that were full of refugees, former inmates released from Nazi Concentration Camps, POW's (Prisoners of War) and hordes of people who had fled from the advancing and rampaging Soviet Army. Richard often visited the DP Camp when he was out playing, "I felt sorry for these poor buggers because without a passport or some sort of official documentation, they couldn't prove where they had come from and therefore couldn't be sent home. So, some of them were still stuck in these camps ten years after the war had ended." Note: The very last DP Camp, located in Austria, was officially closed in 1959.

On arrival at his first posting, in Essen, Sgt Louis Makinson was allocated two top floor flats in a building that looked like an old German Army barrack block. They were allocated two flats because the Makinson family was so large. "Apart from me mam and dad, there was, David who were born in 1943, I came along in 1947, Louie were born in 1948, Patricia arrived in 1950, then Graham were born in 1952, Tony in 1953, and Rosie were born in 1955. Elizabeth were the youngest in our brood but she were born in Scarborough in 1958 after me dad had come out of the army." Richard remembers his dad being taciturn with everyone whilst he was growing up, but that didn't stop him from having a very happy childhood. Just outside their married quarter was a tram stop where Richard would catch a tram and head off into town with his German friends, "Me brother David used to say I could speak better German than I could English when I were growing up." *Authors note: Because you're from Yorkshire Richard, I can honestly believe that.*

In 1957, Sgt Makinson was one of 13,000 Signalmen who were discharged from Her Majesty's Armed Forces on Redundancy.

This was the lead up to National Service being scrapped and the British Army, Royal Navy and Royal Air Force began restructuring into the volunteer Fighting Force that it is today. Louis Makinson received a redundancy payment and pension on his discharge from the army and in 1958 he used the money to buy a Bed and Breakfast business near Scarborough in North Yorkshire. Unfortunately, in 1960 the bottom fell out of the UK holiday market and people took advantage of cheap air travel and flew to Spain instead. Sun, sea, sand and sangria were preferable to a cold choppy sea and soggy chips. After four years, Richard's dad sold the B & B business at a loss and started working as relief manager at a Scarborough brewery.

Richard failed his 11+ exams and was subsequently sent to St Peter's Catholic School, "I was quite good at maths but I always did all of the working out in my head, but for exam purposes you had to show the examiner how you arrived at the result. The lack of details on my exam papers caused me to be put in a special class for Dummies." His dad Louis successfully applied for Richard to be moved over to Graham Sea Training School, but after only 2 terms he was kicked out for fighting. Most of the students had been in the school from the age of five and had adapted to the learning structure, "They already knew how to tie knots and use Morse Code but because I were starting at the school aged eleven, I were already well behind the others and received the customary insults and aggravation that were dished out to a late-comer." The Graham Sea Training School was recognised as being a good faculty but the teachers were very physical and the teaching practices were of their time - "What do you mean you can't do it!" Clout! Having said that, Richard's younger brother loved it at the Sea Training School and he eventually graduated into the Merchant Navy. Richard returned to St Peter's Catholic

School and eventually left there at the age of 15, without a single diploma to his name.

After leaving school, Richard proved himself to be a real grafter. He worked as a Barrow Boy for Rington's Tea where he earned £5 a week, £4 of which went straight to his mum to cover his food and board. He also worked in Scarborough's Army Navy Store as a Shop Assistant, and for Scarborough Council as a Life Guard before working in the building industry. In those days, Richard also worked for a Steel Erecting firm where he mitred asbestos sheets without any safety or protective equipment. If you fell off the platform in those days you were simply called a dummy and you climbed back onto the scaffolding. It is supposed that the same ethos applied to working with hazardous materials like asbestos. Switching between the building trade and working as a farm labourer, Richard eventually learned to drive dumper trucks and tractors, without having to take any form of driving test. At the age of nineteen, Richard was earning good money and he had a healthy interest in birds, beer and disco's, but in 1967 he proposed and got married to his girlfriend Joan whom he'd known at St Peter's Catholic school.

To gain even better work and wages, Richard and his dad went on a Government Training scheme in County Durham where they learned how to be Capstan Lathe Setters. At the end of their Training Course they were guaranteed a well-paid job. After successfully passing the Course, both families moved up to Newton Aycliffe in Co Durham where Richard was contracted to work for Eaton Yale and Towne, paradoxically, this firm made engine and gearbox parts that were supplied to the MOD for Military Vehicles.

Joan and Richard had been married for 3 years by now and they already had two children, Richard and Rebecca. After making a doctor's appointment Joan was told she was expecting their third child. Christopher John Makinson was born in February but tragically he had two holes in his tiny heart that couldn't be repaired at that time. Today they would probably be able to operate on him, but this was back in 1970 and paediatric heart surgery was still in its infancy. Sadly, Christopher died on the 7th of August 1970, having lived for only 7 months. For much of his brief life, Christopher had to remain under the care of the local hospital. Richard found it difficult to cope with his sons' death, "I simply abandoned my missus and 2 kids and left them to look after themselves, even though we were both grieving for Christopher, I selfishly ran off and joined the British Army." Every year Joan and Richard still celebrate Christopher's birthday.

Hiding his heartache, Richard entered the ACIO (Army Careers Information Office) in Darlington and asked the Recruiting Sergeant if he could enlist as a Sapper in the RE (Royal Engineers). When told there weren't any vacancies in the RE's he was offered the chance of joining the Royal Corps of Transport (RCT) as a Driver. Richard shrugged his shoulders and unenthusiastically said, "Sounds alright." After telling Joan that he'd joined up, she didn't appear too displease, Richard explains, "We were on good wages at that time but what with losing Christopher, Joan and I felt a total change of environment might be a good thing for our family." In November 1970 Joan moved back in with her parents in Scarborough, whilst Richard travelled down to Buller Barracks in Aldershot by train to start his Basic Training.
Richard's time at Buller Barracks was just the thing he needed, "I quite liked being chased around at the time because I didn't have to think for myself, I just

> ARMY CAREERS OFFICER
> ARMY CAREERS INFORMATION OFFICE
> 148 Northgate, DARLINGTON
> Telephone: Darlington 4530
>
> Our reference:
> Your reference:
>
> 28th October 1970.
>
> Mr R.A. Makinson,
> 44 Ashfield,
> Newton Aycliffe,
> Co. Durham.
>
> Dear Mr Makinson,
>
> Reference your application to enlist into the Regular Army.
>
> I regret to inform you that there are no vacancies as a Marine Engineer in the Royal Corps of Transport, but they are prepared to offer you a vacancy as a Potential Driver in the R.C.T.
>
> If you are willing to accept this vacancy, would you please inform this office soonest.
>
> Yours faithfully,
>
> Joseph Sgt
> Army Careers Staff
> Darlington.

Richard Makinson's offer of a placement as a potential Driver in the Royal Corps of Transport, sent from Darlington ACIO (Army Careers Information Office) and dated 28th October 1970.

had to do as I was told."" Even doing Guard Duty at Christmas didn't faze him. As a child Richard used to bull his dad's boots for him when he was in the R Signals and so the bullshit of basic training and army life all seemed to fall into place. The final Driver Training phase also seemed a natural and easy progression for Richard and within a week he'd passed his HGV 3 test in a Bedford RL. All that tear-arsing around farms and building sites was obviously a good precursor for him. Because of a co-incidental death in the Makinson family during his Basic Training, no-one came to Richard's Passing Out Parade, but he was philosophical about it, "I were disappointed no-one could turn up, but let's face it, shit happens. I also can't remember doing any NBC (Nuclear Biological and Chemical) warfare training at Buller Barracks. Most of my NBC training were learned during my first posting, to 10 Regiment RCT." The Cold War and threat of a Chemical and Nuclear war was still very much in evidence during the 1970's.

A 'bundle' of Drivers accompanied Richard from Buller Barracks to 10 Regiment RCT in Bielefeld, West Germany. Drivers Glenn Maple and Bill Proctor were also posted into the same Troop as Richard. The three of them were sent to C Troop, 9 Squadron RCT, where they met their OC (Officer Commanding) Major Husthwaite and TC (Troop Commander) 2/Lt (Second Lieutenant) Dale Hemming-Tayler. Major Huthwaite gave Richard the impression of being, "More of an Office Wallah than an experienced Squadron Commander," and Richard also thought that 2/Lt Hemming-Tayler (known as H T to all his friends) was a typical over-enthusiastic subaltern, "He were very intelligent but unfortunately wanted to be included on everything that were happening. Even if it had nothing to do with him." Every Driver who was sent to C Troop had to have a one to one interview with H T to explain where they'd come from, what experience they'd had, and what job they would possibly like to do within the Troop.

At the time, no-one wanted to be the OC's Driver and so Richard volunteered, with a certain amount of trepidation, because he wasn't sure exactly what the job involved. He soon discovered that the job included an early start and late finish almost every day. At 0730 hours every morning, Richard had to collect the OC from his Married Quarter and drop him back home again whenever 'the boss' had finished work. Depending on any CO's conferences and Officers' Mess functions, the finishes often went into late evenings and/or the early hours of the next morning. On the plus side, Richard never had to do Guard Duties or Working Parades and unlike other OC's Drivers he wasn't treated like a batman. On several occasions, Richard also drove for Brigadier Attack, the Brigade Commander, if his own Staff Car wasn't on the road.

Richard's opinion of his OC changed one night when 9 Squadron RCT was returning to barracks after an Exercise. The weather was foul in the extreme and after hitting black ice, the Squadron G1098 wagon careered off the road and tipped over. Two cooks who were travelling in the rear of the truck were injured and all sorts of military equipment was strewn everywhere. Major Husthwaite RCT jumped out of his Land Rover, rolled up his sleeves and immediately went to work. He organised the First Aid treatment and evacuation of the two cooks, and then he got his hands dirty by helping the lads manually cross-load the spilled military equipment onto another truck.

In 1972 Richard initially seized a Private Hiring in Stukenbrock so Joan could come over to Bielefeld and join him, at that time MQ's were in very short supply, which resulted in Richard and Joan moving into an Army Hiring in Augustdorf, before finally being allocated an Army Married Quarter in Asemissen. Consequently, Richard handed over his job as the OC's Driver because it was deemed unfair for an OC to keep a married soldier at his beck and call all times of the day and night. Richard took his HGV 2 Driving Test in an "Old knocker" before completing his B2 Drivers Course. He then joined 9 Squadrons' Servicing Bay Team. He also hired a car from a firm at Seiker lights so that he could get into work from his isolated Married Quarter Accommodation. Being an RCT Driver, Richard selected a real beauty as well, a 1.6 Litre Mk 1 Ford Capri GTXLR, apparently it moved like, and I quote, "Shit off a hot shovel."

In his new Servicing Bay job, Richard and two other Drivers worked under the direction of Cpl 'Robbo' Robinson RCT, where fundamentally the three Drivers were simply 'Grease Monkeys'. 'Robbo' had been involved in an accident a few years previously and as a result he had a badly deformed hand. With typical RCT wit and cruelty, he was always referred to as, 'The Claw.' As far as Richard could tell, the Servicing Bay job was a dead-end employment and so he decided to become a Rad Op (Radio Operator) in the hope of increasing his chances of promotion. SSgt (Staff Sergeant) Jimmy Bridges RCT was the RSI (Regimental Signals Instructor) at 10 Regiment and he primarily changed the Regiment's Field Communications set-up and its Operating Procedures. Richard sarcastically states that, "Jimmy was a Rad Op through and through. He started as a Rad Op when the British Army were still using pigeons." At the time, 9 Sqn, 17 Sqn and 36 Sqn each had control of their own Rad Ops and these teams were severely undermanned. Jimmy spoke to the Regiment's Commanding Officer, Lt Col (Lieutenant Colonel) Jenkins, and asked if he could reorganise the Rad Ops and place them all under one roof. Jimmy wanted to designate the new organisation as Radio Troop and he would be their sole commander. The Colonel gave him the go-ahead and Jimmy started trawling each Sqn for volunteer Radio Operators. He needed a minimum of three Rad Ops per Sqn and at that time some of them only had two.

After volunteering, Richard did the B3 Radio Operators Course which was conducted by Jimmy himself in 10 Regiment's Training Wing. The four-week course involved the care, maintenance and use of the C12, C13, C42 (VHF), C45 (VHF) radios and the A41 man packs which were rarely used in the Regiment. The candidates on the Course had to learn how to tune each radio in to a given frequency, how the exterior box on vehicles worked and how to connect them to the VHF radios, how and where to connect antenna's, voice procedure, fault finding, Morse Code, accurately and neatly recording messages on Log Sheets, and a host of other security information. There were twelve candidates on the Course and they all passed every test. Richard explains, "No-one failed the Course because SSgt Jimmy Bridges had designed it so everything was easily learned. He really knew his stuff did Jimmy."

Richard found the VP (Voice Procedure) part of the Course relatively easy but he struggled a bit with the Morse Code. To qualify as a B3 Rad Op, each candidate had to be able to send 8 words a minute in code and on the B1 Course that went up to 12 words a minute. During the course, Jimmy deployed the entire course onto Stukenbrock Training Area where the candidates broadcasted to another Rad Op Course being held at Buller Barracks in Aldershot. SSgt Jimmy Bridges RCT was a gifted and very motivated Rad Op and instructor, so much so, that he finished his army career at the RCT Training Base in Leconfield,

East Yorkshire as the WO1 in charge of all Rad Op Trade Training for the entire Corps.

When Radio Troop was finally up and running, Jimmy had plenty of Rad Ops at his disposal in 10 Regiment, and when they deployed on Exercise he alone decided which Rad Ops were assigned to which Sqn (Each Rad Op remained with their designated Sqn) and in which of his FFR (Fitted For Radio) Land Rovers they would be deployed. When 10 Regiment deployed on Exercise there were three Radio Operators to a Crew at various key points. The CO had his own radio crew and each of the Sqn HQ's also had a radio crew. He also had to provide crews for the DP (Distribution Point), RP (Replenishment Point), XP (Exchange Point) and Ops (Operations).

During the 1970's, the British Army had to constantly 'make do and mend' simply because there wasn't enough money available for new equipment, spares, or even to provide enough troops for every commitment around the world. Let's face it, in 1969 'The Troubles' erupted and BAOR had to supply enough soldiers to try and keep the peace. So, when a unit was sent to Northern Ireland, every other unit in BAOR had to pick up the shortfall and cover their commitments, Radio Troop in 10 Regiment was just another example of this British Army's 'make do and mend' policy. Richard can clearly remember when units from 3 Division in Duisburg deployed to the Province and 10 Regiment had to cover the Comms (Communications) aspect of their Exercises. Whilst on Exercise, Radio Troop organised their own working practices and never did stags on guard; they had to organise their own stags listening out on each network and recording every message on a Log Sheet. Richard eventually became a B1 Rad Op and qualified as an RSI (Regimental Signals Instructor. He failed on his first attempt at Buller Barracks but ultimately passed the RSI Course at Leconfield.

Richard eventually did three tours of duty in Northern Ireland (1972, 1976 and the winter period of 1977/1978). The first, in 1972, was by far the worst. To remember his time on that tour, Richard only needs to flick through a copy of David Barzilay's book, **The British Army in Ulster Volume 1**. On pages 108 and 110 there are pictures of two casualties that Richard transported to the RVH (Royal Victoria Hospital) in Belfast, driving his Saracen ambulance. The soldiers were members of either the 1st 2nd or 3rd Battalions of the Royal Green Jackets (RGJ), who were deployed to Belfast at that time. One photo shows a soldier with a shell dressing wrapped around his head, but still wearing his RGJ beret whilst kneeling by a fence and holding his SLR (7.62mm Self Loading Rifle). The other photo shows a Green Jacket helping an injured comrade into Richard's Saracen Ambulance and he clearly has a steel nail protruding from under the skin of his right forearm. Unfortunately, the publishing agent of David Barzilay's book no longer exists and I cannot include the pictures in my book without their, or David Barzilay's, permission, even though both photographs were taken on the same day by an RGJ CSgt (Colour Sergeant).

Just prior to deploying to the Province, 10 Regiment RCT was told that their presence as individuals wouldn't be required in Northern Ireland, yet four weeks later Richard was told that 9 Sqn was going to deploy as a complete Sqn. "During the early days of Northern Ireland our pre-deployment training was piss poor. We had no idea about the political situation and had never heard of riot control techniques. We didn't even know what sort of vehicles we'd be driving and so couldn't do any Driver Training. We had absolutely no idea of what we were going to face. A cease-fire was in place when we arrived in Belfast and everyone was bimbling about in open-topped Land Rovers." The truce was used by all the troops in that area to show RCT Drivers like Richard around the local area, "We thankfully found our way around Andersontown and recced the whole area without anyone shooting at us."

When 9 Squadron finally arrived in Northern Ireland, they were the first designated APC Sqn to drive Saracens on the streets of Belfast. These vehicles were a mixture of green and sand colours because they were being made ready for use in the Middle East. At that time, the IRA began using Tungsten Tipped Armour Piercing Ammunition and an Infantry Cpl from Mulhouse Location was the first to be killed by one. He had been travelling in one of the more lightly armoured Humber 1 Ton 'Pigs'. The MOD cancelled the Middle East order and re-directed the more heavily armoured iconic vehicles to Belfast. Other than the Humber 'Pig' and Alvis Saracen, the British Army had a limited selection of APC's (Armoured Personnel Carriers) at their disposal. The small Ferret Armoured car was designed as a four-wheeled reconnaissance vehicle and could only just manage to hold its crew of two. That left no room to carry any extra troops, the Saladin was pretty much the same. The Saladin was designed to be used as a six-wheeled convoy escort vehicle with a crew of three. The turret held a 76mm QF (Quick Firing) gun and a .30 Browning machine gun. Although the Saladin was designed using the same engine, chassis, and transmission as the Saracen, it couldn't carry any extra personnel inside and was therefore about as much use as an APC, as the Ferret car. The Saracen gave much better protection against AP and RPG (Rocket Propelled Grenade) Ordnance but in the end, if the vehicle was hit in the right place at the right time, then those on the inside were at best going to be severely injured.

When the cease-fire ended, and the bullets again started to fly in Belfast, the City became a modern-day version of the OK Corral, especially in Lenadoon Avenue, which was on the western (*pardon the pun*) side of Andersontown. In 1972 there were some brand-new Protestant occupied council houses in Lenadoon Avenue, (*they were far superior to those where Richard lived in Scarborough*), but the occupants felt threatened by their Catholic neighbours and so they moved out of the area. After removing their personal possessions, they then set fire to the houses so that the Catholics couldn't inhabit them. These incidents are what caused the ceasefire to break down. When Richard first started patrolling Andersontown, the army mobile patrols often stopped at Catholic houses and used them for 'Tea Stops.' "We were apparently in Belfast to protect the Catholics and because of this we were often spat at by the Protestant faithful. It were a very confusing time." It wasn't long before the juxtapositions changed.

During those hectic days, Richard was moved to several different locations using a 'Pig' ambulance from Musgrave Park Hospital. His memory about those places is a bit hazy, but he does remember being based at Glenn Road in White Rock, Oliver Plunkett School and Andersontown Bus Station, as an Ambulance Driver. Although not trained to drive a Saracen, Richard had to take one of the APC's to Moscow Camp so that it could be converted into an ambulance. He had to stay on HMS Maidstone for four days whilst the stretcher racks, blue light and Klaxon horns were fitted, he also had to wait for the sacrosanct white background and red crosses to be painted on the front, sides, and rear of the vehicle. Whilst waiting for the APC to be transformed into an ambulance, Richard was given his initial Driver Training on the Saracen around Belfast docks using a spare vehicle.

When the Saracen APC had finally been transformed into an Ambulance, Richard drove it to his new location at Andersontown Bus Depot on the Falls Road. The Regimental Medical Officer (RMO) he worked with was Captain Ken Brown RAMC, a local man who had originated from Belfast. The two of them were going to be a very busy team. Apart from the aforementioned Green Jackets who'd been injured in a shrapnel explosion in Beechmount Avenue, Richard also drove Captain Brown to pick up LCpl (Lance Corporal) Dave Card of the 1st Battalion Royal Green Jackets who was shot in Commedagh Drive, one mile from the Bus Depot. Dave Card was only 21 years old. He'd been patrolling on the waste-ground in Andersontown on the 4th of August 1972 when he'd been shot through the neck by a sniper. Richard and Captain Brown both heard the shot and were immediately dispatched to the incident just in case they were needed. Apparently, the other soldiers in the four-man patrol couldn't rescue LCpl Card because he was on open ground and no-one knew from which direction the shot had come. On arrival in Andersontown, Richard parked up the Saracen Ambulance and was told by the RMO to stay in his driving seat because the Green Jackets were carrying Dave Card to the Ambulance. After gently placing Dave's body onto the ambulance stretcher, Captain Brown examined his casualty and saw that the bullet had gone through Dave's flak jacket and that he had an awful and very bloody injury to his neck. It turned out that the round had bruised Dave's spinal column, which had consequently been ruptured. Richard heard Captain Brown say, "There's not much hope."

With the blue light flashing and Klaxon Horns wailing, Richard screamed through the Saracens five gears in the hope of getting LCpl Dave Card to the hospital alive. Half way back to the hospital Captain Brown shouted for Richard to stop because the movement was hampering his attempt to use the foot pumped suction apparatus. Two minutes later the 'Doc' shouted, "Right, carry on!" Sadly, by the time they arrived at the MPH Captain Brown informed Richard that LCpl Dave Card of 1 RGJ had died. Both Richard and Captain Brown were distressed by Dave Card's death, simply because although they wore different cap badges, they still knew most of the Green Jackets and his death felt like they'd lost a close friend. Unbeknownst to those who have never been on a team trying to save a real casualty, the team involved could often feel guilty if the casualty couldn't be saved. Richard also had the extremely unpleasant task of cleaning out the back of his ambulance, "There were so much blood everywhere, it took me ages to clean it all up."

Over the next few days Richard pondered about the MO's problem when he tried to use the foot pump suction kit in the back of the moving ambulance. Using his engineering type brain, Richard came up with an idea. The windscreen wipers on an Alvis Saracen were vacuum operated using power from the engine. Richard simply connected the suction kit up to the windscreen wipers vacuum system and, hey presto, constant suction was available that could be used on a bleeding or choking casualty. After sterilising the whole 'gizmo' it was ready to go to work. Unfortunately, Richard didn't have any windscreen wipers whilst driving battened down, but then again, it wasn't a perfect world. By the time Richard came to the end of his first tour of Northern Ireland, he'd heard a lot of gunfire and seen a lot of blood split, a lot of it from civilian as well as military casualties. Not long after the cease-fire was broken, Andersontown was flooded with about 600 soldiers trying to quell the violence. On one day alone, three soldiers and eight civilians were shot. It was during this period of fighting that Richard first heard the sound of a Thompson submachine gun being fired, "I'll never forget the sound as rounds flew over the top of our heads, it were a whirring sound rather than that of a high-powered assault rifle which were more like the crack of a whip." At night, he also heard the discreet 'phhtt' spitting sound of a pneumatic weapon. Using a .22 rifle, the 2i/c of one of the Green Jacket Battalions shot out the street lights in his area. He didn't see any sense in providing IRA snipers with a clearer night-time target of his soldiers! The 1972 tour of Northern Ireland was probably the toughest of every British Soldiers' tour in the Province, and for several reasons. One: It was a new conflict and the British Army had yet to learn how to effectively operate in its new UK Internal Security role. Two: There were more deaths and injuries to both British security forces and civilians in that year. Out of about 500 individuals being killed during this period, 148 were believed to be British Security Forces (SF). The most appalling amount of deaths in Northern Ireland was only exceeded during Richard's second tour in 1976. While on his post tour leave, Richard's son Christopher was born on 22nd December 1972.

Between the tours Richard had been promoted to LCpl but for his next tour in Belfast, again with 9 Sqn, he was promoted to full Corporal. This time Richard wasn't going to be up at the sharp end though. He was 2i/c of the Servicing Bay in Moscow Camp under Robbo the Claw. In preparation for the forthcoming tour he was sent on a course to Bulford Camp in Wiltshire, where he learned how to service and maintain Saracen's and Humber 1 Ton 'Pigs.' It was a constant battle trying to keep these old vehicles on the road, and not just because people were shooting and throwing things like bricks and petrol bombs at them. Every grease nipple on the underside of a Saracen APC was the same size, but the different components and mechanisms didn't use the same sort of lubricant. On arrival in his Servicing Bay, Richard inspected one of the units Saracens and found an incorrect heavy grease had been used in the six-wheeled drive units which could have seized up the vehicle. He wanted to VOR (Vehicle Off Road) every one of these APC's, but that would have brought the entire British Army in Northern Ireland to a standstill. Instead, every time a wrongly lubricated Saracen came into his Servicing Bay, he had to melt out the heavy grease and refill the drive units with the correct liquid grease. Each servicing was a very messy and time-consuming task. It was lucky that Richard enjoyed doing that sort of work.

When 9 Sqn RCT returned to Bielefeld on completion of their tour in Belfast, Richard went back into Radio Troop. After his post tour leave, it wasn't long before SSgt Ken Franks RCT took over from Jimmy Bridges as the RSI, it also wasn't long before Richard was kicked out of Radio Troop. Nearing an Endex (End of Exercise) the Sqn was heading towards its next field location. On the Orders Group (O Group) prior to the Sqn move, all Rad Ops were ordered to keep radio silence whilst mobile. The OC of 17 Sqn obviously hadn't read the same script as everyone else and after he broadcasted on the network, Richard in no uncertain terms gave the OC a bollocking over the air. "Hello Sunray One Seven this is Zero! Read your current Signals Instructions! No comms whilst on the move! Out!" At the very next rest stop, the OC decided to hold an emergency O Group where he vented his anger on Corporal Richard Makinson RCT.

After an indignant outburst by the OC, Richard lost the job he loved doing but, luckily, he wasn't busted in rank and was temporarily moved into HQ Troop 9 Sqn as an Admin NCO. Both of Richard's promotions had been awarded by 9 Sqn's OC, Major Charles Colvin RCT (*The very same Officer involved in Bob Birrell's Crocodile Abercrombie farce*), after strong recommendations from Jimmy Bridges. Richard still believes to this day that SSgt

Ken Franks RCT didn't defend his Rad Ops vigorously enough. In 10 Regiment there was a high turnover of Junior NCO's and Richard was subsequently posted into D Troop 36 Squadron as a Section Commander.

Members of Richard's Section were labelled a bunch of misfits within 36 Sqn because of Richard's recent undignified departure from Radio Troop, that and the Section being full of renegade RCT Drivers like 24316645 Driver 'Skin' Collins. In 1976 the author can clearly remember when 'Skin' was preparing his AEC Mk 3 Militant 10 Ton Truck for an up and coming Exercise. 'Skin' illegally removed the Governor from its engine FIP (Fuel Injection Pump) which allowed the 'Millie to far exceed its limited safe maximum speed of just below 50 mph. On the plus side, it would also allow 'Skin' to speed past all the other 'Governed' RCT trucks on the road. During one neck-breaking episode on a German road, 'Skin' was very surprised when the pistons on his...now ungoverned engine, suddenly and violently appeared in the cab of his truck... through the engine cover. Oh those 'not so' halcyon and happy days! 'Skin' replaced the Governor on the FIP and pleaded ignorance about what had happened to the engine to his Troop Commander, 2ndLt Collinson and his OC Major Freddie Crabbe. Regardless of other soldier's attitude towards his Section, Richard thought they were a great bunch of lads and he stayed with them until he was transferred into B Troop 17 Sqn for his third tour of Northern Ireland. A Cpl who was already on pre-Northern Ireland training for the Christmas tour in South Armagh had broken his arm and Richard was nominated to replace him as the RCT Section Commander in Bessbrook. LCpl 'Ginge' Cyril Tickle was Richards' Section 2i/c and their small RCT detachment was manned by excellent, and slightly strange nutcases, like Driver Bill Baker and Johnny Walker. Johnny was moved into the Forkhill and Bessbrook areas to replace Driver

Mark Schmitz, who had been injured during a recent mortar attack. *Note: You can read about the full Military Careers of these eccentric and extraordinary RCT soldiers in my other books called, 'Rickshaws Camels and Taxis' and 'Most Roads Led to 10 Regt'.*

The author was on the same Christmas tour as Richard but was stationed in Newry location. One day, the author had to drive a Saracen for 3 miles up to Bessbrook, not long before his birthday on the 7th of December. Richard and Cyril had an illicit stash of alcohol in the RCT accommodation and whilst waiting for his Infantry Section to return, the author was given a tumbler filled with a celebratory birthday brew. The 'Micky Finn' style drink contained a mixture of Whisky, Asbach Brandy and Bacardi Rum…. with just a dash of lemonade. Brian (Harry) Clacy wasn't allowed to leave the RCT room until he'd consumed every drop of the concoction. If he'd been caught by the RUC (Royal Ulster Constabulary) whilst driving the RGJ Section back to Newry, he'd certainly have failed a breathalyser test.

Richard was posted to 60 Sqn RCT in Catterick on completion of his South Armagh tour with 17 Sqn. On arrival, he was given the job as RSI, which he continued to do throughout his tenure with 60 Sqn. In the winter of February 1979, Richard was posted back out to BAOR but this time to 4 ADFA (Armoured Field Ambulance RAMC) in Minden, and after leaving Catterick Garrison he and his family headed for the Port of Hull in their Opel family car. North Yorkshire Council workers were on strike at the time and so the roads in Yorkshire hadn't been snowploughed or gritted. At the time, it was so cold that Richard describes the roads around Hull as being like an ice-skating rink. The climate in Germany wasn't much better and even the Germans were struggling to keep the main roads open. The extreme weather at times slowed Richard's journey down to a crawl. He decided to call into 10 Regt RCT in

Bielefeld to telephone his new unit in Minden and inform them that he was going to be slightly delayed.

The sentry on 10 Regt's gates told him that it had been snowing in BAOR for quite a few days and that apart from the Duty Driver's Land Rover, no other vehicles had left the camp. Undeterred, Richard decided to press on with his journey to Minden which was now only about 30 miles away. Because of the winter conditions, it took Richard and his family over two hours to finish their expedition. The guard on the gate at Kingsley Barracks was a Sapper in the Royal Engineers and he was incredulous that Richard and his family had just travelled the 300 miles from Zeebrugge to Minden in those awful conditions. Richard sardonically told the young Sapper, "Well, there are drivers....and then there are RCT Drivers."

Whilst serving at 4 ADFA Richard consecutively deployed on **'Exercise Spearpoint'** in BAOR during 1980 and on **'Exercise Amber Express'** in Denmark in 1981. After returning from Denmark, Richard failed a BFT (Basic Fitness Test) for the first time in his army career. During the 3-mile run, he found it increasingly hard to breath and he couldn't finish the 2nd part of the test in under the minimum 11 minutes required. Richard was ordered to attend remedial PT (Physical Training) lessons and when he failed another BFT several weeks later, the Commanding Officer of 4 ADFA interrogated him in his office with the intention of metering out a verbal warning. In the British Army, every soldier must personally maintain his own physical fitness so that he is always fit to fight, at all times. During the formal interview without coffee, the RAMC Lt Col decided to examine Richard in his office to see if he had any underlying medical problems. He diagnosed Richard as having the medical condition Asthma. The condition was again confirmed at BMH

(British Military Hospital) Rinteln a few days later and for Richard the news was devastating. He would sadly have to leave the British Army having only served in its ranks for 12 years.

In October 1982, Richard, Joan, and their three children were posted back to the UK where they were allocated a married quarter in Driffield, East Yorkshire. Eight weeks later Richard was unceremoniously discharged from the Royal Corps of Transport and the British Army.

After being discharged from the British Army, Richard worked as a Dray Man and eventually spent Seventeen and a half years with Greaves Printing Factory as a Book Binders Assistant and Press Room Assistant. For the last 5 years of his working life, Richard worked as an independent Taxi Driver around the Scarborough area. He and his wife, Joan, still live in the area and are now fully retired. Richard is the eldest Makinson in Scarborough heading a family of four generations as his grandchildren are now married with children of their own.

24267087 Warrant Officer Class 1 Chris Iddon
RCT and RLC - (1972 – 1996)

Chris Iddon's dad was conscripted into the RAF to do his 2 years National Service in 1948. (*National Service began in 1948 and ended in 1960, however, it wasn't until May 1963 that the last National Serviceman was finally discharged from the Armed Forces*). "My Dad was an MT Driver during his time in uniform and in two years he drove larger and more varied vehicles than I did in my 22 years' service in the RCT." Chris continues, "I don't know why I didn't join the RAF like my dad did really." After leaving the RAF, Hugh Iddon married Maggie Laycock and was then offered an internal job move with Imperial Chemical Industries (ICI), from Hillhouse (near Thornton Cleveleys just outside Blackpool) to Barnet in North London, and from there to a new manufacturing plant in Welwyn Garden City, where Chris Iddon was born in the Cottage Hospital in 1956.

"I was considered to be a bright lad, but in all honesty, I had no interest in anything academic and so I left school at the first opportunity without any qualifications. My attitude over school-work put me into a bit of conflict with my mum and dad." Chris was more interested in playing football, smoking cigarettes and messing about with motorbikes. He spent a lot of his spare time scrambling in the local woods on some motorcycles that he and his mates had cobbled together. Chris was reading a copy of the 'Victor' comic one night when he noticed a cut-out application on the back page. The advert offered a free booklet about the British Army for anyone completing and posting off an attached form. The notice instantly grabbed Chris's attention and so he completed the form, cut it out and and sent it off.

Several weeks later Chris was down at the local boys' club having a laugh with his mates when his Dad walked in and called him over, "What the heck have you been up to now son?" Whilst racking his brain about which of his most recent misdemeanours might have come to light, Chris's Dad continued, "There's a bloody big Army sergeant sitting on our sofa at home and he wants to talk to you." It was a dark November evening and Chris started walking home with his Dad whilst pushing his bike. Hugh told Chris, "You don't want to keep someone like that waiting son, I suggest that you put your bike lights on and get going."

As Chris entered the Iddon family sitting room, a tall, imposing, and very smart Grenadier Guards Senior NCO stood up and firmly shook Chris's hand, he then briefly interviewed Chris before handing over some army information leaflets and bumf. Before leaving the Iddon's home, the impressive military man told Chris that in a couple of weeks he would be sent to the Army Youth Selection Centre at Corsham near Bath. Chris eventually went to Corsham and watched a lot of Army recruiting films telling him about the different Corps and Regiments of the British Army. After completing a plethora of written tests and physical assessments, Chris decided that he wanted to join the Royal Electrical and Mechanical Engineers (REME) and train to become a Vehicle Mechanic (VM). During his interview for this book, Chris told the author, "I liked messing about with motor-bikes and engines and so I thought it would be nice to be able to fix stuff properly."

Disappointingly, the Selection Staff at Corsham told Chris that there weren't any vacancies available for REME VM's at that time, instead they offered him the opportunity to join the Junior Leaders Regiment of the Royal Corps of Transport (Jnr Ldrs Regt RCT). Chris didn't have a 'Scooby' what the RCT was or what its soldiers did for a living. When told that they drove all sorts of army vehicles, including motor-bikes, Chris very nearly bit the Interviewer's hand off for a placement. After returning home, Chris later received another letter from the British Army inviting him to St Albans Army Careers Information Office (ACIO) to attend for his Attestation (*that's when a potential recruits' scatter-brained interest in becoming a soldier starts to get a bit serious*). Each applicant has to state their name, and swear by Almighty God that they will bear true allegiance to her Majesty Queen Elizabeth the Second, Her heirs and successors and that they will as in duty bound honestly and faithfully defend Her Majesty, Her heirs and successors in Person, Crown and Dignity against all enemies and that they will observe and obey all orders of Her Majesty, Her Heirs and Successors and of the Generals and Officers set over them. Chris signed on the dotted line to become a Junior Leader at Norton Manor Camp in Taunton, Somerset. The bumf at the time indicated Norton Manor Camp was, 'The home of the future Senior Non-commissioned Officers of the Royal Corps of Transport'.

On the 9th of May 1972, Chris met another RCT recruit at Paddington Station and they both travelled down to Taunton together. Chris couldn't remember his travelling companions name but recalled that, "He went into 'A' Squadron and eventually jacked it in before completing the training syllabus. He'd decided the RCT wasn't for him and so transferred into the Royal Military Police (RMP), that young lad went on to become a bloody military copper." *Authors note: Such is the RCT soldiers disdain for 'Redcaps' - Military Policemen, even after the passage of 45 years.*

The next few weeks were like a whirlwind for Chris. He remembers reporting to the Quartermaster's Stores and being given a mattress cover in which to carry all his newly issued clothing and equipment. The severe-looking Staff Sergeant behind the counter wore black rimmed glasses and spoke with a gruff Scottish accent, "My name is Staff Sergeant McDonald and I'm the Squadron Quartermaster Sergeant; you lot will all call me Staff!" Having not been exposed to too many Jocks and their particularly aggressive accents, Chris initially referred to the SQMS as, "Stuff!"

Back L to Front R. J/Sgt Ray Ractliffe, J/Dvr Billy Burke, J/Cpl Chris Iddon, J/Dvr Martin 'Skin' Keen, J/Cpl Ron Campbell, J/Dvr Steve Bull, Sgt Jasper Davy, J/Dvr Steve Gibbs. 10 Tors 1973.

Chris was assigned to Connaught Troop in 'C' Squadron. Junior Lance Corporal (J/LCpl) 'Gaz' Merrills led the new intake over to their spider hut accommodation, where they met up with their Troop Commander, Captain B A Lucas RCT and their Troop Sergeant, Sergeant Tony Ward RCT. Chris describes Sergeant

Ward as being an awesome soldier. Unfortunately, Sergeant Ward was posted back to a working unit halfway through Chris's training schedule and was replaced by Sergeant Davies, another first-class RCT soldier who went on to become a commissioned officer. Sergeant Davies recommended and secured a promotion for Chris up to Junior Sergeant (J/Sgt), even though they had a love-hate relationship like most of the other trainees and instructors in JLR, proving that Chris must have been a keen, smart, and quick-witted Junior Leader.

Captain Lucas eventually took command of the External Leadership Wing (EL Wing) and he in turn was replaced as the Connaught Troop Commander by Captain G (Graeme) Morrison RCT. Captain Morrison (later Lieutenant Colonel) was a superb Officer who was held in the highest regard by everyone in the Corps. He was an avid horse rider who'd had his bottom lip bitten off by his own horse. The lip had been sewn back on of course, with Chris casually describing the repair job as, "It looked in fairly good order actually."

Chris would bump into Graham Morrison several times during his career when the 'Galloping Major' was posted to Headquarters 1st (British) Corps (HQ 1 (BR) Corps) at Bielefeld in West Germany and as the Second in Command (2IC) of the Jnr Ldrs Regt RCT at Colerne, Wiltshire where Chris was to become a Troop Sergeant (Tp Sgt) in 30 Squadron later in his career.

Meanwhile, back in 1972, on his last day at home before heading off to Taunton to start his recruit training, Chris went into his local Barber's and had his hair cut very short, he wanted to be ahead of the game when he arrived at his very first unit in the British Army. He was a bit taken aback when, on arrival and displaying his one-day-old shearing, the Barber there stuck him in the chair and took off even more hair from his head.

During Chris's first 12 months at Taunton he didn't do much socialising and remained a quiet member of the troop. He was glad to get away from school and was a bit annoyed when he discovered that a substantial portion of the weekly training programme at the Jnr Ldrs Regt RCT consisted of classroom work. English was swapped for Communication Skills and Maths became known as Military Calculations.

In the second year of his training, Chris progressed on up into Senior Troop (Snr Tp) where he started mixing with the likes of Drivers Ray Radcliffe, Roy 'Chalky' Proffit, and 'Skin' Keane, devil-may-care soldiers who would soon put a stop to his cautious nature. Ray Radcliffe had been C Sqn's Junior Squadron Sergeant Major (J/SSM) when Chris had been presented with his J/Sgt stripes in Connaught Troop. During his leisure time, Chris started dating a young girl whose father was a member of the Trades and Labour Club in Taunton. "There was plenty of cheap beer on tap every Saturday night and so, after getting a late-night pass, we four used to go down there and regularly got absolutely legless. That first night though, we returned to camp and signed back into the Guardroom and tried to walk down the camp's main road in a straight line whilst drunkenly laughing our heads off. Oh, what happy days."

Chris states honestly, "In Senior Troop I really under-whelmed myself. My Dad had already taught me the basics of driving and so when I miserably failed my first dual test in a Bedford RL truck, I was upset and very disappointed in myself. I bounced back though and pissed through the re-test." On completion of their training at Taunton, Chris, Chalky Proffit, and 'Skin' Keane were all posted to 10 Regiment RCT in Bielefeld, West Germany (Chris and Roy were posted to 36 Sqn and 'Skin' Keane went straight into 9 Sqn). Ray Radcliffe, on the other hand, was posted to RAF Thorney Island for RCT Air Despatcher Trade Training. He eventually failed the Air Despatch Training because he was more interested in beer and women than pushing pallets out of the back of an RAF C 130 aircraft.

There were legends at the Jnr Ldrs Regt RCT like Geoff Marley and his brother Bob, who were both believed to be 'well hard' by everyone who knew them. As it turned out, they were 'well hard' and still are. They were absolutely brilliant blokes who became great friends when they were posted to 10 Regt RCT at the same time as Chris. Shortly before giving his interview for this book, Chris met up with the Marley brothers in Plymouth for a night out. *Authors note: You can take the boys out of the RCT, but not the RCT out of the boys.*

On arrival at 10 Regt RCT, Chris and Roy Proffit temporarily went their separate ways from 'Skin' Keane, and for the next six months the pair drove ambulances for the HQ 1 (BR) Corps Medical Centre in Ripon Barracks. Ripon Barracks was located just a couple of miles along Detmolder Strasse from 10 Regt and was home to HQ 1 BR (British) Corps, 14 Sqn RCT, and a Royal Signals Sqn. The big attraction for a couple of 18-year-old lads was that a number of these units had girls of the Women's Royal Army Corps (WRAC) lodged in the Barracks. The female soldiers worked mainly in the Communications Centre (COMCEN) and the Telephone Exchange.

On completion of their attachment to the Medical Centre, Chris and Roy had truly taken advantage of the hospitality offered by the girls and firmly established themselves as regulars at the

NAAFI bar in Ripon Barracks, The Jimmy Club (4 Sig Sqn), The Waggoner's (14 Sqn RCT) and HM's, the German civilian bar just outside the back gates of Ripon Bks! The two ne'er-do-wells had adopted a similar lifestyle to the one Ray Radcliffe was enjoying back in the UK at RAF Thorney Island. After staggering back to their room one-night, however, Chris switched on the light and was astounded to discover someone was sleeping in his bed. A hand-written note at the foot of the bedstead stated, 'I've come to join the boys'. Ray Radcliffe had put in a posting preference to follow his friends to 10 Regt after failing the Air Despatchers Course and had been posted to 9 Sqn. He'd arrived late at night and decided to hijack Chris's bed until the 9 Sqn QM staff could allocate him a bed-space the following morning. It looked like fate had put the happy band back together again.

The Ambulance Troop of 36 Sqn (*which included Chris and Roy Proffitt*) was eventually attached to 9 Sqn for their forthcoming operational tour of Northern Ireland, but the Troop was destined never returned to 36 Sqn, becoming C Tp, 9 Sqn on return from Northern Island. This led to Chris, 'Skin' Keane, Ray Radcliffe, and Roy Proffit all ending up together in 9 Sqn RCT and doing a couple of Northern Ireland tours together. Chris went on to complete four tours of duty in Northern Ireland during 1975, 1976 1977/8 and 1979.

On the 2nd of January 1975 Chris flew out to Belfast with his Section Commander, Corporal Tommy Dunlop, and Drivers Dez Hall, Sid Jasper, and John Owen. During their four-month tour at McRory Park they were operating in support of 2nd Royal Green Jackets (2 RGJ) and 1st Royal Welsh Fusiliers (1 RWF). The RCT Drivers were there to drive the locations Humber 'Pigs' and Makrolon Land Rovers for the Infantry on mobile patrols in and around West Belfast.

There was a cease-fire bubbling around Northern Ireland at that time and much of the hostility suffered by the RCT lads only came from 1 RWF. The 'Taffs' had a habit of calling all the non-Welsh RCT Drivers, 'Limeys,' a nationalistic slur that had probably been misappropriated from our North American cousins. *(In the mid-1800's the North Americans used the derogatory term 'Limey' against the sailors serving in His Majesty's Royal Navy. A dose of lime juice was given to Royal Navy sailors along with their daily ration of grog (rum) to prevent them suffering from scurvy).* But, nonetheless, they were a good bunch and generally got on well, their secret weapon and the RCT's own Welshman, John Owen, even won the 'Leek Eating' competition on St David's Day! When the Sqn returned to Bielefeld, Chris was sent on a Saracen and 'Pig' Instructors Course at the Army School of Mechanical Transport (ASMT) Bordon, in preparation for instructing other 10 Regt Drivers for future Northern Ireland tours.

During one of the accommodation moves in early 1976, everyone in the Troop became labourers and moved the unit furniture from one Sqn block to the other. When Chris picked up a chair and tried to carry it on his head, the lifting action resulted in him ripping away the muscles that were joined to his spine. "That was the most painful experience of my entire life," said Chris, "I ended up being taken by ambulance to the British Military Hospital (BMH) at Rinteln and was made to rest on a board for the next 10 days. The Medics thought that I'd never walk properly again for the rest of my life. It wasn't until the early 1980's that my spine finally got back to being completely healed." His hospitalisation in BMH Rinteln was followed by 4 weeks light duties, during which period Chris idled away his time in the Women's Royal Voluntary Service (WRVS) Club. The injury also resulted in his transfer to the unit tyre bay for the forthcoming tour of Northern Ireland being cancelled. Chris's spine wouldn't be able to cope with the heavy lifting and so he was given a different job to do in Belfast.

On his next tour of the Province, Chris was based in Moscow Camp, Belfast where he drove for Commander APCs at HQ APC Staff. In that job he drove an assortment of civilian cars, ranging from Vauxhall Chevettes to Mk3 GT XLR Ford Cortina's. The cars were painted a variety of weird colours that any decent and self-respecting RCT Driver wouldn't be seen dead in. On the plus side, Chris wore jeans to work every day and grew his hair to a length that gave WO2 (SSM) Ken Maher heart palpitations. Every time Chris drove out of the Moscow Camp gate, he was tooled up with a Browning 9mm HP (Hi-Power) Pistol tucked down the back of his jeans. When Chris wasn't driving the Commander APCs around the Province, he often worked with George Best's Dad. The famous Manchester United player's father worked for HQ APC Staff as a civilian storeman in Moscow Camp, and when they weren't working, Mr Best often took Chris for a drink in some of the Rangers Supporters Clubs in Belfast's Protestant areas (it must have been a heck of a way to spend that long hot summer of 1976)!

Chris got married immediately after this second tour of Northern Ireland and asked his best mate, Driver Roy 'Chalky' Proffit, to be Best Man at the wedding ceremony. Chris was disappointed when 'Prof' turned him down, but it transpired that he just didn't fancy giving a speech in front of all those wedding guests. Driver Colin Webber *(the very first RCT soldier that Brian (Harry) Clacy hero-worshipped in 10 Regt RCT)* stepped up to the mark. Colin was a young lad who originally came from Birmingham and, in the author's opinion, was the ultimate RCT 'Truckie.' Chris says of his friend, "Colin was a complete character, a really great lad." Lance Corporal Linda Hewitt WRAC and Driver Chris Iddon RCT both 'tied the knot' on the 10th of September 1976 (*Authors note: Linda's name comes first because she outranked Chris*). The wedding was a great few days because Dvr George Goreman (*who had also moved to 9 Sqn from 36 Sqn*) got married the day after Chris and Linda, George's wedding was a very posh affair. It was a marathon 'session' of stag and hen do's followed by Reception parties.

Back in Germany, Chris and Lin then went to live with friends for four months whilst waiting to be allocated a Service Married Quarter flat at 3/2 Florence Nightingale Strasse in Oerlinghausen.

Later that same year Chris was promoted to Lance Corporal (LCpl) which was much against the wishes of his Tp SSgt, Brian Young. *Author's note: Brian has written a book about his 27-year career in the Royal Corps of Transport, it's entitled, 'As You Were.'* Brian Young was often referred to as 'The Boy General' by the Junior NCOs and Drivers in the troop. Chris states, "To be fair, I liked him when he was my Staffie because he brought a modern approach to soldiering. He wasn't all about screaming and shouting and was different from many of the other SNCOs in 10 Regt. Staff Young wasn't happy about my recommendation for promotion though and to his credit, he was upfront with me about it and told me so to my face." Nevertheless, despite SSgt Young's reservations, Chris was promoted to LCpl and did several jobs within 9 Sqn where he became a Section 2i/c and Don R (Despatch Rider) before training to be an Eager Beaver Operator.

In the 1970's the official description for the Eager Beaver, in army jargon, was: 'Tractor, Wheeled, Fork Lift, 4,000 lb, Rough Terrain Vehicle.' In the days before Health and Safety (H & S), Eager Beaver Ops drove the vehicles without the benefit of a protective cage around the driving seat. These versatile vehicles were used to load and unload trucks of their palletised cargo both in barracks and on Field Exercises. When driven on tarmac roads, the Eager Beaver bounced around like the Lunar Roving Vehicle used by NASA Astronauts on the moon landings in the 1970s. Chris operated an Eager Beaver in Load Transfer Areas (LTAs) on Field Exercises, transferring loads between an assortment of trucks. Chris followed two 'Beaver' legends in 9 Sqn who went by the names of LCpl Ian 'Beaves' Beaver (that really was his name) and Colin 'Hibby' Hibbert. Those two RCT legends could cross-load a couple of 10 tonners faster, and more accurately, than anyone Chris knew, and he wanted to be at least as good as them.

Life in 10 Regt became a constant turnover of BAOR Field Exercises, Northern Ireland ('OP BANNER') Training, 'OP BANNER' tours, more BAOR Field Exercises, more Northern Ireland Training, ad infinitum. All of this was laced with a busy social life and the constant search for the next fast car, and there were a few of those knocking around 9 Squadron at that time. On Chris's next OP BANNER tour (1977/1978) he was sent to Mulhouse location which was a spit away from the infamous Falls Road, and just around the back of the Royal Victoria Hospital. On that tour the soldiers from Mulhouse experienced the delights of having fridges and washing machines thrown at them from the top of Divis Flats. One good thing did come from this tour though, Chris was promoted to full Corporal when the Squadron returned to Bielefeld.

On promotion to full Corporal, Chris applied to be an instructor in 10 Regt's Training Wing. The Training Wing was run by a larger than life, burly black SNCO called Sergeant Tony Morris. "Tony was a really nice guy and he taught me a great deal," said Chris. Cpl Ron Bly and Chris both worked in the Training Wing as instructors, running B3 Continuation, B2 and B1 Courses, with the odd Motorcycle and Eager Beaver Course being thrown in for good measure. At some stage during each Course, Chris and Ron would take their students up to the Servicing Bay and teach them how each type of vehicle in the Regiment should be serviced. They had to scramble about under the vehicles in the inspection pits to teach the Drivers how much of which oil, or grease, went into each part of each vehicle, students also had to identify every grease nipple on all types of vehicles. During the courses, Cpl 'Rob the Claw' Robinson or Corporal Richard Makinson kindly vacated their Servicing Bay and left the Training Wing Instructors to get on with teaching their students.

It wasn't long before Chris went back on yet another 'OP BANNER' tour, where this time he was sent to Ballymurphy (The Murph), in West Belfast, as a Section Commander. On the four-month tour C Tp, 9 Sqn supported 1 Kings and then the Argyll and Sutherland Highlanders. In the last few weeks of their tour and fortunately before they arrived, 1 Kings had five of their soldiers shot by the IRA, two being killed by only one round. The bullet entered the Saracen through its open back doors and bounced around the inside of the Armoured Personnel Carrier (APC). Lance Corporal Rumble and Kingsman Shanley were both unfortunately killed. "We had an awesome tour with the Argyll's," said Chris, "The OC of the Company at Ballymurphy was Major Cameron Campbell and he went for it big time because their Regiment needed to take back control of their Area of Operations. Major Campbell was a fantastic soldier supported by Company Sergeant Major Hogg, (*known as Boss Hogg because of the Dukes of Hazard TV show*) and a Second in Command who had actually served in the Regiment in the final days of the Second World War!"

Chris's friend, LCpl Stan Taylor, was appointed the RCT Section 2IC for the 1979 tour in 'the Murph'. Stan ultimately went on to become the Regimental Sergeant Major (RSM) of the Defence School of Transport (DST) at Leconfield, East Yorkshire before being posted to a Liverpool TA unit. "Stan was a real Jock comedian" says Chris. Unfortunately, Stan died of a kidney problem in 2012. His sister had donated one of her kidneys to him for the necessary transplant some years previously, but it all went wrong when Stan was infected with a bug which sadly killed him, a real tragedy.

During the Section's time in 'the Murph', their Troop Commander, Lt Paul McMahon and SSgt Brian Young paid them a visit one Saturday afternoon whilst the lads were watching the wrestling on TV. They were waiting for the big finale between 'Giant Haystacks' and 'Big Daddy' to start, when a double tap was heard from somewhere in 'the Murph' area. Chris explains, "We had 8 lads in the section, 5 Saracens, and 1 'Pig' in the location, and so in the event of a shout some of us were not going to get to drive an APC."

On hearing the shots being fired, all the Trog's/Trogg's sprang into action, falling over each other striving to grab their own flak-jackets, rifles and helmets, they all then charged out of the door in the hope of grabbing a driving position in one of the APCs. "SSgt Brian Young and our Troop Commander didn't have a clue what was going on," said Chris, "They just sat there gawping." Chris tried to be polite to his RCT bosses as he dashed out of the door, he then bumped into the OC and Boss Hogg. The Infantry CSM shouted out to Chris, "Corporal Iddon, with us, NOW!" Chris jumped into the back of the OC's Land Rover and deployed onto the streets with the Company Commander. Chris recounts, "Because one of their boys had just been shot, every street in

West Belfast was flooded with Argyll Infantrymen. The injured soldier was bundled into the back of LCpl Stan Taylor's Saracen and he quickly drove round to the Royal Victoria Hospital (RVH). The soldier survived and made a full recovery but the whole Company remained on the ground for many hours before being stood down. The Tp Comd and SSgt Brian Young had both left long before Chris had got back to location.

In a later incident, an earth-shattering bomb had exploded near the Ballymurphy location and at the same time Driver 'Mac' McCabe RCT went missing. It was initially assumed he was playing cards in one of the Grunts' (Infantry soldiers) rooms, but after a couple of hours he still hadn't shown up and Chris became concerned. He reported to the 2IC in the Ops Room, "Sir, one of my lads is missing." A thorough search of the location was organised and Driver 'Mac' McCabe was eventually found, semi-conscious in the RCT garage. When the bomb had exploded near the garage, the shock-wave had caused an array of heavy-duty shelving and tools boxes to collapse on top of 'Mac' and he couldn't extricate himself. Luckily, he only suffered some minor abrasions and bruising.

Considering all of the shootings, bombings and general aggro that happened during that particular tour of duty, in true RCT fashion Chris said, "That was the best Northern Ireland Tour ever, no one on our watch died, except for a Labrador dog called Rhubarb. He attached himself to the lads and was often seen accompanying footsies (foot patrols) in the Murph. Sadly, it is assumed, this was noted by the local residents and one day Rhubarb disappeared."

When the Sqn returned to Bielefeld, Chris was selected for a posting to the British Military Mission (BRIXMIS) in Berlin. These

British Military units operated behind the 'Iron Curtain' in East Germany during the Cold War. The BRIXMIS teams drove around in civilian cars and essentially did a bit of spying on our potential enemies, i.e. the Russians and East Germans. SOXMIS was the Soviet version that carried out similar sorts of missions in Western Germany. RCT soldiers selected for an attachment to BRIXMIS had to prove themselves to be of the highest calibre that the RCT could provide. Chris was really excited about being a driver on a BRIXMIS Team and couldn't wait to get on with the Driving and Intelligence Training courses. Believe it or not, Chris was disappointed when RCT Manning and Records promoted him to Sergeant and cancelled his posting to BRIXMIS. Instead, they posted him to the Jnr Ldrs Regt RCT at Azimghur Barracks in Colerne, Wiltshire, as a Troop Sergeant (Tp Sgt).

On arrival at Colerne, Chris was appointed Tp Sgt of Herring Tp in 30 Sqn. Once again, he was disappointed because he wanted to be Tp Sgt of Connaught Tp in 90 Sqn, the same Tp and Sqn in which he'd done his own training at Taunton in 1972. *Note: By the time the RCT JLR had moved from Taunton to Colerne, its Sqn's had been changed from 'A' Sqn, 'B' Sqn and 'C' Sqn to being actual numbered Sqn's. 'A' Sqn was now called 30 Sqn, 'B' Sqn 57 and Chris's old 'C' Sqn was now 90 Sqn.* Chris was still very young to be a Training Sgt Instructor (h*e'd only left the Jnr Ldrs Regt RCT at the end of his training some 6 years previously*) and with hindsight he felt slightly intimidated by some of the other older Permanent Staff members who saw him as 'another Junior.'

To try and get some extra 'Street Cred', Chris grew a moustache as fast as he could. The SSM of 30 Sqn was WO2 Dave Turner-Swift, who would shortly to assume the appointment of Regimental Sergeant Major of the Regt. Dave Turner-Swift treated Chris like he was an adolescent child. Not everyone was

(WO2) Terry Cavender RCT. Terry was the Regimental Chief Clerk and wasn't the sort of soldier who took life too seriously. He was a definite advocate for having fun in the WO's and Sgts' Mess and at work.

Chris remembers one particular Regimental Dinner Night when Terry Cavender was the main performer in a short skit held on an improvised stage. He was acting the part of a Sqn OC and another Mess Member, Squadron Sergeant Major WO2 (SSM) Andy Cornet, was playing the role of his SSM. The skit portrayed two soldiers on OC's orders for minor misdemeanours. When the curtains were drawn back Terry was sitting behind a desk covered by an Army blanket (the desk, not Terry) and the SSM was standing to the side of him.

Terry: "Morning Sarn't Major, what have you got for me this morning?"

SSM: "Two Drivers sir, both up in front of you on AF B 252 charges. One for failing to get a haircut when ordered to do so by his Troop Sergeant, and the other for not turning up for his Guard Duty."

Terry: "Right, march the first guilty bastard in Sarn't Major."

The SSM marched the first offender in front of the OC's desk.

Terry: "Good morning young man. Now, kindly, explain to me exactly why you failed to get a haircut when ordered to so by your Troop Sergeant?"

Dvr 1: "I've no excuse sir, I simply forgot."

Terry: "Well, to stand there in front of me blatantly stating, 'I forgot Sir' is completely unacceptable. Every soldier should carry out the orders of his Troop Sergeant without fail. I find you Guilty and award you a fine of £60. March him out Sarn't Major and march the other culpable bastard in."

After marching the first Driver out, the SSM marched the second reprobate in front of the OC's desk.

Terry: "Well Driver, can you tell me why you failed to turn up for your stint on Guard Duty?"

Dvr 2: "I'm really sorry sir, I simply forgot all about it."

Terry: *(Outraged)* "YOU FORGOT! Do you think that is an acceptable excuse for failing to turn up for Guard Duty? You've let me down, your Troop Sergeant down and more importantly, yourself and your comrades down, you should be ashamed of your blatant lack of attention to detail. I find you Guilty and award you a £180 fine and 7 days Restriction of Privileges. March him out Sarn't Major!"

The second Driver was marched out of the office, Terry then thanked the SSM and stood up. The SSM looked down in horror when he noticed that Terry wasn't wearing any trousers.

SSM: "Fuck me sir, you've no trousers on this morning."

Terry: "Oh my word Sarn't Major.....Sorry about that, I completely forgot!"

Terry Cavender told the Author: "You probably had to be there. I do recall some 'wag' shouting – "The last time I saw a pair of legs like that they were hanging out of a nest!"

Life in the WOs and Sgts Mess was always fun when Terry Cavender and Andy Cornett were around. *Authors note: Terry has written a book about his amazing career in the Royal Corps of Transport, he rose through the ranks of the RASC and RCT from Junior Private to eventually being a commissioned officer. The book is entitled, 'A Boy from Nowhere' and is available on Amazon.*

Chris was sent on a Unit Expedition Leader (UEL) Summer Course up in Scotland, "I really enjoyed that Course, because years earlier I'd read 'Everest The Hard Way,' by Sir Chris Bonington (a former Royal Tank Regiment officer). I had a desire to get qualified so I could spend time doing some mountain climbing," said Chris "and I later got the chance to do a Winter UEL Course as well. The Winter Course was obviously much more challenging and serious." Whilst on the Winter Course, Chris met an ex-Royal Marines Commando who was putting together a month-long Combined Services Expedition to Canada. The ex-Commando told Chris, "If you can be bothered to write me a letter when you get back down south, you can apply to do the selection week and I'll consider you for a place on the expedition."

Major J C G (John) Hall RCT was the Officer Commanding (OC) of 30 Sqn at Colerne and when Chris reported to him and gave a brief account of his UEL Course, he fleetingly enquired about his chances of going on the 4-week expedition to Canada. The OC stated, "You can definitely go on the selection phase but I think the Commanding Officer (CO) will object to you going on the expedition itself. It will all be about the cost I'm afraid." Chris excelled on the selection phase and was told there was a place on the team if he wanted to go. But, as Major Hall had predicted, the CO refused to give his permission for Chris to join the excursion. To circumnavigate the CO's objection, Major Hall proposed that Chris fund his part of the trip himself. Chris pointed out the fact that the CO still might not give his authorisation and he therefore couldn't possibly go. Major Hall reassured Chris, "Leave it to me Sergeant Iddon. You fund the trip and I'll inform the Colonel of your departure after the plane has left the runway."

Sgt Chris Iddon, Summit of Mount Andromeda, having completed 'Sky Ladders' a 3,000ft snow & ice face

The expedition team of ten Servicemen and women flew to Calgary in Canada on an RAF VC 10. The journey necessitated a short refuelling stopover in Reykjavik, Iceland. Those other team members on the expedition included, Billy Scott, a Sergeant serving in the Royal Scots Regiment, two (Women's Royal Air Force) WRAF Servicewomen, and Sergeant Farrar-Hockley Royal Army Medical Corps (RAMC), the expedition team medic was the nephew of General Sir Anthony Farrar-Hockley, GBE KCB DSO & Bar MC. General Farrar-Hockley was famously nicknamed 'Farrar the Para' because he had served in the Parachute Regiment during the Second World War.

The team spent an overnighter at Calgary before moving on to the Adventure Training Centre at David Thompson Resort (DTR), which was used as a Base by soldiers from British Army Training Unit Suffield (BATUS). The team stayed there for about a week, climbing some local mountains before picking up a stack of British Army 10-man Ration Packs for the rest of their expedition. The large ration packs were very heavy and DTR loaned the team a Bedford MK four tonner and driver to take their rations up to the Columbian Ice-fields in Northern Alberta. Although the team were travelling in two huge gas guzzling American Station Wagons, complete with imitation wooden panelling on the sides, they didn't have enough room in the cars to carry all their ration packs and personal equipment.

For the next ten days, the raison d'être of the expedition would dictate that the team climb the 'Big Stuff' around the Columbian Ice-fields, sometimes at heights of over 12,000 feet. When they set up camp, Chris shared a tent with Billy Scott, which was sited next to Sergeant Farrar-Hockley RAMC, the team medic's tent, and his bivouac was next to the two WRAF girls who were also sharing their own canvas shelter. After only a few day's climbing the team returned to a closed camp-site where the Rangers told them that grizzly bears had been spotted roaming around the camp-site and it was therefore deemed a very dangerous place for people (particularly those sleeping in tents) to stay, the team were advised to move on to another area.

That evening as Chris poked his head out of the tent, he witnessed the problem the Rangers had warned them about. He saw an old American guy in his pyjamas and dressing gown shuffling towards the washrooms, the old feller was carrying a toothbrush, complete with a dob of toothpaste on the bristles, and not fifteen feet behind him was a fully grown adult grizzly bear. The old bloke was oblivious to his Yogi-bear stalker who seemed to be following him. Chris and Billy were no more than 30 feet away from the old man and they went into silent convulsions of laughter at the scene, the two British soldiers were worried about two possible consequences of making a loud noise. One, if they laughed out loud the massive predator might become so alarmed and excited, it might result in the old man getting attacked. Two, if they shouted a warning to the geriatric Canadian, he might turn around, see his stalker and might suffer a heart attack. It all ended well though and the octogenarian Canuck wasn't savaged to death.

On another night, a female Grizzly Bear with two cubs found a box of the expedition's British Army Compo Rations and whilst the bears were having their midnight snack they awoke Sergeant Farrar-Hockley RAMC. He poked his head out of his tent and roused Chris and Billy, "Fuck me! There's fucking bears everywhere, and they're eating our fucking compo!" Not the language that one associated with the well-spoken F-H at all! Chris replied, "Yeah, yeah, just go back to sleep." At that point Chris himself was suddenly startled into consciousness by a spine-chilling, throaty roar. "I thought to myself, 'Fuck me! I'm lying here with only two thin pieces of tent cotton and an Army sleeping bag for protection against, what could possibly be, an 8-foot, 50-stone, fearsome, British Squaddie eating, fucking psychopath." By that time, Sergeant Farrar-Hockley RAMC was starting to get on Chris and Billy's tits when he shouted, "Can you hear that chaps, can you hear it?" Chris lost his composure slightly when he shouted back, "Of course we can fucking hear it, we ain't bloody deaf."

Unbeknown to the lads, one of the two RAF Servicewomen had decided to sleep in one of the expedition's massive station-wagons because she was so terrified about the thought of prowling grizzly bears. She'd prudently locked all of the cars doors. It was at this point that Sergeant Farrar-Hockley RAMC made a heroic dash to the said car, in the hope of saving himself from a mauling by an enraged grizzly bear. Now, said WRAF Servicewoman in said car was rudely woken up by said heroic medic trying to open the locked door. She looked out of the car window and saw him was standing there in his enormous, white, Y-front underpants whilst breathing heavily and whispering, "Let me in, will you?"

Thinking the medic was trying to get his leg over, the virtuous WRAF bird replied in a lady-like fashion, "And you can fuck off!" Sergeant Farrar-Hockley pressed his case to be let into the car, "For goodness sake let me in there will you?" He then made the mistake of telling the WRAF bird, "There are fucking bears out here!" The WRAF bird recoiled in horror and went into a dizzy fit, "Tell me there aren't any bears out there!" Farrar-Hockley replied in a slow, frustrated, and slightly nervous voice, "Ok, there's no bears…. now open this fucking door will you!" Chris and Billy nearly pissed themselves laughing at this Brian Rix style farce, but discretion being the better part of valour, they both also heroically dashed to the car where all four of them then spent the remainder of a rather uncomfortable night, watching the 3 bears trash the next-door camp which was occupied by a couple of Americans.

The whole team then packed up and ventured off to Mount Lyell for about four days. To get there they had a 20-mile walk in; every team member was loaded up like a pack mule with tents, doss bags, spare clothing, cooking equipment and rations. Chris had seen a 100-year-old photograph of the exact same place where they would set up camp on the shore of a massive lake, the photograph incorporated a British Explorer gazing wistfully up at the mountain. Apart from the explorer, the place looked exactly the same as it did in the century-old picture. In anticipation of other bears coming into their camp to scrounge for food, the team placed their rations into large plastic bags and pulled them up into the trees using some spare rope. Unfortunately, the team ended up staying in situ for the full four days because the weather was so piss-poor.

The two ex-Royal Marine team leaders were later joined by two Canadian climbers and their climbing instructor, the five of them having previously made plans to climb the North Face of Mount Robson. At 12,972 feet it is the highest mountain in Canada. As with Mount Lyell, it was another 20 miles walk in and so Chris, Billy, and two pack horses helped them transport all their equipment and rations to the North side of Berg Lake, below the North Face of Mount Robson. It was there they set up camp. Chris described his view of the mountain from the camp-site as, "The most beautiful place I'd ever seen in my life; a glacier was draped down the side of the mountain and it tipped into the edge of the lake. Icebergs that had broken off the glacier were gently floating about on the water." Over the next week, Chris and Billy spent their time at the camp-site doing some walking and climbing, before finally helping the climbers carry their kit to the start point on the North side of the mountain, they then sat and watched them do the climb.

On negotiating a long narrow ridge near to the summit, the mountaineers came upon two cornices, each cornice was an overhanging formation of hardened snow on the edge of a rock face. These naturally made structures formed a bridge over an immense drop. Had it collapsed as they crossed it the climbers would all have inevitably fallen to their deaths. The route to the summit was now untenable so the climbers had to abseil back down the rock face, a 21-rope length drop that had to be completed in several phases. It was mid-day by this time and the sun was beating down on the group. The heat, combined with a very complicated abseil route, resulted in the party taking longer than anticipated returning from the climb; they walked back into the campsite at 0730 hours on Saturday. Chris and the team had to be in Calgary Airport on Sunday afternoon to check in for their return flight to the UK. They'd all been on the go for over two days and had been existing on Dextrose tablets and biscuits dead-fly (Army compo biscuits containing currants). They literally had nothing left to eat as they packed up their camp and started on the 20-mile trek back to Jasper. The Royal Marines were so exhausted that Chris and Billy had to carry some of their kit for them. The four-day strenuous excursion had extended into a gruelling seven-day, and ball-breaking, undertaking.

When they arrived back at the car-park in Jasper, the ravenous party spotted a sandwich wagon where they could buy Canadian/American style BLTs, something that Chris had never before experienced. His more worldly-wise companions ordered

BLTs and so Chris went along with their choice from the menu. On biting into the massive sandwich Chris became aware of what the L and T meant in a BLT and loudly expressed his indignation, "Why the fuck have you put vegetables in a bacon sandwich? A bacon sarnie contains bread, bacon, and brown sauce. Period. You do not put fucking vegetables into a bacon sandwich!" However, Chris ate every last morsel of that BLT, which he described as being, "Awesome." After finishing their fast-food, the team then drove into the centre of Jasper and booked into a log cabin for the night before heading out for a gigantic meal that Chris described as "Amazing." In the morning the lads had just enough time to drive to Calgary and hand in the car before checking in at the airport, so ending Chris's, "Fantastic and life-changing experience."

When he got back to Colerne, Chris received a glowing report about his contribution to the expedition. Eventually Chris was recommended for a move from 30 Sqn to the Regiment's EL (External Leadership) Wing as an Instructor. If accepted, Chris would be taking the Junior Leaders on Adventure Training to places like the Brecon Beacons, North Wales and the Lake District. For a week at a time, Junior Leaders would participate in activities such as hill walking, abseiling, caving, rock climbing, skiing and canoeing. This was potentially Chris's ultimate job as a soldier and in January 1982 he was posted from 30 Sqn to the Regimental External Leadership Wing as an Instructor, so beginning one of the most enjoyable phases of Chris's military career.

Two years later, Graeme Morrison (the Galloping Major) who was now the Regimental 2IC at Colerne, was instrumental in Chris being given a prestigious posting to the International Motor Pool at Supreme Headquarters Allied Powers in Europe (SHAPE) in

Belgium. Chris worked as a dispatcher in the Motor Pool, dealing with all of the VIP transport and he worked alongside soldiers from all NATO member countries. The CO was a German Officer called Busch, Major John Taylor RCT was the 2IC of the Motor Pool and they were supported by an RAF Warrant Officer who was the MTWO. Chris's immediate boss was an old Belgian Para, who was a real character, with a tale or two to tell of soldiering in the Belgian Congo.

Sgt Steve 'Ossie' Osborne & Ssgt Chris Iddon, 2 Sqn, 1 ADTR, off for a Bratty and Chips!

In 1986 Chris was posted to 2 Sqn, 1st Armoured Division Transport Regiment (1 ADTR) in Bunde and was succeeded in Shape by Sgt Bob Russell, an old colleague from his JLR days. Chris was promoted to Staff Sgt for the posting and eventually served as the Tp Staffie in A, B, and C Troops and in the Transport Operations Office. Chris became heavily involved in the unit's Northern Ireland Training programme soon after he had arrived at Bunde. His previous experiences in the Province were an invaluable asset in that he could pass on his knowledge to those who hadn't previously experienced an Operational Tour. Sgt Stephen 'Ossie' Osbourne RCT worked for Chris as his Tp Sgt and ultimately went on to become the RSM of 27 Logistic Support Regiment RCT. After leaving the Army, 'Oz' wrote a book about his career in the RCT which he called, 'Always Believe in Yourself.' "Oz was a cracking Tp Sgt," remembers Chris, "his enthusiasm and self-confidence were inspirational for the lads." During the NI Tour, Chris and 'Oz' became known as the SSAFA Sisters (Soldiers, Sailors, Airmen and Families Association) because with a Troop of almost 80 men to deal with and an absent Tp Comd (Lt 'Woody' Woodford was off working closely with the Infantry at this particular time) they seemed to have more than their fair share of domestic incidents to deal with. During the tour the 'SSAFA Sisters' had to travel all over the Province by helicopter to visit some far-flung locations like Crossmaglen, Forkhill and Londonderry.

Chris was eventually posted from 1 ADTR and went to MoD Army Management Service (AManS) on promotion to Acting WO2. AManS was the British Army's own Internal Management Consultancy Service, Chris being the logistic expert for the team. Predominantly Army personnel, there were also a number of civil servants on the team. Initially, Chris was the most junior rank in the organisation but his appointment to the substantive rank of WO2 was quickly followed 2 years later by a further promotion to WO1. The whole team was made up of WO1's, Majors and Lieutenant Colonels. The job initially entailed Chris spending 14 weeks on a Course at the Royal Military College of Science (RMCS), Shrivenham in Wiltshire and thereafter he spent the next five years on a number of other (often extremely boring) courses.

Army Management Services and its personnel were Army trouble-shooters that would visit MOD establishments and examine many of the operational and administrative challenges these units were experiencing. They would then come up with solutions for these complications and present their proposed solutions to their sponsors.

These are just some of the tasks that Chris was personally involved in whilst serving at AManS:

1. Planning for the British Army draw-down from BAOR.

2. The refurbishment and building of Barracks and Married Quarters in Catterick and Tidworth Garrisons to house the returning BAOR Troops.

3. The logistics involved in moving these soldiers and their unit equipment and vehicles back to the UK.

4. The 'In-Service' planning for the Apache Helicopter.

5. He also visited DCBRN Centre at Winterbourne Gunner, where the Defence Chemical, Biological, Radiological and Nuclear Centre needed advice on ways to improve their administration.

6. On another job he spent 9 months at AMF (L) (Ace Mobile Forces (Land)) in Bulford, researching how to improve the logistic support required by AMF (L) when they deployed to Norway and Turkey, to practice their operational role. This extended from Memoranda of Understanding between NATO and host nations, right down to simple things like the boxes they used for packing their equipment.

Chris learned so much about the wider British Army during his time at AManS and of course it offered him the opportunity to work closely with civilians and improve academically, it was the perfect pre-release course! Iddon's first comment about this phase of his career was that, "this was when they took the cabbage out and implanted a brain." The changeover from RCT to Royal Logistics Corps (RLC) went almost un-noticed by Chris because he spent most of his time at work wearing a suit.

If you think that Chris has had an impressive, if somewhat different, military career then wait until you read about how he has spent his life since leaving the Army!

He worked on:

1. The Planning and Emergency Services for the Farnborough International Air Show from 1997-2000.

2. He was the Operations Director for the Dutch Temporary Structures Company, De Boer, for 4 years until 2005 and spent a lot of time at the firm's headquarters in Holland.

3. Whilst working for himself he project-managed a job at the Chelsea Flower Show.

4. He has also worked and lived in Barbados whilst organising the temporary infrastructure for the 2007 Cricket World Cup. During this time, he took over 130 flights in 10 months because it was such a massive logistics challenge, the competition was held at 13 venues on 9 different islands.

5. He was responsible for developing the Health and Safety policy for temporary works at the Beijing Olympics Equestrian venues in Hong Kong.

6. He went to Johannesburg in South Africa to set up and deliver the temporary infrastructure for the 2009 FIFA Confederations Cup and 2010 FIFA Football World Cup and whilst doing that he was commuting back and forth to Delhi in India, where he advised a team doing a similar job for the 2010 Commonwealth Games.

7. He then went on to spend 6 months in Doha, the capital of the peninsular Arabian Gulf country of Qatar, working on the Asian Football Cup.

8. And last, but by no means least, Chris managed a team of up to 600 people installing temporary grandstands and tents at the London Olympic Games, in 2011 and 2012.

His work schedule had been immense, and he finally ran out of steam, the stress of working on the London Olympics finally putting him into hospital for a brief period. Chris did the right thing in the end and walked away.

He now lives in Epwell, Oxfordshire with his beautiful wife Linda where he runs his own Company, Timeline Events Services (TES) Partners, from where he acts as an advisor to the International Olympic Committee on temporary infrastructure and services, as well as working with a number of companies in the global event industry, the most recent of which is planning to deliver the first National Youth Games in the fast-evolving Saudi Arabia.

Chris confided in the author, saying, "Harry, believe it or not, I'm not a people person. I'd often rather turn the other way than speak to people. I really do suffer with my self-confidence. I know that about myself, but when the shit does hit the fan I can take 5 minutes out before I constructively run around getting the problem sorted and for sure, I could never have achieved all that I have in the last 20 years, had I not had the training and experience that my time in the Corps has given me, or for that matter without the support that Lin, my long suffering wife has quietly given in the background for over 40 years. *Authors note: if only you'd manned up Chris, just think what you could have achieved.*

24484265 Warrant Officer Class 2 Ted Fost
RCT and RLC (1978 – 2002)

Ted Fost's life has often been dragged into an ugly and convoluted world of violence, be that as a child, soldier, boxer, and finally as a civilian truck driver. Throughout his life, Ted Fost has never turned his back on a fight, and in 2011 he became embroiled in an ugly and vicious brawl with three other men who he describes in his usual indomitable way, "*One was as big as me, but the other two muppets were fuck all.*" Ted had been discharged from the Army some 9 years before this public punch-up took place, and after he'd completed 24 years' of 'Exemplary' service in the Royal Corps of Transport (RCT).

Ted said to the author, "*You have to bear in mind that I was an old man when this ding-dong kicked off, (49 years old to be fairly precise), but I still stayed on my feet against these fuckers for about 10 minutes before they managed to get on top of me.*" When Ted says that they'd 'got on top of him,' he means that he ended up in hospital for a week after suffering from some appalling injuries. Ted suffers from an impaired memory because of what he calls, "That good kicking". *(Authors note: I've never understood what a 'good' kicking is like. Each one I've ever received in the British Army was always a bloody dreadful experience).* After reading this chapter, any ex-RCT soldier who served alongside Ted and is disappointed that he (or she) didn't get a mention in his story, they might now understand why he probably won't remember them or anything they did together. The exact details of this melee come from Ted's own words, "The first guy hit me with a piece of wood and then out of the shadows came a couple more. They laid into me and I had my back to my wagon whilst trying to keep on my feet. The first blow from the piece of wood cut my head and split my ear. I kept up the good fight for about ten minutes before I was knocked out cold and I believe they stamped on my head a few times. My injuries consisted of a split eye, my ear hanging off my head, and a fractured jaw which resulted in me losing three teeth. I spent a week in hospital and two weeks recuperating at home before I was fit enough to go back to work."

Ted's family's military history contains some venerable military chronicles, his Great-Grandfather was born in 1854 and he eventually went on to serve in the 9th Battery of the Royal Artillery, which at one stage was based on the Devonshire Coast. Gunner William Fost was a typical young soldier of that time who probably joined up to get away from the boredom of living at home. He may well have wanted to grab some adventure in an otherwise dull, monotonous, and austere existence. Many young lads of the time probably imagined the life of a Victorian soldier to be a glorious and exciting way of life. The Recruiting Sergeants of the day wore smart red tunics with large white chevrons on each arm and children were attracted to the Recruiters like moths to a flame. British Army Recruiting Sergeants have always been able to spin great yarns about what a grand life it is serving in the British Army, and Gunner William Fost of the Royal Artillery (RA) may well have been enticed into the Army after being regaled with stories of soldiering in India and South Africa. He certainly wouldn't have been told about the poor pay, awful rations, boring stints on guard duty, and the harsh military discipline which involved some very brutal punishments.

The Cardwell Reforms that were introduced by the British Government in the 1870's, however, did a lot to improve the pay and rations of the average Victorian British Soldier. And in 1881 the British Government added another bonus for the British Army, the British Army was forbidden from administering flogging as a form of punishment to its legendary Red Coats. The archaic and sadistic whippings were replaced with a new military penance called Field Punishment No 1, the changes incorporated a convicted soldier being tethered to a field post or gun wheel for a designated amount of time each day, until his sentence had been fulfilled.

Ted has some proof of his Great-Grandfather's Service in the Royal Artillery. He has a couple of trophies that Gunner W S Fost had been awarded for his excellent shooting skills using the Mk1 Martini Henry rifle *(The rifle had been adopted by the British Army in 1871 and remained in service until the bolt action Lee Enfield took its place)*. Ted still proudly displays these awards in his home; they are endorsed with the following inscriptions on a goblet and clock.

Goblet
1st DVA
Prize presented by the Mayor.
April 2nd 1877
Won by Gunner Wm Fost

Clock
Presented by Lieut F R Bonberie.
Shot for by the 15th Batt 1st HAV.
Ranges 100 200 &400 Yards.
Won by Gunr W S Fost.
May 12th 1882

Ted's Grandfather on his mother's side of the family was WO1 (RSM) Board who served in the 1st Battalion Dorset Regiment for 40 years, during that time he soldiered in Africa, India and throughout the First World War. Another of Ted's relatives had enlisted into the Royal Navy during the Great War and served on HMS Invincible during the Battle of Jutland.

Lewis Fost, Ted's dad, was born in Stratton village a few miles North West of Dorchester and he served with the Royal Air Force durin the late 1950's in Holland, Germany, and the Middle East. He was also attached to the British Army on numerous occasions, but his service records remain a bit sketchy on exactly what he was doing at that time. Lewis Fost served with the British Army during the Aden campaign (14th October 1963 – 30th November

1967) and he was attached to famous Infantry units including the Ghurkha and Dorsetshire Regiments. Exactly what Lewis was doing during these attachments remains a mystery to Ted, even today. After returning to the UK, Lewis served for 30 years as a Civilian Police Officer and spent much of that time as a 'Copper on the beat' when he was based at Paddington Green Police Station in London.

Ted has three siblings from his mum and dads' marriage, he has a 5-year older Brother who is called Lewis after their Dad, a 2-year older Sister called Rachael, and another sister, Justine, who is 4 years younger than Ted himself. No-one knows what goes on in a child's head at times, but Ted was obviously a very disturbed and angry little boy. He was constantly involved in fights on the way to school, during lessons at school, during playtime at school, on the way home from school, and that often spilled over onto his free-time fights during his evenings on the streets of North London. Ted explained, *"In the end I became a right hooligan and assaulted anyone who looked at me the wrong way, and that included policemen."* Life at school in North London was a very tough experience and Ted often kept himself to himself, but when he saw a school bully tormenting a female friend of his, he felt compelled to intervene. Ted knocked the tormenter senseless and the school staff had to telephone for an ambulance to take the tyrant to hospital and from this point onwards, Ted joined a local gang of hoodlums and he often had to bailed out of trouble by his dad.

The British Heavyweight boxer Henry Cooper unwittingly became an influence on Ted Fost's life when they met at Vale Farm Boxing Club near Wembley. It was after meeting the famous British Fighter that Ted started training in that club when he was about 12 years old. The boxing training progressed onto Ted representing the Hendon Police College Boxing Team and he fought for them on a couple of fixtures. It was perfectly legal for family and friends of Policemen to represent the college at fight-meets. Meeting Henry Cooper and participating in boxing tournaments cemented Ted's life-long love of the sport, however, it didn't stop him from getting into trouble with the law!

When a slightly older previous school-friend, Martin (Spike) Langford, was home on leave from the Army, he chatted to Ted about what life was like when serving in the British Army, "*In the Army we play lots of sport and have nice clean rooms to live in, we also get plenty of food three times a day, all you have to do is queue up for scoff three times a day and when you get to the front of the line, they pile loads of it onto your plate.*" Ted enquired of his friend, "*So it's a bit like Butlins then?*" The sport and food alone encouraged Ted to try and join the British Army, but the Recruiting Sergeant had some rather bad news for him. "So, *you've been in trouble with the police have you son? Then I'm afraid we can't accept you into the British Army, those are the rules I'm afraid.*" After being rejected by the Army, a colleague of Lewis decided to speak up and vouch for Ted down at the Army Careers Information Office. The military recruiters relented on their objections and after doing his entrance exams and physical tests, Ted was told he could join the Junior Leaders Regiment of the Royal Corps of Transport, which was based at Colerne in Wiltshire. Whilst awaiting his Army joining instructions, a forward-thinking Ted decided to get some experience working as a Labourer for an old civilian truck driver in anticipation of his forthcoming career as an Army truck driver. When Ted originally asked his Dad about which part of the Army was the best to join (Ted had already expressed an interest in becoming an Infantry soldier), his Dad told him, "*Don't join any of that lot because when you come out of the Army you'll end up selling televisions for Radio Rentals. If you join the RCT though, you'll get qualifications and a trade that Civvy Street really needs.*" Ted decided there and then, he was going to be as a soldier in the Royal Corps of Transport.

The Junior Leaders Regiment RCT (Jnr Ldrs Regt RCT) which was formerly based at Norton Manor Camp, Taunton in Somerset was initially established to train soldiers of the Royal Army Service Corps (RASC), the unit then rebadged into the Royal Corps of Transport (RCT) in 1965 but remained at Norton Manor Camp in Taunton. By the time Junior Driver (J/Dvr) Ted Fost turned up for his Junior Leaders training in June 1978, the regiment had moved to Azimghur Barracks near Colerne Village. At least 40% of the young men who entered those gates at Taunton and Colerne went on to become either Commissioned Officers, or Junior/Senior NCO's and Warrant Officers of the RCT.

Ted was put into Gloucester Troop in 30 Squadron under the guidance of WO2 D A Turner-Swift RCT who was 30 Sqn's Squadron Sergeant Major (SSM). Ted Vousden was Ted's Troop Sergeant in Gloucester Troop, Sgt Vousden would eventually attend one of Ted's future wedding ceremonies. The Junior Leaders that Ted trained alongside were young men like Junior Driver (J/Dvr) Bob King, (who would eventually be promoted to Warrant Officer Class 1 Junior Regimental Sergeant Major (J/RSM)) and included Rosie Rosarto, Lennie Bantleman, and Pete Iheagwaram. *"They were all great RCT soldiers in the making,"* said Ted. In fact, by the end of their army careers, Lennie Bantleman, Ted Fost and Pete Iheagwaram would all eventually rise to the rank of WO2 (SSM). Pete would ultimately finish his RCT career at Colchester whilst serving in 16 Air Assault Regt RLC before then having a successful career in the Civilian Police Force. During his training at the Jnr Ldrs Regt, Ted expanded on his boxing experiences and fought several other Junior Leaders, both in and out of the boxing ring, but the one opponent he could never best was Bob King. *"Bob boxed at a heavier weight than me and he was just too strong, I was never tough and resilient enough to beat him. Bob King was a great Army boxer and is still a very valued friend."*

When Ted progressed into Senior Troop, he eventually 'Passed Out' of Colerne and submitted his preference of postings, "*I knew that 10 Regiment RCT was the home of our Corps boxers and so I put my name down to be posted to Catterick Barracks in Bielefeld.*" The Mixed Services Organisation (MSO) coach that transported the new arrivals from RAF Gütersloh to their various units in Bielefeld, had a mixture of RCT, R Sigs, REME and Stackers (RAOC) on board. The 10 Regt RCT soldiers were deposited in the Taxi Rank on the opposite side of Detmolder Strasse, Bielefeld and after crossing the busy four lane road they were met by Lance Corporal (LCpl) Johnny Walker RCT who was the Duty Regimental Policeman that night, "*Alright then lads, who have we got here then?*" Johnny was both an accomplished 10 Regt RCT boxer and an unaccomplished comedian.

Ted was put into C Tp, 9 Sqn where his Troop Staff Sergeant was SSgt Pete McCartney, and his Troop Sergeant was Sgt Tommy Docherty. Things started going wrong for Ted not long after he'd arrived within the Sqn, mainly because he wouldn't back down when threatened by other more senior soldiers who wanted to assert their authority over the recently arrived Nig's (*Nig's was a derogatory term used by RCT 'old sweats' for recently arrived Drivers who were, **N**ew **I**n **G**ermany*). Ted was ordered to report to the tool store and sign for a set of coveralls. The stores were located in the cellars underneath HQ 9 Sqn's corridor. As Ted descended the stairs into the basement, a big LCpl from C Tp sneered at him and said, "*Oy, fucking Nig, come here.*" Ted took great exception to the big LCpl's derisive attitude towards him and dragged the JNCO into the cellar where he knocked him out with a couple of punches. Word spread very quickly around the Sqn about this audacious Nig who had punched out one of 9 Sqn's supposed hardmen. A congregation of soldiers, including LCpl Phil Stonier and Drivers Sandy McPhail, 'Hippo' Hughes, Keith Willoughby, and 'Snigger' Flitcroft all gathered at the top of the cellar stairs to discover who the upstart was.

Sgt Docherty came down from the HQ corridor and started shouting the odds, "*Driver Fost! Get in my office, NOW!*" Ted's Tp Sgt bollocked him all the way as they strode into C Troop's empty office, "*I WON'T HAVE DRIVERS IN MY TROOP BEHAVING LIKE THE SQN FUCKING CORRIDOR IS A FUCKING COWBOY SALOON. WHO THE FUCK DO YOU THINK YOU ARE, GET IN MY OFFICE, NOW!*" Sgt 'Tommy' Docherty then slammed the door behind them and continued to scream and shout at Ted, he then quietened down and told Ted, "*Fucking well done young Fost, you have no idea how many times I've wanted to fill in that twats' face. Good on you my son.*" 'Tommy' then opened the office door and shouted, "*Now get out of my office!*" The charade had convinced everyone in the Sqn corridor that Ted had just been given the bollocking of his life. The incident didn't end there though because later that night a heavily outnumbered Ted (10 to 1) was dragged from his bed by the big LCpl and some of his mates. He was man-handled into the washroom where they broke his knuckles over a basin using a spanner taken from a 10 Tonner tool-kit. "*The beating was a punishment for giving their mate a hiding, and there was no point in putting up a fight,*" said Ted, "*I was up against about eight big lads and if I fought back, it would only have made it worse for me.*" Ted even remembers the name of the RCT soldier who broke his knuckles, but for legal reasons the author can't include it in Ted's chapter. Sgt Docherty moved Ted into a room with LCpl Gus Gleed so that the two of them could keep an eye on each other, he also put Ted on his HGV 2 driving course as soon as his hand had healed, (you needed strong hands to turn the steering wheel on an AEC Mk 1 Militant).

Word had got around 10 Regt about the fact that Ted had got some 'previous' in and around a boxing ring and he was told to report to SSgt Tony Morris in the unit gymnasium for a 4-week fitness and boxing assessment. Tony Morris managed the 10 Regt RCT Boxing Team. The reason Ted initially asked for a posting to 10 Regt was because of the units' prowess in the boxing ring, "*But

I didn't realise exactly how good the 10 Regt boxers were. When I boxed, I just piled through who was opposite me in the ring." Ted was brutally honest about his boxing appraisal in front of SSgt Tony Morris and some of the other RCT boxers, "*I was eating a lot of leather and hitting a lot of air in the spaces where my opponent used to be, they were fucking good boxers at 10 Regt.*" Ted actually sparred against some of the 10 Regt greats like, Charlie Allman, Joe Leeds, Reg Locker, Baz Mayhew and the resolute Cpl Phil Lewis. "*I did some sparring with a couple of the 10 Regt boxers during my appraisal in front of Tony Morris and then went into the ring against Cpl Phil Lewis. It was like going up against a locomotive, Taff Lewis railroaded me, and to all intents and purposes, he beat me up, but I didn't fall down at any stage.*"

At the end of his four weeks assessment, Ted was called into the Gymnasium Office for an interview with SSgt Tony Morris who told him, "*You're not quite what I'm looking for at the moment, you can report back to 9 Sqn now.*" Although slightly disappointed, Ted went back to working on the Vehicle Park feeling that he'd learned a lot from his time training with the 10 Regt boxers. Within two months Staff Morris collared Ted on 9 Sqn's Vehicle Park with a proposition, "*I've got a fight coming up, are you interested?*" Did a bear shit in the woods? Ted was taken over to the Gym to be weighed and he told Tony that he hadn't done any serious training for a while. It was while being weighed that Ted was given the full story of why he'd been called up for the team, "*Phil Lewis has been arrested by the Royal Military Police for being drunk and fighting, I need some-one at Phil's weight for a charity boxing match in Osnabrück tomorrow night.*"

Ted first public appearance as a 10 Regt RCT Boxer was at that charity fight in Osnabrück where he was up against a 'Tankie' soldier from the Inniskilling Dragoon Guards (IDG) who was shortly to leave the Army after serving in his Regiment for 22 years, and it would be his last ever boxing match for the IDG. On seeing his opponent for the first time, Ted thought the 'Tankie' had to be at least twice his age. As his opponent entered the ring Ted could feel the ground shake under his feet as the Inniskilling 'Tankies' started stamping their feet whilst shouting, "*TANK! TANK! TANK! TANK!*" Ted's opponent ran straight over towards his corner as soon as the bell rang to start the 1st Round. He was probably using shock tactics in the hope of putting Ted on his back foot; it didn't work. Ted boxed the 'Tankie' out of the ring and stopped him in the 2nd Round. When Driver Ted Fost got back to Bielefeld after the match, he found that he was now everyone's mate in 10 Regt.

Over the next few months Ted went to an Army training camp in Rhyl where he did some sparring with the Welsh ABA Boxing squad, he also boxed a bloke who the previous year had been a semi-finalist in the Nationals and Ted stopped him in the 1st Round. Ted also stopped a Royal Artillery Gunner in another BAOR competition just before Phil Lewis reported back for duties on the 10 Regt Boxing Team. Taff Lewis's return to the team meant that Ted had to return to 9 Sqn's vehicle Park. It was around that time that Ted was promoted up to LCpl by the OC of 9 Sqn.

After watching the Television reports about the Falklands War in 1982, Ted felt that he needed to increase his soldiering skills before trying to attempt selection for Special Duties with 14 Intelligence and Security Company (14 Int). From the early 1970's onwards, '14 Int' was established by the British Military to fight a Counter Terrorism War in Northern Ireland. The unit worked closely with all sorts of Special Forces Groups and even had its own intense and very physical selection process. Its soldiers were selected from the four major British military Forces Groups and was involved in dangerous 'reconnaissance' duties in Northern Ireland. The unit was made up of four Detachments that were based in Antrim, Londonderry, Newry and Belfast, the four detachments were commonly referred to as 'The Dets.' I knew then that I wanted to attempt special duties. I spoke with my Sqn

Ted Fost on the Beat Up for the 14 Int Selection.

SNCO's and they organised for an attachment to 3rd Battalion Grenadier Guards at Kiel in North Germany. This is where I did my beat-up training and improved my Infantry soldiering skills. I spent 3 months with some brilliant lads, one of them offered me a Grenadier Guards beret, which I gratefully accepted but refused to wear. Ted described the very basic camp as being, "*A fucking scary place.*" For three months he was run ragged every day on long runs through the woods, intensive weapon training on many types of firearms he'd never seen before, how to build a surveillance hide that would be invisible to the naked eye, and a thousand other 'sneaky beaky' subjects. On a final Surveillance Exercise, Ted was put into a Recce Troop and the other soldiers in his Section offered him the chance to wear one of their Berets. An outraged Ted told them, "*I can't wear that, if my RSM sees me wearing that thing he'll go fucking ballistic.*" Authors note, such is the phobia in the British Army of upsetting your own Regimental Sergeant Major.

On completion of the attachment Ted was told by the Gren's staff that he was going back to 10 Regt with a glowing report. The Staff gave him the following non-committal bit of advice, "*Keep up your fitness training and we may be in touch.*" It was months before Ted was posted to '14 Int' and he is reluctant to say too much about what he had seen and done in the Province. However, what you are about to read shouldn't set the MOD lawyers onto him. Ted was inducted into the unit and sent away for 5 weeks of additional training in the UK. His first job when he reported back to his Det was duties with the Devon and Dorset (D&D's) Regiment. My first job in the province with the D&D's and the second with 3rd Battalion Light Infantry, after that phase was completed, I went back to the UK. My next job was working as a service mechanic at Newtownards. The team got the target they wanted, and Ted was then sent back to the UK again before reporting back to his 'Det' with long hair and a scruffy beard. His next job involved him working as a Service Mechanic in a Ford garage where he observed a certain individual for quite a long period of time, reporting any relevant information back to his Operation Team Leaders.'

Ted explained that everything he did with '14 Int' wasn't all, "*Bodie and Doyle type stuff.*" The Det had safe/observation houses all over the Province and sometimes Ted was sometimes used for the routine maintenance duties on these places. Two electric heaters had been left in a safe house that wasn't being used for a while, and Ted was detailed to take an unmarked car to collect the radiator heaters and return them to the Quartermaster's stores. Unbeknownst to Ted, a team of 'friendly' Operatives were using the place when he tipped up to collect the heaters. As he entered the house Ted was set upon by four 'Cloak and Dagger type' agents who had seen him get out of the car and watched him walk up the front garden path. Unfortunately, the 'Operatives' manning the OP in the house had never seen Ted before and because of his long hair and beard, assumed he was one of the bad guys. With four burly men holding him down and twisting one of his arms up his back, he also had his face pushed down into the hall carpet and heard someone say, "*Who the fuck are you?*" Without giving his identity away, Ted mumbled something about only being there to pick up some electric heaters, it took the 'Men in Black' several minutes to check-out Ted's identity and after making a couple of calls, he was given the all clear. This was after they had tied him to a chair and scared the shit out of him.

Ted isn't too sure of how many details he can give about another incident he was involved in, so the dates and identity of the people involved are kept to a bare minimum. Some soldiers had been shot whilst on a stake-out one night and one of them had died at the scene, another had been severely wounded and was clinging onto life in hospital, Ted was detailed to pick up the wounded soldiers' wife from Belfast Airport and take her to the hospital where her husband was being treated. Ted was tooled up with a collapsible shotgun and a Browning 9mm HP pistol. Whilst on route to the hospital Ted was hemmed in by an illegal Vehicle Check Point (VCP), manned by IRA henchmen. The wife in the back of the car had been sobbing all the way from Belfast Airport and after spotting the VCP Ted thought to himself, '*Fucking hell woman, you are going to have to man up a bit for a while, we could be in some deep shit here.*' The IRA gunman was wearing a British Style army combat jacket, a pair of jeans and had a full-face balaclava on his head, even more worrying was the fact that he was also carrying an AK 47 Rifle. When Ted pulled forward, the gunman shone a torch directly into his face and demanded to know where he was going. Ted showed the gunman his doctored driving licence and very quickly adopted quite a convincing Northern Irish accent, the terrorist then noticed the woman crying in the back of the car.

Gunman: *What's up with her?*

Ted: *Apparently, she's wailing on her husband.*

Gunman: *Why?*

Ted: *He's got a cancer or something and I'm taking her to the hospital.*

Gunman: *What?*

Ted gave a very convincing portrayal of being a bored and exasperated Irish taxi driver nearing the end of his shift.

Ted: *I'm taking her to the hospital because her husband is fucking dying. Can you let us get on now!*

Gunman: *Oh aye, on you go then.*

A very relieved Ted drove his passenger onto the hospital and left her there with someone else taking over his 'Baby-sitting' duties. On debrief the following morning, Ted's RSM, who was a Para Regt soldier, told him, *"Fucking hell Ted, good one mate."* Because of Ted's unflappable reactions, the RSM recommended Ted for a post as a batman/driver for 'Colonel C' who was serving in the Province at that time. The Colonel was big mates with General Peter de la Billiere and Ted was instructed to report to the Colonels safehouse the following night.

Ted walked up the path and knocked on the front door, the Colonel answered the door himself and was wearing a dressing gown and slippers.

Colonel: *Ted?*

Ted: *Yep.*

Colonel: *In you come.*

Ted: *But I thought...*

Colonel: *In you come Ted!*

Ted: *I thought I was …..*

Colonel: *Get in the fucking house will you Ted!*

Colonel C then briefed Ted on what he needed him to do the following day. Firstly, he needed to be driven to the Maze Prison, after which, he had an appointment at an RUC Station near etc. Ted eloquently explained to the author that, "*For the next five weeks I was the Colonels bitch, and all I had to do was drive him and Peter de la Billiere (who was Director SAS at that time and on more than one occasion I drove him around the Province). One of my jobs at the time was to keep my fucking big mouth shut.*" When the Colonel C had finished with Ted's services he told him, "*Thanks for everything you've done for me Ted, you're a good man. You'll be going on holiday for the next three weeks.*" Generously, the Colonel had organised, and paid for, Ted to have a Saab hire car for his three weeks leave in the UK.

On his last assignment, Ted was given over to 9 Ulster Defence Regiment (UDR) and when he arrived at the location, he was told that an Irish UDR Corporal would be commanding their patrol. The stroppy UDR Cpl vociferously laid down the law to everyone in a threatening manner, including Ted. The patrol wasn't good from the very start and Ted had a feeling it wasn't going to end well. There seemed to be a lot of hostility and aggression directed towards him from the other soldiers in the patrol because he was a 'Brit.' Halfway through the duty, one of the UDR soldiers spat in a woman's face and she called him a dirty bastard. The soldier then back-handed her and another soldier kicked her shopping trolley over and then threatened her with his rifle.

The patrol was eventually debriefed in a canteen in an old Nissan hut. As some Officers entered the room, Ted took the UDR Cpl who'd commanded the patrol to task over the back-handing incident.

Ted: *What the fuck was that all about?*

Cpl: *It has nothing to do with you, you fucking prick, she was just a fucking Taike bitch.* (*A derogatory expression used in Northern Ireland about Catholic women*).

Anyone who knows Ted Fost will appreciate that the Cpl was on a road to perdition by using this sort of language towards him.

Ted: *What? Like my Mum? I'm a Catholic you know.*

When the Cpl concurred with Ted about his Mum, a fight broke out in the de-briefing room between him and the other soldiers from the patrol. Ted smashed a chair over the Patrol Commanders back and he chinned a Rodney (Officer) who stepped forward to come to the aide of his NCO. Ted revealed on his interview, *"There was no way I was going down in front of these fucking muppets."*

Ted was sent back to HQ '14 Int' where he tapped the boards in front of the CO (Colonel C had left by this time) who told him, *"You're going on enforced leave now Ted, you're too angry to continue in this sort of job."* Ted agreed with him and told the Colonel, *"No problem Boss, I'm ready to go now anyway."* An RE clerk gave Ted his posting options after he'd left the Colonel's office; he could take a posting as a Staff Car Driver in Washington DC, Hong Kong, or Singapore. Ted enquired why 10 Regt RCT wasn't on the list of possible postings available to him? Before leaving the unit, Ted was presented with a unit plaque and a souvenir tankard, embossed with a personal quotation taken from the Holy Bible. Every soldier who has ever served at 14 Int Coy in Northern Ireland has traditionally been bestowed with similar types of gifts. Ted's tankard has the following words inscribed on it:

'Luke XIV Verse XXIII (King James Version)'

And the whole multitude of them arose and led him unto Pilate. And they began to accuse him, saying, we found this fellow perverting the nation, and forbidding to give tribute to Caesar, saying that he
himself is Christ a King.
And Pilate asked him, saying, Art thou the King of the Jews? And he answered him and said, Thou sayest it.
Then said Pilate to the chief priests and to the people, I find no fault with this man.

A very sad footnote about Ted's attachment to 14 Int happened after he had eventually returned to 9 Sqn RCT in 10 Regt. Ted watched the harrowing news broadcast about the murders of Cpl's Derek Wood and David Howes in Anderson Town. These young Royal Signals NCO's were dragged from their unmarked car after being blocked in by an Irish funeral procession, the mourners believing that they were members of an opposing terrorist organisation. Derek and David were both armed with 9mm Service pistols but neither of them fired any rounds towards the baying mob who attacked them. They were both stripped of their civilian clothes before being pitilessly, and inhumanely, executed on some waste ground.

Ten years later *(The butchers were supposed to serve 25 years in prison)* the British Government kindly released Derek's and David's execution squad under the Good Friday Agreement, and yet those same politicians are still hounding some of those British Soldiers who stood between the Northern Irish warring factions from 1969 - 1998. The bitter irony of this story is that whilst a distraught Ted Fost watched the news report like many other Servicemen (*the author included*), he had a lot more to be upset about than the average incensed British Serviceman. Ted was very good friends with Cpl Derek Wood and had worked closely with him on many occasions doing 'Top Cover' whilst out on relay duties.

After a month stop-over in Buller Barracks, Aldershot, Ted then flew back to BAOR and reported to SSgt Phil Stonier in A Tp 9 Sqn and within 6 months of being back in 10 Regt (1987-1988) was promoted to full Corporal and made a Truck Transporter Fuel (TTF) Section Commander. One of the soldiers in his Troop was Driver Richie Temple (*Richie's full story is the penultimate chapter in this book*), Ted terrified the life out of Richie from the day he was put into Ted's Section, which is unsurprising really, because they both come from opposite ends of the personality spectrum. "*Richie was a good Driver,*" said Ted, "*And he was obviously bought up by good parents. He wasn't a rough-arsed Council Estate scrote like a lot of us were. He was a very pleasant guy who'd obviously had a good education. He was a bit more up market than a lot of the guy's in my Section and more suited to be an Officer and a Gentleman than a Driver.*" Driver Gringo Green, also on the other hand, was a wheeler and Dealer within Ted's TTF Section, and when Richie and his room-mate were discussing that it might be nice to have a couple of Budgerigars in their room, Gringo took them at their word and tipped up the following day with a couple of Budgies, cages, and enough seed to feed them for the next 6 months. There were others in Ted's Section who did achieve distinction within the Corps though, Driver Dave Holyoak went on to become a WO 1 (RSM) and Driver Dave Goodchild rose through the ranks and eventually was granted the Queen's Commission within the Corps.

When the First Gulf War was looming on the horizon, 10 Regt RCT was warned that they were going to be a key element in the Third Line Logistic Supply System for 1 (UK) Armoured Division. 9 Sqn would be supplying the fuel in their TTF's and UBRE's and 17 Sqn would be shifting the ammo etc, in their General Transport vehicles. Lt Col P (Phillip) Chaganis RCT was the Commanding Officer of 10 Regt RCT when the Regt deployed out to Saudi

Arabia. He made the decision to withdraw Ted from his TTF Section in 9 Sqn, promote him to Sgt, and put him in RHQ's. I was put into RHQ as the Ops Sgt, working for Major Harvey Ops doing security with the then RSM WO1 Ian MacLachlan, a brilliant guy. The CO knew my reputation and that I was a handful at the best of times. I believe that he wanted me on his staff in case things went wrong and we needed to fight. Ted eventually did 10 months in the Middle East because he was on the Advance Party with the first Officers to deploy and was one of the last to return when it was all over.

Ted Fost in Bahrain whilst on a Close Protection duties.

Whilst out there he provided CP for Lt Col Chaganis and his Adjutant, Captain Macnish (later Lieutenant Colonel) (*Cameron Macnish's Chapter is also included in this book)* the Padre and the RSM. He had to accompany them when they went on meetings with the Egyptian Army, were briefly attached to the 1st US Marine Corps and visited the Scots Dragoon Guards and a Royal Artillery (RA) unit that was equipped with the new Multiple

Launch Rocket System (MRLS). 17 Sqn would be one of the RCT Sqn's doing the ammunition re-supply runs for those units. The CO detailed Ted to accompany an MOD Civilian VIP to the airport for his return journey to the UK. The senior civil servant was wearing a Saville Road pinstripe suit and carried a briefcase and umbrella. After safely dropping his charge off at the airport departure lounge, Ted went to a nearby shopping mall to buy some slabs of soft drinks for the boys back in the unit. A scud missile landed not far from their Land Rover and blew it onto its side rupturing a lot of the fizzy drink cans that spewed out their contents. Ted was covered from head to foot in a mixture of sweet sugary fluid and sand, the sticky mess plastered onto everything, including their weapons. The three lads then lifted the Land Cruiser back onto its wheels and briefly inspected it for any damage, Ted gave it the once over said, "*Yeah, that'll be alright*." before they headed back to 10 Regt's location.

A lot of Ted's deployment during the Gulf War saw him hanging around various high-level command centres and working with RMP's and CP trained soldiers who were conveying VIP's all over the theatre of war. At one of the Brigade Headquarters, (Bde HQ's) Ted was watching some RAF bods pinning an overlay on some maps when General Peter de la Billiere walked in. The General was Commander-in-Chief of all the British Forces in the Gulf, and Second in Command of the entire Multi-National Forces. As he was walking past he stopped and said to Ted, "*Don't I know you?*" Ted replied, "*Yes Sir!*" and before the ex-SAS Directing General walked off he told Ted, "*Nice to see you again Sergeant*." One of the RAF bods said, "*How the fuck do you know him?*" Ted replied, "*Just some stuff I did in Ulster*."

When the war was over, Ted was utilised by the powers that be to check areas that had been used by their coalition forces and make sure that they hadn't left anything 'naughty' behind, especially weapons and ammunition. Ted checked out a previously used unit location that had some caverns to its rear.

He was unarmed and working on his own at the time when he entered those caves. As he went further and further into the darkness, he was met by some growling animals who were protecting their young. Ted thought to himself, *"Shit, I always thought that when I was killed as a soldier, it would be by being shot on the battlefield on the end of a bayonet, not by catching rabies from a wild fucking dog."* Ted slowly and safely backed out of the darkness and returned to his HQ. It wasn't long after this incident that Ted flew back to BAOR.

Ted Fost in Baldrick Lines Al Jubayl 27th November 1990.

After he'd returned to Bielefeld from the Gulf War, Ted's recollections about the dates and timings of his army career start to get a bit hazy. He does remember being asked by WO 1 (RSM) (Roger) Cass RLC if he wanted to go back to the UK with 10 Regt RCT when it moved back to Colchester Garrison. Ted decided to remain in Bielefeld and became a part 7 Regt RLC when the new unit moved into Catterick Barracks. A Staff Car pulled up next to Ted as he was marching up Column Road one day. A Senior Officer climbed out of the rear of the car and asked, *"Sergeant!*

Would you be kind enough to direct me to the NAAFI?" Colonel (later Brigadier) Stern recognised Ted as soon as he clapped eyes on him, *"I know you, you're a boxer. It's Sergeant Fost isn't it."* Colonel Steirn had seen Ted box on a few occasions, including when he was a lad and he'd fought for the Hendon Police College. *"I've got a proposition for you Sergeant,"* he said.

That proposition resulted in Ted being promoted to SSgt, and he started selecting, building and running 7 Regt RLC's future boxing team. Just as the late, lamented SSgt Gary Fuller, when I was a young boy in JLR RCT Gary Fuller was my boxing coach for the 18 months that I served there. He would often hold my whole head in one of his massive hands, lean in close and whisper in my ear, "Fost, you're a fucking wanker. Even when I boxed in competition and won he would always repeat those words to me. I love that guy". Ted started trawling the new RLC units to muster the best boxers the Corps had, in the hope of assembling yet another comparable boxing team. Drivers Micky Ord, Chris Stock, Jim Garvie, and LCpl Nigel Evans were all legacies of the boxers left behind in Bielefeld when 10 Regt departed for Colchester and they all helped to recruit and set up the new team. The only difference was that these lads now had the new RLC rank of Private, as opposed to their old RCT equivalent rank of Driver. Ted explained, *"The last Logistic unit that had achieved anything in boxing was the mighty 10 Regt RCT, the loss of SSgt Gary Fuller, Micky Gannon, Stevie Johnson, and all the other super stars from that era sadly saw the demise of RCT dominance in boxing after 1977."* Ted wanted to have an ultimate team of thirty RLC boxers to work with and after gaining others from 3 Tank Transporter Regiment RCT, he often got near to that desired figure.

It must have been daunting for SSgt Gary Fuller back in the early 1970's when he started assembling, what ultimately became, the famous 10 Regt RCT Boxing Team. Ted explained how it was for him when he started building his team, *"At 7 Regt RLC, our boxing team of Chef's, Drivers, and a few bottle washers would be up against Major Infantry Units like the Queens, Kings, Guard's Regiments and Para's, but when the team started training I thought to myself, 'Fucking Hell, this team is good.*' Within three weeks of creating the team, Ted and his lads in 7 Regt RLC progressed into the BAOR Semi-Finals against 2nd Bn Royal Anglian Regiment, The Royal Anglians were current champions and favourites to take the competition title. After the penultimate fight the score was 4 – 4 and in the last round of the final bout, Private 'Scouse' Eddie Edwards RLC was beaten on points.

The following year, Ted got his team to the finals against the Parachute Regiment but unfortunately lost to the Paras at RAF Aldergrove. Over the next 5 years on the trot, under the guidance of SSgt Ted Fost RLC, 7 Regt extraordinarily won the BAOR competition five times. Ted was eventually posted to the Scottish Transport Regiment as a SSgt and Cpl Jim Garvie took over from him running the 7 Regt Boxing Team. In future competitions, Jim's 7 Regt teams beat 2 Para in the semi-finals but was beaten by 1 Para in the final, (Cpl Jim Garvie RLC beat both Paratroopers he faced though). Ted wants to state that, "Colonel Steirn was a massive influence on him taking over and running the 7 Regt boxing team and if he hadn't had the help from him and Kevin Bennett, Jim Garvie, Nigel Evans, Jim Crilly, Micky Ord (who Ted states was an absolute fucking nightmare to try and control), 'Scouse' Eddie Edwards and the rest of the team, he couldn't have achieved anything. "*They'd all had mottled army careers and most of them had been locked up in a Guardroom at some stage or other, during their time in the Corps most had been a problem of some sort to their Commanders. But they were all very fit hard-nuts who had a determination to win, a lot of 7 Regt's wins came down to sheer guts and attrition.*"

"I would like to pay tribute to a few names who are complete and utter fucking legends".

Kevin Bennett
Jim Garvie
Nigel 'Big Daft' Evans
Jim Crilley
Mick Rutherford
Chris Howie
Troy Watkins
Malc Earl
Stevie Gallea
Micky Ord
Davie Brown
Deano Hill
Chris Stock
Eddie 'Scouse' Edwards
Steve Sutton
Dave Downing
Mick Keane
Richie Gooderham
Davie Hewlett

There are too many others to mention, but they gave me their all and served the Regt well and with courage.

The RLC swapped Ted with the RQMS at the Scottish Transport Regiment (STR) and so he went off to Edinburgh as a SSgt (SQMS) for the next 18 months. Ted's boss was WO2 Graham Jack RLC, who he described as being, "*A brilliant bloke who took me under his wing, I needed it as well because I wasn't the best SNCO in the Corps, I was very confrontational and got in everyone face if they annoyed me, no matter what their rank or position.*" At that stage of Ted's Army career, he'd been married twice and was the father of 4 children, (Heather, Iona, Eilleen and Gregor – their brother Luke as born later). Gregor was taken ill one night, and Ted was advised to take him to the hospital in Edinburgh. Ted decided to bring his eldest (8-year-old Iona) along with him, so that she could hold onto her brother as he drove the car. After giving his son the once over, the Doctor gave Ted some medical instructions and asked him to bring Gregor back in the morning to have him looked at again.

As the three of them walked back to the car park, Ted saw his car was being wrecked by five drugged up yobbos who were all from the same family, they were well known to the Edinburgh police. Ted's car was the only one in the car park that night and he screamed at the hooligans, "*Get off my fucking car!*" At the same time, he passed his car keys to Heather and asked her to, "*Get Daddy's club out of the boot of the car for me will you darling, and no matter what happens, make sure you put it into my hand.*" After knocking out one of the thugs with a single punch, Ted then set about the other four and their American Pit Bull Terrier, utilising a hockey stick that he'd misappropriated from the SQMS Sports Store. The incident had been spotted on local CCTV and the local constabulary dutifully turned up and arrested Ted not long after he'd dealt with the hoodlums. The police watched the hospital CCTV and deduced that Ted was defending his family and was also trying to protect his car.

The following morning the police contacted Ted's boss, WO2 Graham Jack RLC, and informed him of what had happened to Ted. They told him, "*We've come to a quick conclusion on this incident but need to interview SSgt Fost before we close the case.*" Graham collared Ted as soon as he walked into the Headquarters building that morning and told him, "*There are two coppers in the bosses' office and they want a word with you in front of me and the old man.*" One of the policemen said, "*Although it was very dark last night, the CCTV verifies everything you put in your statement and you were clearly defending yourself, and I have to say, that was the best bit of CCTV footage I have ever watched. You proper went for it my man, that was very impressive, what the fuck did you use to hit them with?*" When Ted told them that it was a broken hockey stick that he'd been meaning to dispose of, the policeman said to Ted, "*Put this in the boot of your car my man,*" and he handed over a police-issue riot control baton that had a right-angle handle, *"Use this next time you have any wee bits of bother, it'll be better than any hockey stick. Oh, and by the way that CCTV footage is going viral round all our Police Stations, we've been after these bastards for a while."*

WO2 (SSM) Ted Fost 3 CS Sqn RLC.
Within a year Ted was promoted to WO2 and posted down to 3 CS Regt RLC at Abingdon as 35 Sqn's SSM, a job that Ted

described as being, "*The worst fucking job in the world, it was so naff. No-one wanted to be your mate anymore and all the SSM's were in a competition to be the smartest and shiniest Sarn't Major in the Regiment.*" Accordingly, Ted stated, "*The only other Trog in the unit was a great lad called WO2 SSM Al Tindale RLC, the rest of them were all stackers (Ex Royal Army Ordnance Corps).*" Ted started applying for MOD jobs just before he was discharged from the Army and each reply came with a disappointing, but polite, letter that said, 'Thanks, but no thanks.'

Ted bought a house in Cleethorpes near Grimsby. He and the family all moved in and one day he had a brain-freeze, he deserted his wife and children and moved down to Andover. For a short while he lived at his brother's house whilst waiting out his probation period to join the Hampshire Police Force. During that period Ted beat up a Police Sergeant and was given the option of resigning from the force, or having criminal charges brought against him. Ted resigned. Friends he was living with asked him to leave and he ended up living in his car near the Humber Bridge. Ted thought that he was destined to drink himself to death.

Whilst drinking in a bar one night, Ted met the pub barman, Chris Denford, who offered Ted a room to stay for a while until he sorted his life out. Over the next few months Chris used his contacts to get Ted some jobs, "*Let's face it,*" said Ted, "*My London accent didn't cut me any favours up here in Grimsby*." He worked on the docks for a while and did some labouring before getting himself into yet another fight, Ted threw the bloke into the dock and the management asked him to leave. Over the next few years Ted worked with a Dutch firm after driving trucks for a nice guy called Chris Ridley.

He came home one day to find his partner had left him and taken everything with her, including his son. Ted started working on the continent for a Swedish Company and didn't take a day off, or return home, for the next three years. When he did get back to

Cleethorpes, it was to a still empty house. He took up an offer of a job in Tampa Bay in Florida and just before leaving he visited his son who sobbed and told Ted that he didn't want him to leave. The departing words haunted Ted so much that he decided to return to the UK after just three weeks.

Ted lost his father 2 years ago and still misses him terribly. "My Dad was my best mate as well as my Father. I spoke to him a couple of times a week and he would always listen and give me good advice, because normally I would have fucked up somewhere and attacked somebody. But he never judged me, not once, because he loved me. Luke, my youngest son, got on with my Dad like a house on fire. Luke also loved him dearly".

Ted continues to live in Cleethorpes and still drives articulated trucks for a living. On a recent trip Ted was taking a break when a tanker driver came over to his cab, banged on the door and they had the following chat:

Tanker Driver: *I know you.*

Ted: *Oh yeah.*

Tanker Driver: *Do you know who I am?*

Ted: *Some nobber who drives a tanker for a living. What the fuck do you want?*

Tanker Driver: *You're Ted Fost, and you frightened the shit out of me when I was in 10 Regt, you made my life in the Army a fucking misery.*

It was at that point in their conversation that the complainant got back into the cab of his tanker and drove away. As he drove off Ted thought:

Ted: Ah good, another satisfied customer.

Ted is due to marry Lisa Marie Fennessy in May 2019, she is the granddaughter of Roy Gilbert, the owner of Verna Bier Quella, Roys Bar across the road from 10 Regt's Camp in Bielefeld. Ted met Roy as a young RCT soldier on the many occasions he would drink in the Quella bar and played cards. This was the first time and place that Ted met Lisa all those years ago, he describes Lisa as being his whole world, and more. They are planning to use their wedding reception in sunny Cleethorpes as a 10 Regt and 7 Regt reunion.

24627424 Driver Tim Butterworth
RCT 1982 – 1987

Tim and Russ Butterworth with their Mum and Dad (Sgt Butterworth, Duke of Wellington's Regt).

Most of the RCT soldiers (Trog's/Trogg's by nickname) who have volunteered to be interviewed for inclusion in any of my books are, in the main, sons of soldiers. Tim Butterworth is not only the son of a soldier but is also the brother of a Trog soldier.

Tim's Dad, Denis 'Butch' Butterworth, grew up in Leeds and on 7th May 1959 and he enlisted into the British Army's legendary 1st Battalion Duke of Wellingtons Regiment (Duke of Boots). He was one of the last recruits to complete his training at the Regimental

Depot in Wellesley Barracks, Halifax, West Yorkshire. From the 6th of August 1959 all further 'Dukes' Infantry training courses were conducted at the 'Kings Division Depot' at Queen Elizabeth II Barracks, Strensall, near York. When Denis joined his Battalion, he was placed into the Battalion's Somme Company and ultimately worked his way up through the ranks to become the Anti-Tank Platoon Sergeant. When the Battalion was stationed in Halifax, Denis met, fell in love, and married June Marie Slattery. They enjoyed a brief attachment to an RE unit at Chattenden in Kent where Dennis was an instructor on Lodge Hill Camp Firing Range.

By 1980, the 'Dukes' Battalion was stationed in Minden Garrison West Germany, and it was there at British Military Hospital (BMH) Rinteln that Denis was diagnosed with having two brain haemorrhages. The RAMC Doctors ultimately sent Denis back to the UK and he was admitted to BMH Woolwich on the 1st of September 1980 for further diagnosis and treatment. June Marie Butterworth obviously wanted to accompany her husband back to the UK but she didn't want Tim to go through any further emotional trauma, and so it was decided that he should stay in Minden. The 'Dukes' Welfare Officer thought that Tim, who was only 14-years old at the time, would be better off staying with a family serving within the Battalion. Tim on the other hand though, wanted to stay with his best friend, David Ainsley. David's Dad was a serviceman in the Corps of Royal Signals and wasn't even attached the 'Dukes.' The Ainsley's were more than glad to have Tim stay with them and help the Butterworth family get through the emotionally charged and distressing period of Denis's illness. Tim remained in Minden whilst his mum and Dad flew back to the UK and at the time, he thought it was all a bit of an adventure; subsequently Tim realised that his mum had a lot to deal with at BMH Woolwich, and so in reality it was probably for the best that he did initially stay in Minden. The Members of the Battalion's Wives Club kindly cleaned Denis's and June's MQ for them to get it ready for handover back to the ASU

(Accommodation Services Unit) in Minden. Tim said, *"There weren't that much to do anyway because as far as me mam were concerned, Cleanliness were next to Godliness."*

Tim's brother, Russell, was serving as a Driver in A Troop 17 Squadron, 10 Regiment RCT which at the time was located in Bielefeld, about 30 miles away from Minden. 'Russ' used to nip over and visit his family whenever he had any free time and just before he deployed to Northern Ireland on an OP BANNER Tour a couple of years previously, he tipped up at the family's Married Quarter in Minden with a Saracen APC. He was doing his NI Driver Training in preparation for 17 Sqn's Christmas deployment to the Province (Oct 1979 – Feb 1980); a young Tim was given the privilege of sitting in the Driver's seat for a short while and he daydreamed about driving a Saracen APC himself one day. Meanwhile, Denis and June went to see a top Neurological Surgeon who was based at another London hospital. The Surgeon told them that Denis had suffered two haemorrhages in his brain, one on top and another deeper into the brain itself. The medics gave Denis an estimated 50/50 chance of surviving the complicated and very dangerous surgery he was about to undertake.

The 'Dukes' moved back to the UK and took up post in Catterick Garrison. Tim travelled back to the UK with another family who were also serving in his Dads' Battalion. He met up with his mum at their allotted Married Quarter, located just behind the line of white shops in the middle of Catterick Garrison. After 6 months in hospital and several brain operations later, Denis's condition had considerably deteriorated both physically and mentally, so much so, he was never going to get back into the Battalion. Having served with the 'Dukes' for just over 21 years, Denis was being discharged from the British Army and his beloved Battalion. In 1981 Sgt 'Butch' Butterworth of the 1st Bn Duke of Wellingtons Regiment was Medically Discharged from the British Army. He hadn't completed his full 22 years service but his

Regiment, and the MOD, wangled it so that he would receive a full 22 year's gratuity and pension.

Denis, June, and Tim moved into a council house in Halifax and after living in Married Quarters for nearly 22 years, Prime Minister Margret Thatcher decided that because of his time and money he'd spent paying to live in Service Married Quarters, they could buy the Council house at a more affordable price. June used the money from Denis's gratuity to completely pay off their mortgage. Tim started attending the local Secondary Modern School in Halifax and considering he'd attended four different Services Children's Schools (SCS) over the previous few years, he still claimed CSE passes in History, Geography and Maths.

After leaving school, Tim joined the Army simply because his Dad had been a soldier, his brother was a soldier, and for years he hadn't considered doing anything else. At the Army Recruiting Office the Recruiting Sergeant was from the Duke of Wellingtons Regiment (Halifax was a big part of the Regiments' catchment area). "*Before I went down to the Army Careers Office I asked me Dad, coz he could still talk at that time, what he thought I ought to join.*" He told me, "*If you're going to join up lad, then you need to get yourself a trade.*" "*I also recalled when 'Russ' came to visit me in Minden when he were doing his Northern Ireland Training in 1980, he pulled up in an Alvis Saracen Armoured Personnel Carrier (APC) near me Dad's married quarter. I were allowed to sit behind the steering wheel of this fantastic APC and I remember thinking to me self, 'I'm going to drive one of these beauties' one day'.*"

Bearing all this in mind, Tim told the 'Duke's' Recruiting Sgt, who knew Tim's Dad from when they served in the battalion together, "*I want to join the RCT.*" The Sgt continued to try and coerce Tim into joining the 'Dukes' but Tim was adamant, "*I simply wanted to drive Army trucks like me brother.*" At Harrogate Selection

Centre, Tim put in his three choices of which regiment or Corps he'd prefer to serve in:

1st choice: RCT
2ND choice: RCT
3RD Choice: RCT

The Selection Staff suggested to Tim that he might consider joining the RCT.

Tim got off the train at Bath Railway Station in September 1982 and, along with the other recruits, climbed into the back of an Army truck and they were transported to the Junior Leaders Regiment RCT at Azimghur Barracks, Colerne. At the camp reception centre Tim was collected by his Troop Instructors, Sgt Gibb and Cpl Don Morgan, and taken over to Clayton Troop in 57 Sqn. Corporal Morgan was a black soldier who was always immaculately turned out. He recognised the Butterworth name and asked, *"Have you got a brother called Russ?"* When Tim told him that Russ was in fact his brother he snarled, *"I was in 10 Regt with him and I didn't fucking like him."* Tim thought to himself, *'Ooops.'* From this point onwards, Cpl Morgan was constantly on Tim's back and he eventually made a point of back-squadding him, purely because he disliked his brother. *(The author spoke to Russell Butterworth, who today still lives in Germany, about why Cpl Morgan disliked him so much, and he was none the wiser.)*

Clayton Troop went out on a 3-day Exercise in January 1983 and on the second night they all had to do a night time river crossing whilst carrying a casualty on an improvised stretcher. It was a bitterly cold night and the Junior Leaders had to pack up their kit in black plastic bags before protecting the whole bundle by wrapping everything up in their waterproof ponchos (the package also acted as a floatation device). The temperature was hovering around 0° and as Tim could barely feel his hands, he let go of his floatation device and slipped under the water. Junior

Driver Frankie 'Syd' McCoy and Junior Lance Corporal 'Dinger' Bell both grabbed hold of Tim and pulled him out of the water; Tim's jaw was chattering away ten to the dozen and he began shaking violently. 'Syd' and Dinger unrolled a dry sleeping bag and stuck him inside it to warm him up. *Authors note: This is an indication of the realistic and valuable training that Junior Leaders received in the British Army. Had these two young lads not seized control of the situation, then Tim may well have become severely hypothermic.*

In his second term at Colerne, Tim applied to join the Regimental Sky Diving Hobby Club, because of his age he wasn't allowed to participate during in his first term. The RCT's 'Silver Stars Free Fall Parachute Team' was based in Colerne whilst Tim was doing his training and Sgt Jeff Chandler RCT was their team leader. Under Jeff's instruction and guidance Tim learned how to how to pack parachutes, to safely exit a Cessna aircraft, how to land without doing himself a serious injury, how to remain stable whilst free-falling, and how to turn left and right during free-fall using the air-flow that hits the body and arms. Regardless of his thorough ground training, Tim was shitting a brick on his first of 3 stable jumps using a static line. That meant that after jumping out of the Cessna aircraft, his static line was still securely attached to the airplane and as he plummeted towards the ground, his parachute was automatically pulled out and deployed for him when it was dragged out of his pack by the static line. On completion of that stage of his parachute training he then moved onto doing 3 static line jumps on a dummy pull which involved him pulling a dummy handle on his equipment, even though the static line would deploy his chute for him. The dummy handle was attached to the parachutist's harness by a piece of elastic material so it wasn't lost during the parachute jump. Thereafter Tim had to do three 5 second delayed pull jumps but this was done without using a static line, three 10 second delayed pull jumps, again without using a static line. When they started on the 15 second delay jumps the students began putting into practice on how to turn in the air during freefall.

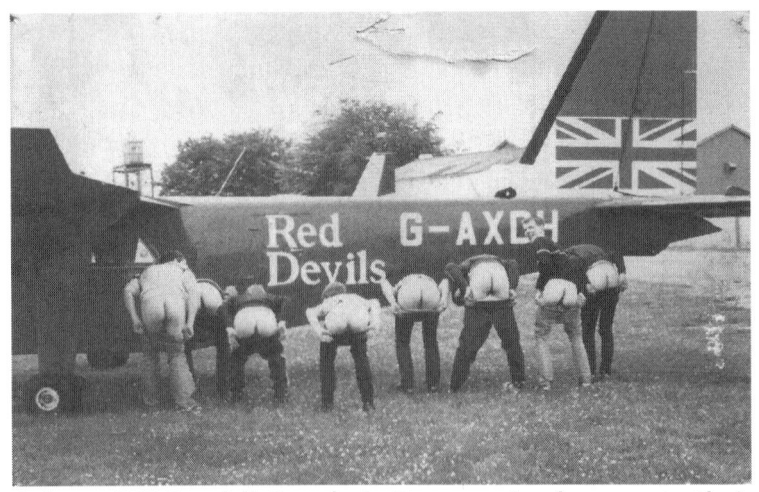

Colerne RCT Freefall Parachute Team paying homage to their Parachute Regiment counterpart team. Tim is 4th from the left.

By the time Tim was ready for his first posting he'd completed about 70 freefall jumps and was at Category 10 level. He was, by then, using square parachutes when he jumped which were much more manoeuvrable during descents after the parachute had deployed. After he was posted to 10 Regt in Bielefeld, Tim did a couple more jumps at the Bad Lippspringe Parachute Club but then gave it up because it wasn't a cheap sport to enjoy. *"Let's face it,"* said Tim, "You could buy a lot of Herforder Pils beers for the price of one parachute jump." Tim knew that his brother was serving in 10 Regt RCT, but he didn't know that 'Russ' had claimed for him to be posted to 10 Regt with him, the OC of 17 Sqn put in the application to RCT Manning and Records that's why Tim ended up at in 10 Regt with his brother. The Junior Leaders from Colerne who were posted to BAOR stayed overnight at RAF Hendon, and the following morning they were taken by coach to Luton Airport. Driver (Later Major - RLC) Mick O'Flynn, Driver's Steve Cruikshank, and A N Other Driver accompanied Tim as they all flew out to Hannover airport. On arrival in Germany they went to the RCT Movements Clerks desk in the arrival area and they were given some railway warrants to Bielefeld. Once outside the airport they caught a bus that would take them directly to the Bahnhof (German Railway Station). The lads hadn't got a Scooby Frigging Doo from which platform their train to Bielefeld would be leaving.

Steve Cruikshank: *Hey Tim, you must know some of that German lingo coz you were born out here, why don't you go and ask someone which platform our train will be leaving from."*

Tim spotted a German lady railway worker wearing a smart uniform complete with a Red 'Twat' Hat. He went over to see if the lady could give them any help. The Bahnhof Official was amazed at Tim's command of the German language and his flawless accent.

Tim Butterworth: *Er...Gerten targ luv.....er.....oh bloody 'ell....er, yer dern't speak any English der yer luv."*

Luckily the lady Railway Official did speak English (and she spoke 'our native tongue' considerably better than Tim could). With typical German efficiency she told Tim, in fluent English, which platform he required, what time the next train was due in, when it would be departing and what time their journey would terminate at Platform 2 in Bielefeld Bahnhof. Tim then walked back to his comrades to let them know what he'd found out:

Tim Butterworth: *Piece of piss that lads, once you've learned a bit of the old German tongue, you never forget it you know."*

The lads hired a couple of taxis to take them to Catterick Camp and Tim proved to the lads that his German vocabulary was improving by the minute.

Tim Butterworth: *Aye oop pal, can yer gerruz all ter Catterick Kasserne bitte please?"*

The four lads were all destined to be put into 17 Sqn and so they headed off to its Headquarters to be processed into the system. Members of the Sqn were hanging out of their accommodation block windows and with no trouble at all, they easily identified the arrival of some Nig's (New In Germany). As the lad's walked past the end of the Sgt's Mess building, Tim spotted his brother 'Russ'. Russell had already told everyone that his brother was being posted into the Sqn and someone shouted, "*Hey Russell, which one's your brother?*" 'Russ' rather impolitely shouted back, "*He's the little one!*" They hadn't seen each other for about 2 years and so gave each other a hug.

It was April 1984 and Tim was put into A Troop where he met his Troop SNCO's, Sgt Seamus O'Callaghan and SSgt Tam Forrester, these two notorious RCT senior ranks treated everyone in their troop fairly, but very firmly. Sgt Seamus O'Callaghan was a famous Corps SNCO who had served as an Air Despatcher during the Secret War in Dhofar; he was also one of the celebrated 10 Regt RCT Boxing team of the 1970's who'd won everything and anything worth winning in Service boxing.

Steve Moulding explained to the author during a telephone interview during the writing of this book, "*I can now understand why Seamus gave a few digs to the men in our Troop, me and Tim were a couple of gobshite's really and we were always late on working parades in the morning. Most nights we were usually pissed out of our heads and Tim was always dropping himself into trouble because he could never keep his big mouth shut. Thinking about it today, we must have driven Seamus and Tam to distraction at times.*" When Tim initially arrived in 17 Sqn, Seamus told him that he'd have to look to his laurels if he was going to match up to his brother Russ who was in B Troop; 'Russ' was working in the motorcycle Training Wing at the time.

Tim was allocated a bed-space and roomed with Driver Keith Haycock, then did a conversion course on how to drive in Germany soon after his arrival. Within a month Tim was put on an HGV 2 driving course in an AEC Mk III Millie with Lcpl Dennis Brown as his Driving Instructor. Tim thought the 'Millie' was a far better driving experience than Bedford TK in which he'd done his Class III training at Colerne.

'Exercise Lionheart' in 1984 was such a massive three-week Exercise that it was divided into two phases, the first stage was called 'Exercise Full Flow' which dealt with the deployment of Allied Forces onto European soil. Stage Two was 'Exercise Spearpoint,' which was the ultimate Field Exercise that followed. 'Exercise Lionheart' incorporated the deployment of over 131,000 UK based Service personnel from Regular, Reserve and Territorial Army units, who deployed into Belgium, Holland and West Germany by land, sea and in the air. It was the largest movement of troops since the Second World War had ended. The Royal Engineers were particularly busy during the Exercise because the planners had written into the Exercise scenario that all major civilian bridges had been destroyed by enemy air assets. The Sappers had to build a lot of temporary bridges so that the units deploying from the UK could reach the Forward Edge of the Battle Area (FEBA). That was where our 17 Sqn RCT hero, Driver Timothy Butterworth, entered the fray.

On the Exercise Tim would be driving his ten ton 'Millie' in support of 38 Engineer Regiment Royal Engineers (RE) which was based at Gordon Barracks in Hameln. He spent a lot of his time being loaded with the necessary bridging equipment and stores which he'd collected from Railheads and Royal Army Ordnance Corps (RAOC) Depots. During the Exercise, Tim found it difficult to adjusting to sleeping during the day and working at night. The majority of military vehicle movement was carried out at night because that's the way the RCT would have worked tactically during wartime; there wouldn't have been any sense in giving the

Tim Butterworth is on the far right and enjoying a few leisure time drinks with other 17 Sqn RCT reprobates.

enemy any easy daylight targets. So, bearing in mind the tactical scenario of RCT Drivers on the BAOR Exercise - and Tim's insomnia problem, it won't surprise the reader that our hero Tim fell asleep at a set of traffic lights one night whilst waiting for the lights to turn back to green.

Tim was very rudely awoken from his slumber by a Deutsche Polizei Offizier banging his truck door and shouting, "*Wach auf Tommy! Sie müssen bewegen dieses Fahrzeug bewegen,*" which roughly translates into English as, "*Wake up Tommy! You need to move this vehicle.*" *Authors note: The German Police Officer probably wasn't being sardonic; the author was often referred to as 'Tommy' by Germans during the 1970's and 1980's.* Tim and his RCT comrades spent longer hours working on the Exercise than most of the non RCT soldiers who had deployed into the field. That was because when Endex (End of Exercise) was called, the RCT Drivers had to return all of the Exercise stores and bridging equipment back to their relevant depots.

On the last day of the Exercise, the OC of 17 Sqn approached an exhausted Tim and asked him how things were going; Tim explained that he'd recently fallen asleep behind the wheel of his truck. He'd been negotiating an 'S' bend that went over a railway crossing on the penultimate day of the Exercise and had hit a lamp post, smashing his truck's wing mirrors. The OC spoke to A Troops' Troop Commander (TC), who detailed Lance Corporal Dennis Brown RCT to drive Tim and his Millie back to 10 Regt in Bielefeld. Tim had fallen asleep on the trucks engine cover before Dennis had got the truck into third gear and woke up just as Dennis was driving through Catterick Barracks' camp gates in Bielefeld. That was a wake-up call for Tim about how exhausting it was for all soldiers on military Exercises, but in particular for the Drivers and JNCO's of the RCT.

When Tim wasn't on Exercise, doing guard duties or working on the vehicle park, he could usually be found down in Bielefeld getting drunk with his room-mate Keith Haycock and their friends, Rob Lawrie, and Steve Moulding. On one particular night they had obtained tickets to get into a discotheque called 'PC 69' which was in Bielefeld town centre. At the time it was a very popular haunt for a lot of 10 Regt soldiers because the establishment sold beer, and every night the place was always full of German girls because the club occasionally hosted live Groups like Oasis, Marillion and Iron Maiden. The band on this particular night was playing Queens' 'Bohemian Rhapsody' when the lads were pulled up onto the stage, and for the next 20 minutes they pretended to be Freddie Mercury. The club Owner was so impressed with the 17 Sqn 'Freddie Mercury' impressionists; he presented Tim and Keith with a bottle of Champagne which turned out to be a bottle of Pomagne, a cheap and nasty version of English Cider. In a good 10 Regt style, the lads immediately popped the plastic cork and drank the whole bottle.

That night 'PC 69' was also hosting a fire-eating act and the entertainer was spitting fire all over the stage and doing a mini burning sword swallowing act. Tim turned to his mate and said, "*Keith, we've got to fucking have a go at that mate!*" The fire-eater wasn't keen on the idea of showing them the tricks of the trade, but after being badgered for 20 minutes he capitulated and the lads went up onto the stage and had a go. "*We did all right actually*", said Tim, "*When we'd done our bit we strode back off that stage and went back to our seats, everyone were amazed that we hadn't got third degree burns or singed bloody eyebrows.*"

The lads then went onto the dance floor where a young man of Turkish descent was showing off his break-dancing skills as he spun around on the floor. Tim remarked to the author, "*By 'eck 'e were good n'all.*" Tim copied what the young Turkish lad was doing but added a couple of back flips before throwing down a challenge to the dancing Turk, "*Go on then mate, top that bugger.*" The break-dancing Turks' sister suddenly ran up to Tim on the dance floor and threw her arms and legs around him and gave him a big kiss. Tim explained what happened next, "*A fight broke out because the Turkish lads weren't happy about one of their own sticking 'er tongue darn the throat of a British squaddie.*" Over the years many 10 Regiment soldiers had become aware that the Turkish community in Bielefeld didn't fight fairly when it came to the art of fisticuffs and bar brawling. The next thing Tim started shouting, "*Keith, Keith. I've been stabbed mate!*" Although the wound was clearly bleeding it turned out that the blade had only penetrated Tim's skin by about a half an inch or so. Keith ripped open Tim's shirt and after inspecting the cut he said, "*Hang on mate, I'll be back in a minute.*" He came back seconds later in possession of an improvised First Aid Kit that consisted of a roll of toilet paper and some Sellotape.

Keith made a pad that resembled a British Army shell dressing out of the bog roll and secured it to Tim's torso by wrapped him up in the Sellotape. Keith reassured Tim when he said, "*Sorted mate.*" The lads then went back to fighting with the angry local ethnic lads. The four of them left 'PC 69' at 0700 hours and walked back to Catterick Barracks in the snow, whilst wearing short sleeved shirts. They couldn't afford a taxi because they were Boracic and Lint (Cockney rhyming slang for skint) having spent all their money on beer and Asbach brandy throughout the night.

On Working Parade the very next morning, the SSM (Squadron Sergeant Major) informed everyone that the next Junior Military Qualifications Certificate (JMQC) Promotion Course was starting that very day, and the Training Wing Sergeant still had a vacancy on the Course for one more Driver from 17 Sqn. The SSM, WO2 Dave Hopper, shouted, "*Right, who wants to step forward and volunteer before I designate someone.*" The drivers started looking around to see which idiot was going to volunteer for this demanding promotion course at such short notice. Drivers who'd already been nominated for the JMQC had already prepared for the course by ironing their No2 dress uniform, bulled their boots, and read up on what was required of them to pass the syllabus. Suddenly, and without any prompting from Driver Tim Butterworth RCT, Lance Corporal Russ Butterworth RCT, yes, his brother, shouted to the SSM, "*Driver Butterworth will do it Sir!*" Tim was astounded at his brothers' impertinent and brassy attitude in volunteering him for further military education. Everyone on the Work Parade, excluding Tim of course, found the whole thing extremely funny. Tim was given the morning off to sort his shit out and get his sorry arse up to the Training Wing. Ultimately, Tim did very well on the JMQC and finished in 4th position overall, but he thinks his high place might have been because he'd only been out of Basic Training for about a year, and a lot of the training information was still fresh in his mind.

One week after the JMQC had finished, Tim noticed on Part One Orders that the Regiment was looking for a volunteer to go on a six-week 'Exercise Med Man' in Canada. It was too good an opportunity for Tim to ignore and so he reported to his Troop Sgt, Seamus O'Callaghan, and put in a bid to be considered for selection. Seamus, rather bluntly, put Tim in the picture as he saw it, *"There are plenty of blokes in this Sqn who have been here a lot longer than you, so no. Go on, Fuck off!"* Tim thought to himself, *'Oh well, fair enough I suppose.'*

Seven days later Tim was back working on 17 Sqn's vehicle park when someone came up from the Sqn Headquarters and told him, *"Tim! The OC wants to see you, get your arse down to Squadron HQ and report to the Sarn't Major."* When he got down to 17 Sqn HQ, Tim was marched in front of the OC by Dave Hopper and was surprised to see that his Troop Commander, SSgt 'Tam' Forrester, and Sgt Seamus O'Callaghan, were also in the office. *"My first thought was, 'Who's fucking died.'* After halting smartly in front of the OC's desk, Tim saluted his Sqn Commander before they started the following conversation.

OC: Well done on passing your JMQC Driver Butterworth, I believe you did very well on the Course."

The OC then stunned Tim by asking him,

OC: Would you like to go to Canada for six months?

Trying to look furtively at Seamus through the corner of his eye Tim replied.

Tim: Flippin' 'eck, er, I mean, yes please sir!

Sgt O'Callaghan: He's supposed to be on his B2 Course next week sir, he's got to do that first, so he can't go.

OC: Can't he do that when he gets back Sgt O'Callaghan? I think Driver Butterworth should be given this opportunity and so I'm going to sanction his detachment to the British Army Training Unit Suffield (BATUS) in Canada. March him out Sarn't Major.

The first-person Tim was going to gloat about the Canada detachment to had to be his room-mate, Driver Keith Haycock. Keith was soon to be going on 'Exercise Snow Queen' in Bavaria and for the last couple of weeks he'd been crowing about it to anyone who would listen. 'Exercise Snow Queen' was a British Army organised skiing trip that was held on the Bavarian mountains. The two-week course/holiday would involve Keith staying in the Corps' very comfortable skiing lodge at Silberhütte and for a fortnight he'd be drinking copious litres of Bavarian Bier in many of the local drinking establishments. When Tim told Keith about his wonderful news his room-mate replied, *"You jammy fucking Nig bastard. How the fuck did you manage to wangle yourself onto that?"* To this very day Tim has no idea why the OC chose him to go on the Canada detachment. Nevertheless, two weeks later Tim caught a plane back to the UK from RAF Gütersloh. After the aircraft had landed at RAF Brize Norton it picked up the UK based soldiers who were also going out to Calgary for 'Exercise Med Man' in Canada.

It was February when he arrived in BATUS and the weather was very cold in the extreme. Tim remembers the temperature in Canada at that time as being a bitterly cold - 20°C! At Calgary airport he jumped onto a yellow British Army owned Greyhound bus with the other newly arrived soldiers and they headed off to their personal accommodation in Camp Crowfoot. The accommodation in Crowfoot was an abomination in comparison to that of the Permanent Staffs' lodgings. The new arrivals attended many safety lectures on what they should and shouldn't do when they deployed out on the prairies. The instructors warned everyone to keep a sharp eye open for rattlesnakes, Tim said, *"Well, that alarming and slightly unnerving bit of news caught my attention straight away.*" During the summer months, rattlesnakes were a constant and nerve-wracking hazard for every soldier who went out on the prairies. The instructors also warned everyone to stay away from the Assiniboia Inn (more commonly referred to as the Sin Bin) in the town of Medicine Hat. The instructors' verbal warning about this den of iniquity only served to make the place an even more attractive proposition to a lot of British soldiers.

Tim was posted into BATUS to replace Driver 'Scouse' Symonds who was also on detachment from 17 Sqn RCT. 'Scouse' sold Tim his massive Chevrolet car for $40 before he flew back to `Germany. The huge car enabled Tim to get away from camp during his time off work. He also used it as a Taxi for the lads on camp and charged them a profitable $5 a head for the 35-minute trip into Medicine Hat.

During Tim's attachment to BATUS he would, in the main, be working with an RE Sapper called Phil. They'd both be working on the mechanical targets on the firing ranges because after each of the Med Man Exercises, the targets were in desperate need of being replaced or repaired. The targets and their operating systems were sometimes brought back into camp if extenuating maintenance was required. Tim and Phil were involved in this maintenance programme and often had to drive out onto the ranges in an MK 4 tonner that had a Ford HIAB crane attached. They often picked up, repaired, or simply replaced many of the damaged targets. Their call-sign when they went out on the training area was' Six Four Delta' and when they went out on a maintenance job, in both Summer or Winter, they had to take some emergency equipment with them. The list of kit included:

A map of the area they were working in.
Short Wave Radio.
Sleeping Bags (these were the 1970's feather filled type).
First Aid Kit.

Two Vacuum Flasks (filled with hot tea).
Rations.
Tool Kit.
Spare Fuel.

The rations that they were provided with consisted of a small RAF style white cardboard ration box (These were utilised by all catering services in the Armed forces when a unit travelled by train, coach or aircraft). At best the box would contain some crappy, curly sandwiches, a Mars bar, can of pop, a bag of plain salted crisps, and the obligatory piece of sour and bruised fruit. Before leaving Camp Crowfoot, Tim would have to book out of the camp so that in the event of an accident or someone going missing, the unit would at least know where to start searching for them. The reader should understand that the Training area in BATUS was the size of Wales. When this particular Battle Group had arrived in Canada it couldn't deploy onto the Training Area because of a severe weather condition called a Chinook Wind (Chinook translates into English as snow eater). The easiest way to explain this weather phenomenon is like this. When a warm, wet, and Westerly wind blows in from the Pacific Ocean and passes over the Rocky Mountains, it can sometimes collide with an icy wind coming down from the Arctic. When these two weather fronts meet it produces a staggering amount of snow which then dumps itself onto the BATUS Training Area.

When Tim and Phil went out on their first foray onto the Training Area in their truck, it was bathed in glorious sunshine, but even so, Tim and Phil still took all the statutory emergency equipment with them in their wagon. *"Me and Phil went out on a detail one morning at 0730 hours. It were a bright and sunny day but by the time we were 20 miles out onto the prairies at 1000 hours, it started to bloody snow. And by 1030 hours we were driving through a blizzard still trying to find a faulty target that were in one of them pit things."* They continued down the track but the whole area very quickly became smothered in deep snow. Even

Driver Tim Butterworth, probably having a premonition about one of the other target pits he was going to fall into in a Bedford MK 4 Tonner. To be fair, the pit he fell into was completely filled with snow at the time.

though they couldn't see much, Tim continued to drive on until the MK suddenly dropped down into a big hole (*like the one above*) in the ground - they'd finally found the Target Pit they were looking for. Tim wasn't injured because he was able to brace himself against the MK's steering wheel but Phil, although not badly hurt, was catapulted forwards onto the windscreen. The MK was tilted down at the front in a 45° angle; it wasn't possible to open the doors because the cab was surrounded by compacted snow in the Target Pit. The only way out was through the cupola cover on the top of the cab. They briefly did that and then quickly closed it again because the cold driving snow was gusting straight into the cab. Phil contacted the camp by radio to let them know what had happened:

Phil: *Hello Zero this Six Four Delta, Over.*

Zero: *Zero, send, Over.*

Phil: *Six Four Delta, this call sign has fallen...I mean crashed.. I mean.... we are stuck nose down, in a target pit, Over."*

Zero: *Zero, Roger that, and what exactly do you want us to do about it?*

Phil: *Six Four Delta, we're going to need vehicle recovery. Over.*

Phil gave Zero the Grid Reference of their location on the prairie.

Zero: *Zero, Roger that Six Four Delta, you are going to have to stay put in that location until we can get a recovery vehicle out to you.*

Phil: *Six four Delta, Roger that, can you give me an ETA (Estimated Time of Arrival) of the recovery vehicles arrival at this location?*

Zero: Zero, negative to that, we're not coming out in this sort of weather.

This was why each crew that deployed out on the prairies had to take rations, sleeping bags and radios with them.

Tim and Phil were finally recovered seven hours later. Whilst they were waiting, Phil got into his sleeping-bag and lay out in the foot-well of the MK's cab, Tim did pretty much the same except that he had to lay on the dashboard/windscreen. They often changed places to try and gain some sort of comfort whilst trying to get some sleep. Tim found that lying with his back on the trucks frozen windscreen was akin to sleeping butt naked on an iceberg. They regularly opened the trucks cupola cover to make sure there was enough fresh air in the cab and by doing so avoid any build-up of carbon monoxide. They were eventually rescued by a recovery crew who had spotted the red flag that Tim had tied onto the top of their truck's radio aerial. It was fortunate that he'd done that because the whole truck was completely covered in thick snow and was virtually impossible to see without that flag. The Recovery vehicle was a tracked 432 APC (Armoured Personnel Carrier).

Tim and Phil were taken straight back to the Medical Centre in Camp Crowfoot and were kept in the Medical Reception Station (MRS) overnight whilst being treated for mild hypothermia. Tim explained, "*We kept asking the medics for more blankets because we just couldn't seem to get properly warmed up.*" The medical treatment for hypothermia includes the fact that the patient mustn't be over-warmed too quickly. If the casualty is covered with too many blankets, then he may start to sweat and that will drop his core body temperature even further. Tim's MK truck was recovered the following day.

Three months into his tour Tim went on his Rest and Recuperation leave (R&R) to Montana Falls, where he also made a point of visiting the Rodeo in Calgary with his recently acquired girlfriend. British soldiers invariably took the piss out of the cowboys but they had to be careful, because there were some big gun-slinging bastards at those shows. Rodeo-shows were attended by all sorts of North American Cowboys and Indians in an array of different clothing. Tim woke up with a stinking hangover in a Calgary motel one weekend and as he tried to gather his thoughts together he suddenly realised he was wearing an Indian chiefs' skin jacket and hadn't got a clue where he'd got it from. He admitted, "*I'd been pissed for the previous two days.*" Tim was following in the footsteps of his Dad Dennis who had been part of a Battle Group during his time with the 'Dukes.' Dennis had also been to the Calgary stampede - but he came home with a cowboy Stetson hat!

On another detail, Tim was driving a truck along a route called 'Rattlesnake,' with a Sergeant accompanying him; the pair of them were heading out onto the training area to do some checks on one of the Firing Ranges. When any vehicle crossed a boundary line in BATUS, the occupants have to radio in and get permission to proceed onto another range area, just in case any live firing was going on at that time. Our two intrepid heroes knew they were crossing into the vicinity of another range by use of simple map reading skills and having a good knowledge of the tracks in their local area. Tim radioed control and was given permission to proceed. After 10 minutes he could hear the crack of rounds flying over the top of his head! Discretion being the better part of valour, Tim high-tailed it back to the 'Rattlesnake' track and headed straight back to camp. Before the Sgt got out of the truck's cab he said to Tim, "Don't mention this to anyone, we must keep this between the two of us."

Tim fell foul of the British Army when he got into some trouble with the camp SSM. He was detailed to drive his MK truck over to the vehicle park in Crowfoot Camp and hitch up to an Operations Box bodied vehicle that had a turntable draw bar system. This sort of trailer is renowned to be extremely difficult to reverse because it has a steering type of axle on the front and a Driver has to adapt to a totally different driving technique when reversing. It took a lot of training to acquire the necessary skills needed to become accomplished at this sort of reversing skill. It isn't something that is often practiced in British Army training, not even in the RCT.

On arrival at the designated range, Tim was ordered to reverse it into a previously dug trench. He had to do this in front of an audience of Brigadier's, Colonel's, and a whole gaggle of other Officers who were standing around and pontificating. It took Tim 15 minutes to complete the difficult reversing job and get it into the correct position, whilst he sweated like a Glass Blowers arse. Tim heard an RCT Sgt say to his mate, "*Fucking 10 Regt RCT, what a bunch of wankers."* A senior Officer who was watching Tim manoeuvre the trailer said, *"Bloody hell Driver, you made hard work of that!"* Tim put the Lt Col in the picture, *"I've never been trained to reverse park a turntable draw-bar trailer ...Sir!"* The Officer suddenly became very interested in Tim, *"10 Regiment, that's the RCT boxing Regiment isn't it, bloody good boxers so I've been told. Anyway Sgt, let's see if you can do any better shall we?"* He ordered the Sgt to take the vehicle and trailer out of its position to try and reverse the truck and trailer himself. The Sgt made a complete hash of the job and Tim was, *"Chuffed to fuck,"* to say the least. The Lt Col looked at Tim, smiled, winked, and then walked away.

During the night everyone watched an amazing fire-power demonstration by British Challenger Tanks but after an hour it just becomes a case of, *"Oh look, more 120mm rounds going down the range. Great."* The following morning Tim took the truck and trailer back to camp where he cleaned, refuelled, and last paraded it before being dismissed from work by a Sergeant. As he was starting to nod off to sleep in his room he heard someone banging on his room door, it was Phil the Sapper. *"Our Sarn't Major wants to see you Tim, you'd better get your arse over to his office now because he's not a happy bunny."* The SSM was a massive six-foot barrel-chested tyrant and he started shouting at Tim for knocking off without his permission. The SSM then started punching Tim in the chest before he finally knocked Tim to the floor and stood threateningly over him. When the SSM had finally stopped ranting and raving, Tim left the office and the RE bully slapped Tim around the head and shouted, *"In my office tomorrow morning at 0745 hours for round two Butterworth."* Tim thought, *'Fuck you mate,'* and went down to his girlfriends' place and didn't come back into camp until the following Monday morning. The SSM put Tim on a charge when he returned to camp and he was immediately marched in front of the Commanding Officer of BATUS. The Lt Col read out the information on the AF B 252 Charge Report and ultimately found

Tim to be guilty as charged. He asked Tim, "*Do you accept my punishment or do you wish to be tried by Courts Martial?*" Tim took the wind out of the RSM's sails when he told the Colonel. "*I'd like to be tried by Courts Martial please, Sir.*"

Tim was immediately marched out of the Commanding Officers office and was told by a slightly annoyed RSM, "*Listen, don't be silly lad, you'll probably only get a telling off or a small fine from the Colonel. I suggest you take his punishment and move on with your life.*" Tim didn't want to go to jail (he'd heard about the harshness of 10 Regt's Guardroom back in Bielefeld). He was then marched back in front of the CO who again asked if Tim was going to accept his punishment, and he did. The Lt Col then stunned Tim by telling him, "*Right, I sentence you to seven days detention, march him out RSM!*" Tim thought to himself, "*Fucking hell!*" The following conversation took place in front of Tim in the CO's office:

RSM: *But Sir, we haven't got a jail here in BATUS.*

CO: *Well make one then!*

RSM: *Out of what Sir?*

CO: *I don't know, just find somewhere to incarcerate him.*

RSM: *Well that's not exactly like sending him to jail, is it Sir!*

CO*:* *Well I don't know; just do something with him will you RSM!*

After further head scratching and RE problem solving discussions, it was decided to send Tim over to the RCMP (Royal Canadian Mounted Police); the confused Canadian Mounties looked Tim and his escort up and down and told the Corporal, "*We don't want him.*" Tim and his escort went back to RHQ where some Royal Engineer bright-spark stated. "*There's a Guardroom down *at Camp Crowfoot sir, we'll use that, shall we Sir?." "By the front, double march...mark time....forward.....mark time!"*

The Corporal in charge of the 17/21 Queens Royal Lancers Guardroom told Tim's escort, *"What the fuck do you want us to do with him? We're part of the Battle Group and we haven't got the time, or facilities, to deal with a Soldier Under Sentence.'* By now, Tim's frustrated and extremely pissed off escort said to the QRL NCO, *"Well he's fucking yours now because no-one else wants him."* The QRL Corporal sighed and said, *"Oh fuck it, right where's all your kit Butterworth?"* Tim told him that everything was still in his accommodation.

A Land Rover was summoned and Tim was chauffeured to his room so he could pick up his bedding and personal kit and he was then driven back to the Guardroom. There were three cells in the building and Tim was offered the chance to, *"Pick a cell mate."* He sat in his cell for an hour before the Padré turned up to give him some spiritual guidance and comfort and made sure he wasn't suicidal. After giving Tim a bit of pious prattle the Padré said, *"Right, I'll be off then."* Anyone who has ever done a bit of porridge in 10 Regiments Guardroom will be shaking their heads after reading this. During the 1970's 10 Regt's Guardroom was run by two RCT Legends called Sgt Jimmy McMahon and Cpl Taff Lewis, both of these incredibly tough and emotionally crippled Corps and Army boxers, had served in 63 (Parachute) Sqn RCT and were a frightening example of how a proper British Army Guardroom was administrated in the 1970's. *Author's note: For further reading on this subject you might want to read Captain Roy McMordie, Driver Eric Walters, Driver Steve Tong, and WO 2 John Wilson's chapters in 'Rickshaws, Camels and Taxis. (Rogues, Ruffians and Officers of the Royal Corps of Transport), but I think Sgt Dave Hand's chapter in 'Most Roads Led to 10 Regt' is the sublime chapter on how soldiers were treated by Sgt Jimmy McMahon RCT and Cpl Taff Lewis RCT.*

The disinterested Cpl in the Crowfoot Camp Guardroom didn't take Tim's bootlaces and stable belt off him to make sure he didn't hang himself, and when it came to mealtimes, instead of an NCO screaming and shouting at Tim whilst doubling him over to the cookhouse, the Corporal came into his cell and said, "*Oy Tim, scoff's on, pop yourself over to the cookhouse for your dinner mate, can you bring me something back on a plate?*" After lunch Tim had to have a kip for about an hour or so, which he followed up with some quiet reading time. It wasn't until the next day that someone, somewhere, decided that Soldiers Under Sentence (SUS's) should, at the very least, be doing some sort of work. Tim's routine during the day composed of, Breakfast, Dixie bash, Relaxation, Lunch, Dixie Bash, Relaxation, Evening Meal, Dixie Bash, Relaxation and Reading. Tim's Canadian girlfriend worked in the cookhouse and so he got to see her every day.

The 17/21 QRL Corporal who was supposedly in charge asked Tim, "*Can your girlfriend get hold of a television set, video player, and some pornography we can use in the Guardroom mate?*" (MATE!!!! Jimmy Mac will be turning in his grave). Tim made the Cpl's day when he told him, "*I'm sure she can, our lass is very resourceful.*" The 'contraband' all appeared in the Guardroom the very next day. On Tim's fourth night in the Clink he asked his girlfriend to bring some beers. The next night she turned up with plenty of beer and was accompanied by four of her very attractive Canadian girl-friends. That resulted in everyone have a great party in the Guardroom. (Cpl Taff Lewis RCT would have been spitting blood). When Tim was eventually released from the, 'prison from paradise', he was appointed as the Duty Driver for Camp Crowfoot and spent his remaining time at BATUS, driving a Land Rover on inconsequential details. Tim's girlfriends' uncle was the owner of a large haulage company in Canada and his niece was absolutely besotted with Tim. The pair of them tried to get him to stay in Canada where the uncle would put Tim through his HGV 1 licence and he could become a family member of the Company. Believe it or not, Tim turned them down because he simply wanted to drive army trucks for a living, and anyway, "I'd had my fill of Canada by then and I just wanted to get back to Germany".

On return to 10 Regt, Tim went through a system of bollocking's from lots of the hierarchy before he was eventually placed on CO's orders and marched in front of the Colonel. Tim was given dressing downs by Sgt Seamus O'Callaghan, SSgt Tam Forrester, his Troop Commander, his SSM WO 2 Dave Hopper, 17 Sqn's OC, and all of this was before he got yet another dressing down from the RSM and CO. No matter what Tim told them about the battering he been given by the RE SSM, they all felt that he'd let himself down and had disgraced the name of 17 Sqn and 10 Regt. He was subsequently placed on a formal Three-Month Warning Order. Tim had returned from Canada towards the end of July 85 and felt particularly disillusioned and aggrieved after being put on, what he thought was, an unwarranted Warning Order.

He worked in 17 Sqn's Servicing bay for 9 months before returning to A Troop in 17 Sqn. The Sqn was due to deploy on an 'OP BANNER' Tour to Northern Ireland and Tim wanted to go, but his application was turned down because of the debacle in Canada. This resulted in Tim never getting to fulfil his desire to drive a Saracen APC like the one 'Russ' drove down to Minden during his previous NI training. Tim put in his papers to be discharged from the British Army and went back to working in the Servicing Bay and on the Vehicle Park bringing the Sqn's vehicles up to scratch for their two-yearly inspections. He was ultimately discharged from Buller Barracks, Aldershot, along with four other Drivers from other RCT units. He then worked for a firm in Halifax called Jackson Foods, but because he was still under 21 years of age he couldn't drive any of their HGV wagons. He worked in their warehouse for a while whilst waiting for the DVLA to issue him his full HGV licence which turned up in the post on his 21st birthday.

Beverley Dawn Bates walked into Tim's life and they got married in 1996 using a firm called 'One Stop Wedding' who did everything for them except find the wedding venue. Tim paid for their wedding services up front, as did a lot of other betrothed couples. The firm took their money and then did a runner to live the high life in Tenerife. BBC's 'Look North' did a feature on the 'One Stop Wedding' reprobate and interviewed him in Tenerife where he said he had every intention of paying every penny of the stolen money back. A warrant was taken out for his arrest and the Police eventually caught up with him in Leicester where he was doing a mundane job. Unfortunately, the case against him was thrown out of court because the media coverage meant that he wouldn't get a fair trial.

Tim now lives happily in his pristine and fashionable house in Halifax, Yorkshire with his lovely wife Beverley, where he still drives HGV vehicles for a living.

Lieutenant Colonel Cameron Macnish
RACT RCT and RLC 1980 – 2010

In 1766 Captain James Cook, of His Majesty's Royal Navy, discovered, mapped and claimed the coast of New South Wales in Australia for King George III of Great Britain and Ireland. Years later, the British Government utilised this sparsely populated and barren continent as a much larger version of Wormwood Scrubs Prison and turned Sydney Cove into a Penal Colony. Since then, the British relationship with our Aussie friends has been from, "Love them, Respect them, Hate them," to the other end of the spectrum, "They piss me right off," relationship.

We respect our antipodean cousins because they are always ready to stand by us whenever the Motherland is under threat, notably in World Wars One and Two, and that little spat we had against Communist China and Russia during the Korean War, from 1950 to 1953. On the other hand, we hate the cocky and smug Aussie bastards for being world beaters at our 'British' invented sports like Cricket and Rugby.

Cameron Macnish was born in Melbourne on the 29th of September 1961, but he happily grew up in Sydney, his mum and dad both worked for IBM (International Business Machines) whilst Cameron studied at Epping Boys High School. He somewhat 'tongue in cheek' declares, "At school I was as thick as mince when it came to Chemistry and Math's, but I was quite good at English, History and German. I refused point-blank to take a French Language Course because it all sounded so 'gay' to me. The German language segment, however, came in handy years later when I spent eight years of my life in Das Vaterland mit der Britischen Armee."

The Macnish family has close links with the British Army from way back in the Boer and First World Wars. Cameron's Grandfather, Kelso Robinson, was born and raised in Battenberg Street which was just a spit away from the Shankhill Road in Northern Ireland. Kelso enlisted into the Royal Inniskilling Fusiliers in 1890 and served in the Regiment for 15 years, including some serious soldiering during the Boer War, before he left in 1912 - having reached the giddy height of Lance Corporal (twice).

When Kelso returned to Ireland he found that life was intolerable for him and his family (like the majority of the Irish Nation) because they were on a borderline starvation diet. He travelled out to Australia in early 1914 in the hope of finding some work, so that he could feed his family. Before his loved ones could join him on the other side of the world though, once again he enlisted, but on this occasion into the Australian Army Service Corps as a 35-year-old soldier, which at that age in modern days, would mean Kelso should have been nearing the end of his military career, not starting it. During his time with the Aussies, Kelso served in Gallipoli, and in France with the 1st Australian Divisional Train.

During his service in France he was awarded the Military Medal for bravery. Whilst under heavy shell-fire, a very brave Kelso of the Australian ASC hooked up with a limber that was travelling in front him, its horses and infantry commander having all been killed. He calmly delivered the extra stores to the same destination as where was heading. Cameron still has his Grandfather's unique medals at home in Australia, unique because the set contains British Boer War Campaign medals, with a further mix of Australian First World War Campaign medals and the hard-won Gallantry Medal. Kelso died in the late 1950's, a short-time before Cameron was born.

On the other side of his family, Cameron's Grandfather Harold, was a Queenslander Infantry soldier who served with the 48th Battalion of the Australian Imperial Forces (AIF). Harold was only too delighted to show his battle scars from the war to his small grandchild, Cameron. Cameron nonchalantly told the author, in that casual macho Australian manner, "Oh, they were only the usual shrapnel type of wounds and a few others, nothing drastic." He explained that Harold had been wounded out in 'No man's land,' and was laid face down in the mud when he heard a clanking sound behind him. It was a Mark IV British Tank. Fortunately, the tank broke down just before it ran over Cameron's Grandfather. "I was lucky enough to have some great chats with him, he was a dirty old bugger, and that must be where I get my background from. After the war he ran a Sugar Plantation in New Guinea before finally settling down in Brisbane."

While still at school, Cameron joined the Scouts and Army Cadets. He liked dressing up in uniform and running around the bush with a Self-Loading Rifle tucked under his arm. "We did a lot of camping back in those days. Let's face it, the Australian weather does make it conducive to living an outdoor life under canvas." On leaving school, some of his friends applied to join the Royal Military Academy in Duntroon on a 4-year degree Course, a choice that would ultimately see them serving as officers in the Australian Army. The Aussie academy is like the United States version of West Point. After completing their degrees in Academics, candidates spend the next year doing purely military training. Cameron wanted to go to Duntroon but unfortunately his Dad was transferred to the US Office in New York, so he spent the last year of his education in an American High School. Cameron said, "It was a bit of a culture shock for me; there were girls available. I'd been at an all-boys school back in Australia, I mean the girls were nice and all that, but I wanted to make some money and so I spent all my spare time flipping burgers."

After 12 months Cameron applied to join the Australian Army and came back to Australia almost a year before his parents did. He was accepted into the Duntroon Military Academy where he studied for his Bachelor of Arts (BA) as an Officer Cadet. Cameron, unfortunately, ultimately failed so badly that the

Duntroon Academy asked him to leave their establishment with the request that he never darken their doorsteps ever again. He explained, "I was good at all the military stuff but was simply hopeless at all the academic syllabus." He went to work in a factory that produced flavored milk which included sugar, milk, flavoring, coloring, repeat, repeat, repeat, and was able to earn some good money, which was great as far as Cameron was concerned.

Eventually he applied to attend the other Australian Officer Selection process at Portsea which was more like the British Mons Officer Cadet School system in England. Unlike RMA Sandhurst, Portsea didn't include any academic syllabi's during training. Portsea was established in 1951 to provide the 'Aussies' with an Officer Training facility for Cadets prior to their being commissioned into the Regular Australian Army. Before the place closed in 1985, Portsea supplied the bulk of the Australian Army with its trained Army Officers, the school motto was, 'Loyalty and Service.' The original RSM's hut that stood on the camp is believed to be one of the oldest buildings in Victoria State. Major Peter Badcoe VC was a graduate from Portsea and is one of only four Australian Victoria Cross winners that passed out of that training camp and onto the War in Vietnam.

Other notable graduates from Portsea are, Lieutenant David Brian KIA (Killed in Action) on the 5th of March 1964, Group Captain Robert Halverson RAAF (later House of Representative and Speaker of the House), Lieutenant Generals Ken Gillespie, Chief of the Defence Staff, David Morrison Chief of the Army, Jerry Mateparae former Chief of the New Zealand Defence Force and later Governor General of New Zealand, and last, but by no means least, Les Hiddins who was the star of the Television Show, 'The Bush Tucker Man'. *Authors note: Great company Cameron.*

Portsea was everything Cameron wanted from a military career and he thoroughly enjoyed his 12 months experience there, right up until the point of the 'Fighting Withdrawal' on the final phase of the two-week Exercise. He and his fellow Candidates had been beasted from pillar to post all day and night without any respite, and near Endex (End of Exercise) the unit started to do a fighting withdrawal from their final location. Cameron was so tired he swore blind that he saw a Troop of African Elephants walking past him. For those of you who don't know, the African Elephant isn't indigenous to the Australian continent.

As the RACT trucks pulled up to take the exhausted Officer Cadets back to camp, Cameron had an epiphany. He saw the RACT Corporal who would be driving everyone back to camp for hot showers, decent food and some sleep, drinking a huge steaming mug of hot coffee. Cameron suddenly smiled as he'd thought to himself, "I never want to do this walking shit ever again, I want to be a Truckie." He said, "My decision to join the RACT was made at that particular moment in my life. I applied for, and was accepted, for a Commission into the Royal Australian Corps of Transport." At the back of his mind, Cameron thought that if the army thing didn't work out, he could always use the transferable 'truckie' skills out in Civilian life - as opposed to the Infantry Trained soldiers who just trained to kill people whilst they're at work.

The Aussie Army was still using the International 5 Tonners that had been successfully used during the Vietnam War, useful as load workhorses and troop carriers. However, before Cameron could get his hands on the trucks he had to complete his TCC (Troop Commanders Course). There was only one TCC Course held every year and the last one had finished 6 months previously. To bide his time, and help him gain some experience, Cameron was sent on an attachment to 1 Tpt Sqn RACT (1 Transport Squadron RACT) as an Admin Officer. 1 Sqn had been equipped with Unimog's, 4 Ton Trucks, and 3 Tonner Mack

Trucks. Within 6 months Cameron was on his way to the RACT Depot at Puckapunyal. The camp had a Training area, (400km2), which was also used by armoured units, very similar to the British Army's Training Area on Salisbury Plain (780 km2). Puckapunyal is an Aboriginal word that loosely transcribes into, 'The Middle Hill', 'Death to the Eagle', 'Place of Exile', 'Valley of the Winds', 'The Outer Barbarians' or 'The Large Hill'. *Authors note: Cameron did say it was a loose translation.* From 1990 - 2000, Kosovan refugees were accommodated in some of the training barracks accommodation at Puckapunyal until the Kosovan situation had stabilized.

In the early 1980's, a trial was initiated using RACT Troop Commanders in Infantry Battalion's to run their MT Sections for the Infantry. It was deemed to be a low-profile punishment job for the subaltern that had, "Fucked up most in the previous year." Cameron applied to be attached to 5/7th RAR which was based in the same area at Holsworthy. He was assured that after this twelve-month attachment there he would definitely be given command of his own RACT Troop.

On arrival at 5/7th, Cameron met his very hard Troop Sergeant, Sgt Dave Willis, who had served in South Vietnam in 1972 as an Infantryman and as the CO's Driver. Dave Willis knew and loved everything there was to know and love about trucks. Junior Officers of the Battalion were shit scared of Dave because he often bollocked them for putting in their Transport requests and Vehicle Returns in too late. One of the Platoon Commanders had a word with Cameron before he went over to introduce himself to Sgt Dave Willis, "Oh shit, you're going to be Dave Willis's Platoon Commander, are you? I wouldn't want to be in your boots mate." Cameron confidently strode into his Troop Office and asked questions like, "Sgt Willis? What is our availability of these trucks?" and "How many of our Troop vehicles are off the road?" Lt Cameron Macnish and Sgt Dave Willis got on like a house on fire, "He was rough as old nuts," said Cameron, "but a top bloke nonetheless."

Sgt Willis drove a Land Rover down to the Sgt's Mess at lunchtime and picked up all the unit spares needed to keep the fleet on the road, he then proceeded to get pissed in the Sgt's Mess Bar before driving back to the Office. When the Troop went out on a training run, no-one even broke into a sweat because they were delayed by Dave Willis who was always at the back of the troop 'bringing up the rear.' Cameron tactfully suggested that his Troop Sergeant and their soldiers might find it more beneficial if Sgt Willis stayed behind whilst he beasted a sweat out of the lads. After a fantastic year with 5/7th RAR, Cameron returned to 1 Tpt Sqn just up the road and reported to his OC, Major Gary Donahue, who had some exciting news for him.

Major Donahue had chosen Cameron from the Officers in his Sqn to go on 'Exercise Long Look' (August 1984), a British and Australian Military exchange programme. The Brit and Aussie selection teams, on alternative years, chose either a Cpl, Sgt, SSgt, or Lt to go on each detachment. Both nations' soldiers flew and met up in Singapore. They then swapped over aircraft for a RAF VC 10 or an RAAF 707 aircraft for the final leg of their journey. After being dropped off at RAF Gütersloh, Cameron was somewhat shocked by the level of security on the RAF Camp, but considering the Cold War and IRA terrorism that was in full flow at that time, the wire, weapons, and precautions shouldn't have been that much of a surprise to him. He was collected in an army car by an RCT Lt, who drove him to 54 Engr Sp & Amb Sqn RCT (54 Engineer Support and Ambulance Sqn RCT) based at Lubbecke. He would eventually live in the beautiful Officers' Mess in Tunis Barracks that had once been home to Field Marshal Bernard Montgomery at the end of the Second World War.

On arrival at the Officers' Mess, Cameron was informed that they didn't have any vacant rooms in the Mess, "But not to worry Lt

Macnish, we've set up some accommodation for you in that 12 x 12 tent on the front lawn over there." Inside the tent was a fully made up 3ft army bed, complete with bedside mat, reading lamp on a bedside cabinet and some wag had even included the obligatory vase of flowers. 54 Sqn was expecting a less experienced officer who would have been more befuddled about the gag, but even though Cameron was, "Jet-lagged to hell," and was also an experienced officer by that stage of his career, he good-naturedly went along with the joke. The OC informed Cameron that 54 Engr Sp and Amb Sqn RCT consisted of five Troops, three of which were designated Engineer Support and the other two were Ambulance Troops. Cameron would be taking command of C Tp which was an Engineer Support Troop, equipped with MGB (Medium Girder Bridges), Bedford MK 4 Tonners, Class 60 Military Runway Equipment and a whole bunch of Tipper Trucks.

The following morning Cameron was informed that it was tradition for the newest subaltern in the Sqn to march onto Working Parade accompanied by 'Billy The Goat', a Sqn Mascot wearing a beautifully crafted blanket that had the Sqn Badges emblazed on each side. The Sqn 'Corporal of the Goat' collected 'Billy' in a unit Land Rover. On first seeing his Parade Partner, Cameron thought that Billy had a confused expression on his face. The goats face betrayed his thoughts and Cameron swore that the goat was thinking, 'This is a bit strange, I've never done this before' and 'What the hell is going on here.' On the other hand, Cameron thought the whole episode was just part of a normal Sqn day. He had an image of himself marching on parade in front of HM Queen Elizabeth II with 'Llewellyn' the Welsh Guards Goat, or the Para's pony 'Bruneval,' and proudly taking the salute in front of his admiring Troops.

Cameron was led like a lamb, (pardon the pun), to the slaughter really because he knew how idiosyncratic the British were, but he fell for the goat fable, hook, line, and sinker. The SSM had warned everyone in the Sqn the night before that no-one was to laugh out loud when Lt Macnish RACT marched up and down the ranks and inspected the Parade They were under threat of extra guard duties if they gave the game away. The reality was that the moth-eaten goat was borrowed from the back of the Officers' Mess where 'Billy' chewed the lawn to keep it short. As for, and the beautifully created 'Goat Coat'.... well, that was hastily constructed by a German Washer Woman the previous night. Lt Macnish RACT was briefed that he had to march on parade at the head of four other Troop Commanders and their soldiers. Once on the Parade Ground, Cameron had to do a smart about turn before inspecting each troop. It was at that point that 'Billy' started to get a bit bored with his new appointment and became very uncooperative and disobliging. After handing 'Billy's' leather tether over to Cpl Alex Haddon RCT, who was standing in as the Troop Sgt, Billy started dragging his heels and violently demonstrated against his duties because he simply wanted to go back behind the Officers' Mess and fill his face with copious amounts of luscious grass.

Later that same day, Cameron had to carry out the Duty Officer's responsibilities and went over to the cookhouse to make sure the Drivers had no complaints about the food at Tea-Time. When he spotted the row upon row of puddings and sweets available to the lads he exclaimed, "Fuck me! I know about you Brits and your love of tea, but the Drivers get a better fucking tea than we do in the Officers' Mess." The Orderly Sgt then pointed out the roast beef on the savory hot-plate and informed Cameron, "This is what soldiers call tea, sir. What you and other Officers call 'Dinner' doesn't exist in the soldiers' world. This is their evening meal." A flabbergasted Cameron exclaimed, "They're have their evening meal at 5 o'clock in the afternoon! They must be fucking starving by 10 o'clock at night." The Orderly Sgt patiently tried to educate Cameron on the differences between the way the Aussies and Brits did things, "Yes sir, we do it differently, but we call it, 'Having some Class,' and anyway sir, what do you think a down-town evening of pizza's, bratties, kebabs, pommes-frittes mit mayonnaise, and beer are for…. sir?"

Cameron fell in love with the whole RCT life-style in BAOR and often went into the lads' single accommodation, after work on a Friday, to quaff a few bottles of Grolsch with his C Tp lads. This often extended to him meeting up with his boys in a nightclub down town, much to the horror of his brother Officers, "You shouldn't go into those sort of nightclubs Cameron, soldiers go into those establishments." Cameron tried to explain the Aussie Officer ethos of life to his uptight and frigid brother British Officers he had to live with at the Officers Mess, Cameron highlighted the benefits of his lifestyle, "That's exactly why I go into these places. Once I've sunk a glass of my own beer, my Trog's buy me another one, then I don't have to buy a single fucking beer all night long."

The sheer size and complexity of the British Army's involvement in 'Exercise Lionheart' in 1984 nearly blew Cameron's mind. At that time the entire Australian Army totalled 33,000 soldiers; the British Army in BAOR alone amounted to a staggering 120,000 soldiers. Cameron's Tp was assigned to work with the Royal Engineers on building military combat bridges for a counter-attack against supposed attacking Soviet Forces. At the climax of the Exercise, Cameron rendezvoused (RV'd) at a proposed river crossing with 12 tipper trucks loaded with hard- core. He entered the RE's command tent to find out exactly where the hard-core needed to be dropped. The following conversation went on between an RE Captain who was the OC, an RE SSM, and Lt Cameron Macnish RACT.

Cameron: G'day Sir, the RCT lads are here with the hard-core.

RE Captain: Thank you.

A Royal Engineer Sarn't Major entered the tent and spoke to Cameron after he'd saluted.

RE SSM: Hello Sir, any of your RCT lads fancy some stickies? *(Soldiers serving in the British Army usually refer to chocolate bars as Stickies.)*

A slightly indignant Lt Cameron Macnish gave the SSM short shrift.

Cameron: I don't think so Sergeant Major! They don't need that sort of thing at the moment. Anyway, I've told them to get their heads down in the cabs of their trucks, they need to get some serious shut-eye, not other forms of stimulation.

RE SSM: Oh, ok then Sir.

(*The SSM looked weirdly at Cameron before retreating out of the tent, his OC also gave Cameron a confused sideways glance.*)

RE Captain: You do realise that my Sarn't Major was only offering your Drivers some Mars Bars, don't you?

Cameron: Oh, fucking hell, Mars Bars! In Australia a 'sticky' is a pornographic magazine… you know…. because the pages are stuck together with… well you know.

The OC raised his eyebrows and said,

RE Captain: Yes, I do know Lieutenant.

Cameron confirmed that he'd thought the Sarn't Major was offering his lads copies of Penthouse and Mayfair glossy magazines, "I was impressed with the British Army because they were so organised, they'd arranged for their soldiers to have porno mags available whilst out on Exercise. I just didn't think that my lads needed the reading material, or that they had the spare time to do any wanking."

When he returned to Tunis Barracks after Endex was called, Cameron visited quite a few RCT units in BAOR and the UK, where each Trog unit seemed intent on getting the 'Aussie' pissed out of his tiny mind. After that, he took the whole of November off before flying back to Australia and re-joining 1 Tpt Sqn RACT in Holdsworthy. There was some disappointment waiting for Cameron when he returned home, the Australian Armed Forces had reneged on their promise to give him command of his own RACT Tp after he'd completed his one year as a Transport Platoon Commander in an Infantry Battalion. Instead he was being posted to the Land Warfare Centre, Kokoda Barracks, near Canungra in Queensland. The Warfare Training Base was located inland from the Gold Coast and South of Brisbane. Cameron was gutted by the Army's decision to break their promise and decided to take matters into his own hands. He immediately visited the Defence Section of the British High Commission in Australia and introduced himself.

Cameron: "Hello. I'm Lieutenant Cameron Macnish, I'm currently serving in the Royal Australian Corps of Transport. I've recently returned from an attachment to the British Army on 'Exercise Long Look' and I was wondering if you had any need for another Lieutenant in the British Army?"

The very polite British Commissioner sprang out of his seat and shook Cameron's hand.

Commissioner: We'd be delighted to have you join us young man, here's some paperwork. Which part of the British Army would you like to serve in?

Cameron: Well I've been serving in the RACT, so I suppose the RCT would probably be best.

Commissioner: Tish Tosh young man! You don't have to join the RCT, we can accommodate you in any Corps or Regiment you'd like, Infantry? Armoured?

Cameron: No thanks, I live breathe and love trucks. I get off on the smell of diesel fumes.

When everything was signed and sealed, Cameron's parents were disappointed he was leaving the country yet again, but they completely understood why he was doing it. Before he left Australia, Cameron received a telephone call from Major Cath McQuarrie in Canberra who oversaw every RACT's Lieutenant's career management. She told Cameron, "You're a really good officer, Lt Macnish and we're very sad to lose you. If it doesn't work out with the British Army though, then give me a call and the RACT will take you back immediately. It'll be the equivalent of an unpaid Exchange Programme. Good Luck."

In September 1986, Cameron chose to be discharged from Perth so that he could catch a free six-hour RAAF flight there. He then hooked up with a UK bound RAF aircraft that was flying some post-exercise SAS soldiers back to RAF Brize Norton. After staying with an old 54 Sqn RCT friend, who was by then a Captain, he headed off to Aldershot and signed up into the RCT before starting his 10-week Captains Course, which was done in both Aldershot, and at Leconfield in East Yorkshire. The content of the Course was very similar to the Aussie Army (Transport Management and Convoy Planning). After passing the Course, Cameron received a posting to 11 Sqn, 4 Armd Div Tpt Regt RCT (4 Armoured Division Transport Regiment RCT – 4 ADTR), based at Minden in BAOR.

Before leaving Aldershot, Cameron received a telephone call from 4 ADTR's Adjutant, Captain (later Brigadier) Sean Cowlam, to ask if he wanted to take part in 'Exercise Subbies Surprise.' The Exercise was an initiative test to recce any Adventure Training facility, anywhere in the World (at their own cost of course) and write a report about that facility which would then be included in the Corps' library of opportunities. Whilst still in Aldershot, Cameron spoke to the RCT Movers and arranged for a very cheap indulgence flight out to the Canadian Rockies. He could then write a report on the BATUS (British Army Training Unit Suffield) rock climbing and skiing events out there.

Within days of arriving at his posting to Minden, Cameron was on a flight bound for Calgary in Canada. He 'phoned the Adventure Training Camp at BATUS and was disappointingly informed, "Don't bother travelling all the way out here Lt Macnish, there is nothing going on now. I'll tell you what, I'll send you some previous reports written by other Officers and you can compile some sort of document from them. You might as well go off and have a good time in the Rockies whilst you're out here though before you head back to BAOR." After doing nearly two weeks of skiing, sightseeing, eating and drinking, Cameron briefly scanned the documents he'd been sent and plagiarized them into his own manuscript, all the time thinking, "This British Army is definitely my type of Army'."

The OC of 11 Sqn RCT was Major Mark Dowdle. "Me and the boss had a clash of personalities I suppose. However, I got on really well with all the other officers, including all four of the other Squadron Commanders and the Commanding Officer. In the Winter of 1986-1987, Cameron deployed on his first major field exercise with 11 Sqn. The weather was so cold that the diesel in the trucks fuel tanks started waxing and every vehicle had to be started up regularly, just so that their engines didn't seize. Cameron asked his Tp SSgt why they were constantly carrying out these engine starts and was told, "In case the Russians attack." Cameron replied, "Oh, that's interesting, I never thought about them attacking us. It all sounds a bit warlike to me." The reality was that Cameron had joined up with the British Army because 'The Brits' had been involved in more 'Punch-ups' than the

Australian Army over the years. The Aussies had been dragged into the Vietnam War by the Americans back in 1972, but the Brits had been fighting in Northern Ireland from 1969 and they'd also had a 'scrap' down in the Falkland in 1982, Cameron felt that it was all real in the British Army.

Whilst on exercise, Cameron was doing a stag on the Sqn radio network, using the sort of communication skills that were still being used by the Aussie Army, codes like 'Playtime' which referred to the RCT, 'Sunray' which identified the Commanding Officer, 'Bluebell' denoting the REME, 'Sunray Minor' meaning the OC, and 'Albatross' when referring to the Sqn's Operations Officer. A Sergeant Radio Operator who was listening in on another set came dashing into the CP and shouted at Cameron, "Sir, Sir, What the fuck are you doing using that sort of language? Stop transmitting immediately!" When Cameron explained that the Aussie Army had been using this sort of language for years and that, "We learned all this stuff from the British Army." The Sergeant shouted back that the Brits hadn't used that sort of dialogue for over 10 years because the Russian monitoring Stations on the Brockenwald knew exactly what it all meant.

Cameron: *Brocken?*

Rad Op Sgt: *Yes Sir.*

Cameron: *What the fuck is a Brocken, Sergeant?*

Rad Op Sgt: *It's a Soviet Forces Listening Station that is based in the Harz Mountains (pointing) - about 20 Kms in that direction.*

Cameron: *Wow, you mean to say that the Russians have been listening to what I've been saying?*

Rad Op Sgt: *Yes Sir. Anything we say on the radio is automatically listened to and recorded by the Soviet Army for future reference.*

Cameron: *That's really is very impressive Sergeant, and quite cool when you think about it. The Russian Secret Services have been listening in to what Lieutenant Macnish of the Royal Corps of Transport has been saying.*

Cameron immediately abandoned the old British, (but up to date Australian radio dialogue) and started boning up on the sort of stuff he could safely use over the airwaves.

In 1988 Cameron was posted to 33 Sqn in Bunde as their TCO (Sqn Transport Control Officer), or as Cameron referred to the job, the, Truck Counting Officer. His new Sqn was just part of a larger unit called 1 Armoured Division Transport Regiment (1 ADTR). The units' Commanding Officer was on leave during an 'Active Edge' an alert Exercise that had been instigated soon after Cameron had arrived in station. 33 Sqns' OC stepped up and took command of the whole Regiment, which left Cameron to take over the reins of 33 Sqn as it deployed into the field on the 'Exercise Active Edge' call out. (*Exercise Active Edge was a BAOR wide Exercise designed to test a units' ability to assemble its soldiers, and vehicles, into a defensive field location before any invading Soviet Forces arrived on the British Army's doorstep in Germany, with all guns blazing).*

After being tipped the nod that a deployment was on the cards within the next 24 hours, Cameron recced a suitable location for the Sqn's 'Stallies' and 8 tonne trucks to deploy into. He chose an area that contained a mass of beechwood trees that he thought would be useful for scrimming up (camouflaging) the units' mixture of vehicles. 3 Sqn crashed out of Birdwood Barracks in the early hours of the morning led by the Sqns G1098 MK 4 Tonners and water trailers, this admin team would laager up first and the accompanying Chefs would provide the following troops with some tea and hot food when they arrived in the location.

Capt Cameron Macnish (2nd from the right) with some of his lads and a Stolly, on a training area in North Minden in 1987. *Thanks to Stuart Brandwood for the use of his photograph.*

Cameron learned an important and very valuable lesson on his very first 'Active Edge' deployment. As the Chefs vehicles drove into the location, they all became bogged in on the location circuit because the ground and tracks were very soft and boggy. The leading elements of 3 Sqns' 4-ton trucks eventually became half submerged in soft mud, so much so that they needed a REME wrecker to extract them.

The Squadron Sergeant Major (SSM) approached the Sqn location in his Land Rover and when he spotted the queue of trucks waiting on the main road outside the hide area, he overtook them and went in search of his temporary OC, Captain Cameron Macnish. He wanted to find out why the Sqns' trucks were blocking the main road and weren't in location by that time and fully scrimmed up.

SSM: Sir, Sir, What the fuck are you doing sir! I thought you had recced this location yesterday. This whole area is covered in Beech Wood Tree's Sir!

Cameron was by now extremely stressed as he tried to work out how to extract his trucks from this rather embarrasing and sticky situation, before his temporary Commanding Officer found out.

Cameron: Sarn't Major! I have no idea what a fucking Beech Wood Tree is; the only beach I know anything about is Bondi fucking beach, and as far as I can recall, it's definitely located on the other side of the fucking world!

The SSM enlightened Cameron about wooded areas that contained Beech Wood trees, those type of trees are notoriously grown in wet woodland areas and RCT units in BAOR particularly avoided using that type of terrain for scrimming up on Exercises. Cameron admits, "I now know a lot more about German Flora and Fauna than I did as a young temporary OC of an RCT Sqn." At the height of this catastrophic deployment, there were sixty RCT trucks lined up outside the location and on the track leading into the hide and their Drivers were knee deep in mud trying to dig the vehicles out.

It wasn't Cameron's finest hour, and to top it all off a Rad Op came over and told him the CO was on the net and wanted to have a quick word. "Hello 33 this is Zero, shall I visit your location now, Over?" Cameron was quick to reply, "Hello Zero, er.. negative to your request, um.. nothing at all to see here, probably be a complete waste of your time, everything is just fine and dandy at this location. Out." On return to Birdwood Barracks after being stood down Cameron was fined four crates of Grolsh

Beer by the Drivers in his Sqn, one for each Driver of the trucks that became bogged down on the muddy track.

The Sqn was deploying on a 4 ½ month 'OP BANNER' Tour to Belfast in June 1988 and Cameron burnt the midnight oil drawing up the entire Training Programme for the Sqn. It included Driver Training, Foot Patrols (Footsies), Public Order Training, First Parade Vehicle Maintenance, Weapon Training, Riot Control incidents etc. An Infantry unit that was stationed nearby, helped out in instructing on Footsies and the Riot Control syllabus. Drivers from the other Sqn's played the part of a very angry CIVPOP (Civilian Population) and the Sqn suffered more injuries from the overzelous Drivers from other RCT Sqns than they did during the entire tour on the streets of Belfast.

Under the guidance of the Trials Officer i/c Lt Alister Davis RCT (later Brigadier), and Lt Peter Lane, Lt Martin Fidgin and Lt Jody Probert, 33 Sqn trialled the British Army's new Saxon APC which was about to be introduced onto the streets of Northern Ireland. Cameron was based in Moscow Camp, as the Ops Officer in the docks area of Belfast and by the end of the tour, he had served 5½ months in Belfast because of the pre-tour recce's and he also attended the handover to the relieving RCT Sqn.

On a visit to Girdwood Park, the resident Infantry Company Ops Sgt asked Cameron where he would like to visit in their Area of Operations. Cameron requested, "Is there any chance of visiting Battenburg Street, my Great Grand parents used to live there." The Ops Sergeant confirmed, "No problem Sir, we'll probably get a decent cup of tea at the same time." As Captain Macnish RCT stepped out of the back of the APC in Battenburg Street, he said that he felt very important as he took a photograph of the house that he sent home to his mum and dad back in Australia.

During the rest of his tour Cameron visited other Belfast locations like Woodburn and North Howard Street Mill, before moving onto Londonderry. Whilst touring the Belfast locations Cameron did top cover for the Driver of the APC (a Humber Pig) and for a laugh, the Driver switched off the ignition whilst the vehicle was still moving up the road and then switched it back on a couple of seconds later. As all RCT Drivers know, this action caused the APC to have a massive backfire that sounded like gunfire and Cameron nearly filled his combat trousers as he shouted, "What the fuck was that?!" The disgruntled top cover then kicked the Driver in the back of his helmeted head.

After leaving Belfast, Cameron continued to serve in 1 ADTR for another two years until 1990 when he was posted to 10 Regt RCT in Bielefeld as the Regiment's Adjutant. He knew nothing about 10 Regt apart from a rumour that the Commanding Officer, Lt Col P Chaganis (later OBE) had a reputation for being a very stern type of Commander, and that his unit was often referred to as 10 Penal Battalion RCT.' Cameron was concerned that his Aussie background wouldn't be a particularly good career move if he went to 10 Regt and he expressed his concerns to Lt Col Gavin Haig, his Commanding Officer at 1 ADTR at that time. Lt Col Haig reassured and advised Cameron about what could possibly lay ahead for him on his career path as an Officer in the British Army, "You must realise Cameron, that to be an Adutant of a Regular Army Regiment, in BAOR, is one of the highest accolades you will ever receive. You are obviously going places. I would wholly recommend that you take up this Post".

As Lt Col Haig had predicted, the move to 10 Regt was definitely a good move for Cameron, and for many reasons. He was now going to be the Commanding Officers right hand man in the biggest Transport Regiment in BAOR, and he would be privileged to have access to a lot of Lt Col Chaganis's innermost thoughts about the Officers and men within the Regiment. On the downside of being an Adjutant, he would have to become more serious about how he conducted himself in his military career, Cameron explained, "I tried to become a more consientious, dilligent and sober RCT Captain when I was both in, and out of, the office, but after four days I gave up and got pissed in the Officers' Mess instead." Another part of his duties necessitated him discussing disciplinary problems with the RSM whose office was next door to Cameron's in RHQ (Regimental Headquarters). Those who have served in any RCT unit will understand that there are always disciplinary problems when truck driving and hard-drinking soldiers are let loose anywhere near civilians.

The HQ of 1 (BR) Corps was just up the road from 10 Regt RCT in Ripon Barracks. Colonel White L/RCT (later Maj Gen CB CBE JP HM Lord-Lieutenant) had requested Cameron's presence to assist on a Staff Planning Exercise for deployment to a far-flung place somewhere around the world. Most people might consider that to be a standard sort of training exercise for those days, but it wasn't, it was something entirely new for a BAOR garrison to get involved in. The British Forces only planning for a long-distance deployment, in recent years, had been for 'OPERATION CORPORATE' back in 1982 when the Argentinian Forces were put back in their place from the Falkland Islands.

Nothing like that had ever been done before in BAOR, but because Saddam Hussain had invaded Kuwait, some sort of armed response needed to be planned and executed to re-establish the Iraqi Forces back where they belonged. Cameron explained, "The scenario we were given was to plan for the deployment of 1st Armoured Division and its Support Elements from BA. The assets would be transported by sea and air out to Saudi Arabia in preparation for a substantial conflict. I worked alongside Majors and Captains from other units and we spent three weeks working on all the details of our proposed deployment scenario, right down to how much consumable stores would be required to sustain and win the entire proposed conflict. We weren't initially given any maps to work with because no-one knew exactly where we were going."

The team worked on the 'Four D's' strategy, Demand, Distance, Duration and Destination. They had to work on the principles of how many trucks a unit would need to move Ammunition and Combat Supplies from Point A to Point B, and the amount of fuel needed to complete each task. Unfortunately, no-one had told them exactly where they were planning to base these troops and their equipment in Saudi Arabia and how far they would be from the FEBA (Forward Edge of the Battle Area).

Note: This planning was different to any other BAOR Cold War Planning which would normally involve the NATO Forces falling back on territory that they already knew very well, and our Lines of Logistics and Communication would decrease as we fell back towards the ports in France, Holland and Belgium. The strategy would then involve NATO's Forces being re-grouped before advancing and pushing the invading Warsaw Pact Forces back towards the East.

When the Planners and Plotters were eventually given the maps they needed, they put military map marking symbols on the charts to designate where they thought each Logistic Transport Regiment and Squadron were best located. The map symbols they used were generic and didn't display any numbers that would highlight which particular unit the symbol was referring to as in either 10 Regiment RCT or 8 Regiment RCT. That was because the military hierarchy at the MOD had yet to assign which units were going to be used on the deployment. As the Plotters placed each sign onto the charts after deciding where a unit would be best placed, Cameron always made a point of putting a number 10 next to the Logistic Transport Regiment marked on the map-board. Eventually, the committee subliminally *(Authors note: My copy of the Oxford Dictionary and Thesaurus reads that the definition of subliminally is – too rapid to be consciously perceived)* got used to the idea that it would be 10 Regt RCT deploying out to Saudi Arabia as the 3rd line Transport Regiment that would be deploying. Cameron feared that 8 Regt RCT, which was based at Münster, would get the job, rather than 10 Regt.

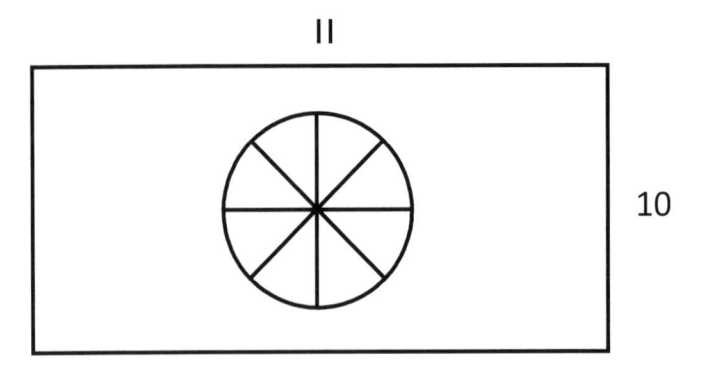

II

[Map marking sign: rectangle containing a circle divided into eight segments (wagon wheel), with "II" above and "10" to the right]

A Map Marking Sign, the Wagon Wheel in the middle denotes an RCT Transport Unit, the II above the flag denotes a Regt and the 10 on the right-hand side denotes the unit as 10 Regt RCT. During the planning phase, all units signs were supposed to be generic, but Captain Macnish RCT kept putting a number 10 on the right-hand side until it was generally accepted that 10 Regt were going to the Gulf. *10 Regt RCT Map marking sign provided by Nicky Clacy.*

It wasn't long before the Planning Committee started saying things like, "So if 10 Regt RCT are located here they can support such and such unit when required." And so, to the other schemers, it became psychologically understood that 10 Regt RCT were going to deploy as the 3rd line logistic element for 'OPERATION GRANBY.'

Part of 8 Regt RCT would also deploy out to Saudi in the form of 12 Sqn RCT which would be attached to 10 Regt. 12 Sqn already had the DROPS vehicles and trained Drivers necessary to complete the logistic line-up required. As the planning developed, Cameron gave 10 Regt's Commanding Officer, Lt Col Chaganis, a few private briefings about what was likely to happen when it all kicked off. When it all did kick off and the units were informed they were going to war, the OC of 36 Sqn RCT (36 Sqn was the only Sqn in 10 Regt not to deploy) was desperately disappointed not to get the chance to take his Sqn on the deployment.

Lt Col Chaganis and his RSM were the first members of 10 Regt to fly out to Saudi Arabia as the Recce Party and Cameron followed on behind as OC of the Main Party, after getting the unit ready to move. He also helped in supervising the convoys of unit vehicles up to Bremerhaven Port in North Germany, so they could be transported by ship down to the port in Al Jubayl. One of the Drivers asked Cameron, "Sir, you're an Australian, what's it like in the desert?" Cameron's answer was succinct to say the least, "How the fuck would I know, I grew up in the city of Sydney, I'm not a bloody Aborigine."

When the Main Party was flying out to Saudi, some of the 10 Regt Drivers started to get a bit boisterous during the flight and Cameron spoke to a female member of the Cabin Crew, "If my lads start getting out of hand then give me a shout will you. I'm the Adjutant of 10 Regt and I've got a couple of tough Sarn't Majors here with me who will definitely get them to calm down." The very pretty Cabin Crew member replied, "Don't worry sir, they are much quieter than some of our passengers on the flights to Ibiza. We're really quite proud to be taking you out there, and we'll be flying you back home after it's all over."

The flight had a brief stop-over in Cyprus before it landed in Dharan Airport at 0200 hours, and even at this time of the night, in October 1990 it was still incredibly hot. Within a couple of days Cameron had swapped his RCT Officer pattern beret for a brand-new aluminum US Army camp cot. Unfortunately, he was unaware that on the American Servicemen's black-market, his British Officer pattern RCT beret was worth at least six US Army camp cots. *Authors note: Bloody gullible Aussie's, still, what can we do with them eh!*

Captain Cameron 'anyone seen my gun' Macnish, Adjutant of 10 Regt, RCT.

The Yank asked what RCT meant when he was talking about his unit and Cameron told the also gullible American Serviceman, "It stands for, 'Recon Combat Troops.' The Yank went off happy in the knowledge that he'd got the beret of some British Army Secret Service Agent who'd covertly served behind the lines during the First Gulf War. Most Officers and Soldiers who served out in the desert during the first Gulf War will tell you that much of their time was spent preparing for the expected up and coming battles.

The actual fighting lasted for only a few weeks because the supreme coalition Air Assets had bombed the crap out of the Iraqi Ground Forces. During his time out in Saudi Arabia, Cameron mainly worked with Sgt (later WO 2) Ted Fost and Major Chris Harvey in the Ops tent, dispatching the necessary trucks, stores and fuel to where it was needed.

Captain Macnish in the Ops Room during Op Granby.

The war in Iraq and Kuwait was over very quickly and the fighting brief, but the whole campaign had been a laborious and horrible event. A lot of soldiers returned home with images in their heads that they wish they'd never witnessed on the road to Basra.

When Cameron returned to Bielefeld he was restored to his normal Adjutantal duties which involved him dealing with the discipline of 10 Regt's soldiers. One particular problem was Driver Mickey Ord RCT who came from the North East of England, Mickey was a tough guy who wouldn't raise a fist to anyone.... that is until he'd put on a pair of boxing gloves, or he'd sunk a considerable amount of alcohol, then anyone and everyone was fair game for a good cuffing around the lughole. Being an RCT Driver, and a 10 Regt boxer, meant that Mickey had a lot of bottle, both in the ring and in the NAAFI bar. One night after 10 Regt had returned to Bielefeld, following the Gulf War, Micky was heading back to his bedspace from the Naafi Bar having downed ¾ of a bottle of whiskey. On his meandering way back to the 9 Sqn accommodation block, he decided to punch the lights out of

13 other RCT soldiers who crossed his path on the way back to his room. The Orderly Officer that night was WO 2 (RQMS) Nobby Saunders, who suddenly appeared on the scene and duly arrested Micky, placing him in the safety of one of the Guardroom Cells. In the morning Driver Michael Ord RCT, woke up with a stinking hangover and had no recollections about any of the previous nights, 10 Regt style, drinking extravaganza.

As the incident had involved a certain amount of drunken violence and indiscipline, Cameron and the RSM were both summond to visit Mickey in his cell first thing the following morning. The 'Adjt' explained to Driver Ord that he was in, "Deep fucking shit Mickey my lad." Whilst trying not to be sick, Mickey explained that he was supposed to be starting his B2 Driver Training Course the following week and that if he couldn't do the Course then he'd think about sacking his whole military career. He didn't want to fall behind everyone else in the race to gaining NCO rank and status. Ultimately, Mickey was given 14 days jail for his misdemeanors and it looked like he was definitely going to miss out on the B2 Trade Training Course, and with that, any posssibility of climbing up the promotion ladder. Captain Cameron Macnish saved the day though. Every morning, the 'Adjt' came down to the Guardroom and personally signed for Driver M Ord RCT and then marched him up to the Training Wing, handing him over to his B2 Instructing Sergeant. Mickey did well on the B2 Course and gained his qualification. Incidentally, Mickey has assured the author that he has never touched a drop of whiskey since that night.

Mickey went on to serve for 13 years in the RCT and ultimately rose to the rank of full Corporal before being voluntarily discharged from the Corps and the British Army. During his service he'd had eight fights for 10 Regt (*this refers only to the official ones in the boxing ring, obviously there were many other unofficial fisty-cuffs in the NAAFI Bar*) and he only lost his first fight which was against Private Schubert of the Princess of Wales

Royal Regiment (PWRR). Mickey fought at Light-Welter weight (64Kg) but his punching power was well above his size and credence. SSgt Ted Fost, the 10 Regt RLC Boxing Coach and Manager, once asked him to step up a weight because he had no-one available to fight at that particular weight. Ted needed Mickey to fight at Middleweight (75Kg) and to gain the necessary lbs required to fight at that weight, Micky used weighted elastic bungees (*Normally used for securing the bottom of soldiers trousers to the tops of their boots*) and wrapped them around his testicles so they weren't noticable during the official weigh in proceedure. Mickey won the fight by a knock-out. His last posting in 2001 was to the Army Foundation College at Harrogate in Yorkshire. He was posted in as a Staff Car Driver and at various times he drove for Sir Geoff Hoon who eventually became the Secretary of State for Transport, Malcolm Rifkin MP, General (later Field Marshal) Michael Walker, and the Commanding Officer of the Special Air Service, when they visited the Harrogate College. Mickey eventually left the army because his wife at that time had recently given birth to his baby son, Toby, and Mickey didn't want to drag them both around various Garrisons to live an unsettling life in the Military.

Life after 10 Regt meant Cameron had to go off to Staff College for a year as a Major, after which he was posted to Wilton to become part of a Joint Planning Team. During his tenure at Wilton he deployed to Norway and Denmark a couple of times. He also deployed to Croatia, Turkey, Greece and Norway. Cameron thought that the Italian Troops were flamboyant but useless, and he started to realise how much the "Greek and Turkish soldiers hated each others guts."

Cameron compiled the minutes of one meeting between the Greeks and the Turks and sent the wrong cryptic and honest notes to both Military Attachè. Cameron was given the bollocking of a lifetime and was informed by the Brigadier that, "The only reason your arse isn't in even deeper shit is because both you and I know that the Greeks and Turks never read anything we send them. The Brigadier sorted the whole mess out for Cameron and organised the right papers were sent to the correct Military Attaché. Strange as it may seem, Cameron was rewarded with a fantastic attachment to Paris where he thought he would be going on the piss every night. It was at the start of the Bosnian and Croatian War and the UN were having all sorts of problems which was why Cameron was sent there to help out with some of the planning issues. He ended up working 18 hours a day. He was sent out to Zagreb for a couple of months, which Cameron sarcastically described as pleasing his wife no end.

Cameron helped in the planning of the Anglo-French Brigade deployment in which the French were providing the necessary Military Police security.

Cameron: The British Army will be providing a Transport Sqn, a Company Headquarters and Two Platoons of Infantry. What manpower will the French be providing to the Brigade?

Miltary Attaché: We shall be providing two members of the Gendarmerie.

Cameron: Ah, good. So you will be sending 2 Company's of Military Police which is about thirty policemen, excellent.

Miltary Attaché: Non!

Cameron: What do you mean Non?! I thought you said that the French Army will be providing 2 Company's of Military Policemen?

Miltary Attaché: Non! I said that we would be providing just two Military Policemen.

Cameron: How can you expect to provide the necessary cover with just two Gendarmes?

Miltary Attaché: You don't understand. The Gendarmerie in my local garrison are complete bastards, they are always arresting my men for doing nothing wrong. They are all bastards!

Cameron: Well, while I sympathise with you and your men, I will need the Gendarmerie to do a lot of the essential route signing.

Miltary Attaché: The 'Route Circuleter' do that sort of thing for the French Army. The Military Police are there simply to do their usual bastard things, like policing and arresting blameless soldiers of the French Army.

And so it proved to be, because when the Brigade eventually deployed onto the ground, Cameron witnessed one of only two Gerndames simply walking around on their beat.

In late November of 1995, 27 Regt RLC deployed out to Bosnia and as the forces ultimately drew down, 8 Sqn RCT was left behind to cover any logistical needs. Cameron left Wilton and took command of the Sqn. The Sqn had two troops of GT (General Transport) vehicles and one Tp of Pioneers. In December 1995 the Force changed over from a UN Power to a NATO Authority and all of the military vehicles had to be painted a different colour. The white paintwork had to go and be replaced with a more suitable NATO Green. The only problem was that the Sqn didn't have the equipment to get the spray-jobs completed so an RLC Cpl haggled with a local Tryre firm that didn't have any anti-feeze that they deperately needed. The Cpl swapped some MOD Anti-Freeze in return for a brand new Spray Gun and some paint brushes. The paint brushes weren't much use because when brushed on the paint, it turned a bright 'Baby Sick' yellow colour.

During this winter period a lot of snow had fallen in Bosnia and the temperature had dropped down to -15 degrees, which resulted in a lot of the Sqn's tentage collapsing, up in the mountaininous areas. Cameron's Staff Sergeant Master Chef had to do a lot of improvising during the cold spell. One day he produced a hot breakfast (albeit) half an hour late, because some of the other chefs had to hold up the Cookhouse tent whilst the others cooked the food. On other occasions the chefs had to use some missapropriated Chobham armour from a Warrior APC to use as a hotplate.

The Chefs Chinese and Italian nights proved to be so popular that the French Brigade Commander, Brig Subero, would always find an excuse to be passing through their location whenever these special dinners were being served. Cameron realised that good food was a real morale builder and that the US Army rations in insulated food containers used to feed the Troops was (technca term here) 'shite.' He stated, "Army chefs are like Premiership footballers, no-one notices them when things are going well, but soldiers always notice when the footballing or their food is of a poor standard."

The Pioneers within the Sqn were told by a Troop Commander, Lt Christopher Williams, that there was a need for some Christmas trees within the unit to boost morale over the Yuletide period. The Pioneers ended up deforresting half of Bosnia, providing one tree for every each tent and department in the entire Sqn. The 'Chunkies' also built a bunker that would provide cover if the unit was being shelled, which it often was. The bunker also provided a great location for the Officers to the Sgt's Mess party. The Pioneers also built refugee camps for Romany Gypsies in Kosovo in 1999 and did some fantastic work, Cameron felt, "They could turn their hand to anything, they were all great lads and my God they were extremely fit. I personally feel that it was a great shame that the RPC was disbanded from the British Army, still, they now add a further string to our RLC capabilities.

I eventually became 2i/c of 23 Pioneer and was involved in building an entire Detention Centre to keep the Albanians and Serbs apart.

After completing his Tour in Bosnia, Cameron was posted with his Squadron to Kinnegar in Northern Ireland where he organised the military training for 200 soldiers, and out of these men there were twenty Nigs *(Authors note: I suppose they should have been called Niks – New In Kinnegar - by rights)* who'd come straight from training and another twenty who had come from 10 Regt. The syllabus was the same as the 1988 training that Cameron had implemented for the Saxon and 'Pig' APC Training back in Bünde with 1 ADTR.

The number of experienced and knowlegable Officers and Warrant Officers in the Corps end up being posted to RLC Career Manning Division (Soldiers Wing) in Glasgow. The same happened to a newly promoted, Lieutenant Colonel Cameron Macnish RLC. He loved the job because he was in charge of putting right RLC soldiers careers that had fallen through the cracks through no fault of their own. Cameron did a lot of road shows and visited an abundance of RLC units. Just one of his successful corrections was a Pioneer Private who was stationed in Cyprus and hadn't been boarded for three years. His Unit had sent an official letter to RLC Manning about why he hadn't been promoted and the letter had ended up in Cameron's 'In Tray.' MRO had been saying that the Private wasn't qualified for promotion because he hadn't yet done his JMQC (Junior Military Qualification Course.

'Sherlock' Macnish discovered that the soldier had successfully completed the course and the Sqn Clerk had published it on Part 2 Orders *(Authors note: Any courses or qualifications that require a change in a soldiers status or pay need to be put on a Part 2 Order to ensurethat the necessary changes are made to a soldiers pay etc.)* but somehow, it hadn't appeared on the RLC system. Cameron made sure the soldier was quickly reboarded, got him 18 months back-pay and granted him immediate promotion to Lance Corporal, "That assignment gave me a good feeling and great sense of satisfaction." He said.

On another mission that involved an Ammunition Technician being aggreived, Cameron was instrumental in granting the soldier a posting anywhere in the world as recompense. He was given the chance to go to Canada within the next 18 months, was delighted with the offer, and accepted it without reservation. Cameron explained, "It took the sting out of the MOD's mistake in the soldiers career management and we sweetened the error by giving him a tasty little morsel. After granting him his wish, it turned out that he'd recently started shagging a German Girlfriend and he didn't want to go to Canada, so the posting was cancelled. Still, it's the thought that counts I suppose."

In 2002 Cameron was posted to a BMATT (British Military Army Training Team) in the Republic of Sierra Leone. The unit had a mixture of 110 Officer and Warrant Officer personnel on its staff and they included Australians, Canadians, 2 Yanks and quite a few British service personnel. The brief they were given was to Train and Develop the Republic of Sierra Leone's Armed Forces because they had not long finished their Civil War. Unfortunately, every civilian walking the streets was armed with their own personal 7.62mm AK 47 Assault Rifle, and some of them (*In particular the Rebels*) didn't quite understand what the English word 'Ceasefire' actually meant. Sierra Leone had an army of 15,000 soldiers and the BMATT Staff were responsible for training, provisioning, and feeding the lot of them.

Whilst there, Cameron worked reasonably long hours playing golf and battling corruption. The locals were stealing the kit that the British Government was donating to them and then sellng it on the Black Market. A Sierra Leone Colonel in charge of the local hospital received a donation of £100,000 worth of drugs but it had all been stolen and sold on the Black Market by racketeers. The only drugs that had been recieved by the hospital were some paracetamol tablets. Cameron visited where the medicines were coming into the country and set up a system where the BMATT collected their own rations from the same place, and collected the medicines at the same time. Each collection was monitored by armed BMATT soldiers and they personally delivered all of the drugs to Lt Col Jonny Lowe who had a firm grip on everything once the stores were safely delivered to him.

Sierra Leone Officers Mess 8th November 2002

The vehicles that were made available to the BMATT were very old 1960's trucks that still had the yellow and blue diagonally split RASC/RCT Corps deignation markings on them and others had the RAOC blue and red Corps markings. The BMATT had to teach the new Sierra Leone Army how to drive and maintain these trucks. The main instructor in the Training Wing was a 70 year old guy who had been trained by the British Army in the 1960's at Borden in Hampshire. The REME guys that came out with the

BMATT said they couldn't teach the old man anything because the principles and techniques he was teaching were still relevent today and that he was doing a great job.

After 12 months working with the BMATT, Cameron was posted to HQ 1 Armoured Div at Herford and the unit was deployed on 'OP TELIC' in 2003 but unfortunately Cameron was dissapointed to discover that he wasn't going with them. He remained behind in Herford to co-ordinate any casualty lists, regularly briefed the wives on what was happening out in Iraq, and kept a firm grip on the ever present rumour control that always raises its head on Rear Party during every British Army Operational Tour. When he wasn't dealing with upset wives, Cameron passed his time in his office by cutting out the nipples and maps of Tasmania (*Authors Note: An Aussie Euphemism for a lady's front garden.*) from Penthouse magazines, he then sent the butchered pictures out to the officers serving in Iraq. A week later he sent out the bits he'd cut out of the soft porn magazines. This kept the 'Aussie' occupied and amused for quite a while.

By 2004 Cameron had left HQ I ADSR to take command of 152 (Ulster) Transport Regiment RLC which was based in Sunnyside Street off the Omagh Road, Northern Ireland. His RSM, (Regimental Sergeant Major) was WO1 Dave Brown RLC who was also a Regular Solder; Dave had previously served at 17 Port and Maritime Regiment and as a Physical Training Instructor (PTI) in 2 Sqn at Bünde. It is alleged that when Dave was Duty PTI he used to turn up the heating in the gymnasium a few hours before 33 Sqn did their circuit training, he says he'd done that purely to help them warm up a bit quicker. Because both Cameron and Dave were Regular Army personnel, they couldn't venture out onto the streets whereas the locally recruited TA soldiers could, which made it a very restrictive posting.

During his tenure as the Commanding Officer at 152 Regiment, Cameron designed and orchestrated a beach landing Exercise that was hopefully going to mirror the opening scenes from the film 'Saving Private Ryan.' A Landing Ship Logistic (LSL) from 17 Port and Maritime Regiment were used for the mini-D Day and the ship was detailed to picked up some Drops Trucks from an RLC unit based in Liverpool. Once loaded, the vehicles were driven on board the LSL which sailed across the Irish Sea heading towards the Belfast Coastline, where the Exercise (Main) would take place. This was no Spielberg cheapskate version either. The Army Air Corps (AAC) provided helicopters to present simulated and impressive air cover, and a Royal Engineers Demolition Team provided Sappers to layout the barbed wire on the beach and simulate a mine clearing task. The Regiments Pipes and Drums Band was detailed to play some stirring music as the vehicles were disembarked from the LSL and driven onto the beach.

The RLC Truck Drivers were warned that their next Confidential Reports depended on them successfully driving off the LSL and making a triumphant and glorious beach landing, mainly because they were doing the whole thing in front of the Brigade Commander.

As D-Day itself dawned, Cameron looked out of his window and saw that an old- fashioned East London 'Pea Souper' fog had suppressed any clear vision down to about 20 metres. The RE's had to hold lights to guide the LSL onto the shore so that they could beach exactly where they were needed. Unfortunately, the 17 Port Regt SSgt in Command of the LSL wanted to get away as quickly as possible after unloading, and so he didn't get as close to the shore as would have been better served for the RLC lads driving the trucks off the ship. As the vehicles came off the ship, the sea-water level came up to the bottom of the trucks windscreens which could have jeopardised the whole Exercise. It would have been a humiliating disaster if the trucks were stuck in the muddy sand on the beach. The Corps' drivers came through in the end, as they always have done; they gunned their truck engines to full revs then skilfully hammered the vehicles until they made it onto the beach and dry land. Cameron became quite emotional after the landings had been successfully achieved. The REME, however, took a dimmer view of what 152 (Ulster) Tpt Regt RLC and 17 Port Regt RLC had done because the trucks had to go through a de-rusting process over the next 6 months.

Cameron enjoyed a fantastic 2½ years Commanding 152 Regiment RLC in Belfast and had upped their manning list to 100%, which in itself was a great achievement considering all the security vetting that had to be completed before the recruits could even begin training.

After leaving Belfast, Cameron was posted to the RLC's DE&S Unit (Defence Equipment Support Unit) at Andover in Hampshire; he was involved in the Defence Operations and Movements where he coordinated the movement of priority freight out to Iraq and Afghanistan and bringing equipment back to the UK. During his tenure in the job he went out to Iraq and Afghanistan several times to visit units. The bizarre thing is that Cameron wanted to go out to these dangerous places because he wanted to see for himself what things were like on the ground and, as he said, "Time spent on reconnaissance is time never wasted."

Before starting a return journey to the UK in a Tristar plane, Cameron was talking to Colonel Alister Davis L/RLC in his office. As they waited to embark for the flight to take off from Kandahar Airport, the two senior officers heard some explosions in the distance and Cameron enquired of his superior officer, in his usual Australian vernacular, "What the fuck was that?" Colonel Davis calmly replied in his usual British Officer vernacular, "I'm not quite sure Cameron; perhaps some of the ATO chaps are destroying some of our old ammunition.". An always forthright Cameron replied, "I don't think they bloody do that at night, do they?" Seconds later a rocket exploded 150 metres away from where the two Colonels were stood, and automatically they dived under a desk. The following words are Cameron's not the authors, "We were big lads with fat arses who needed to get under cover, but there's no rank when it comes to hiding under a desk mate!"

In Iraq a similar thing occurred at Basra Airport and at the Scots Guards Ammo Depot. The Ordnance officer told Cameron, "The Jocks will be really pissed off now because I've only just inspected their depot, and it was immaculate. It's a shame the insurgents didn't hit the Irish depot down the road, their place is in a complete shit-state."

Cameron left the Corps and British Army in 2010 and found his fortune in Pakistan on a US contract. In 2011 he helped set up a Company called 'Arturus International.' By 2013 the firm was struggling like any other new Business, but a year ago they got another big contract and it's been the making of the business. "The workforce in our firm are made up of 98% ex-military people, some have completed many years in the ranks and others not so many, but they're great workers, every one of them."
For the foreseeable future, Cameron is intent on staying in the UK but would like to spend at least a couple of months in Australia every year, he candidly states, "I've now got more friends in the UK than I have out in Oz". *Authors note, "We're more than pleased to take you on board as a plastic Brit... Sir."*

Staff Sergeant Lee Hunt
RCT and RLC 1985 – 2006

Lee Hunt was born in Grimsby in the latter part of 1967, two years later his Mum, Astrid Mary Hunt, and her husband became estranged and so she had to go and live in Scunthorpe. For their benefit, she left Lee and his other brothers in the 'care' of her husband, John Hunt. Unbeknownst to Lee, he'd been surreptitiously given the name Hunt and believed that John was his real father. The reality was that Lee never knew his biological father (Mr Tommon) when he was growing up, and even today Lee doesn't even know his real father's Christian name. The erstwhile Mr Tommon and his brother were both trawler men and they were often away from home for long periods working on one of Grimsby's fishing trawlers. Long after Lee had joined the Army, he tracked down his biological father who was by this time living in Newton Aycliffe, Co Durham. Lee is still unsure of the details of what happened during this period of his childhood and it all continues to remain a mystery to Lee, even today.

When Lee was about 8 years old, he and one of his brothers were ear wigging on the landing upstairs, their parents were noisily arguing in the kitchen about family matters. Lee suddenly heard John shout, "I don't give a fuck about Lee, he's not my fucking son." A shocked Lee already knew his older brother's surname was Davis and that he wasn't John's son, Lee therefore assumed that they both then had the same father. At school the following day, Lee refused to answer the register because he now knew that his surname wasn't Hunt. He also altered the names on all his school books so that they now identified them as belonging to, Lee Davis. When Lee refused to answer his name at registration, he pointed out to his teacher, "My name isn't Hunt, it's Davis." Lee's mum was called into the school to help clear up the matter and she eventually explained to Lee that he had a different father to his brothers.

You, the reader, might think that coming from a troubled home in Lincolnshire, wasn't conducive to Lee getting any decent schooling, but by the time he'd finished his full-time education, Lee walked away with 9 GCE O' levels. He wasn't just a 'swot jockey' either, he also had an avid interest in sports, "I was a bit of a 'Sports Billy' at an early age. Football and running were my particular favourites and at the age of fourteen, I was selected for the Scunthorpe Youth Team Football Club. It turned out to be a bit of a disappointment for me though, because so many of us were on the bench during a match, we only got about 10 minutes playing time." Once he'd finished his education, Lee was put on a Youth Training Scheme (YTS) as a Cabinet Maker. He attended Doncaster College for 6 weeks before working on site at a timber yard and with a Cabinet Making firm. Unfortunately, Lee was simply used as a cheap YTS labourer for the firm, and after a while he started looking for a more lucrative career.

Lee wanted an occupation where he could at least earn a decent wage for the hours he was working, he wanted to move onwards and upwards from his home environment. If possible, he wanted to get away from Scunthorpe entirely because he felt the whole area was smothered with an aura of depression. A lot of his friends from school were either drug addicts, gas sniffers, languishing in prison, or were working at the Scunthorpe Steel Works, and he didn't want to tread down any of those paths. Lee went for an interview with the Humberside Police Force in the hope of at least getting a respectable livelihood. Sadly, he was told that the Police weren't going to be recruiting for another 4 years.

Another option Lee had considered was joining the British Army and so he headed off to the Army Recruiting Office in Scunthorpe, he went there wearing an ill-fitting, cheap, and nasty looking, silver nylon suit. On his feet he wore some even cheaper and nastier looking Dunlop road slappers. In Lee's own words, "I looked like a bag of shit that had been rapidly thrown together."

The burly Cavalry Recruiting Sergeant looked Lee up and down and asked, "What do you want to be?" Lee knew nothing about the Armed Forces and bluntly replied, "I dunno, I just wanna join the British Army." The Sergeant tried to pressurise Lee into joining one of the Horse Guards Regiments, probably in the hope of satisfying his recruiting targets. Lee felt he was being fobbed off by the Sergeant simply because he wouldn't conform to his wishes. The Senior NCO told him, "Anyway, there's nowt on you, you're far too skinny for the Army son. You need to get yourself a few muscles before we can accept you into the British Army."

Lee was very frustrated, "I was already extremely fit and likely as not, in a race, I could have easily out-run that fat fucking piece of shit. But what I thought didn't matter, the British Army made the rules and he enforced them, so I went home empty-handed again, but I thought to myself, I'm not having any of that." Lee returned to his YTS work but in the evenings after he'd left the timber yard, he'd go for a five or six mile run with a rucksack on his back. Inside the backpack he always carried his brothers Fiat X19 spare wheel (minus the tyre) wrapped up in bath towels. Lee went back to the Army Recruiting Office two months later and again tried to join up, this time he was steered towards joining the Royal Signals because, apparently, there were great chances of promotion as a Linesman. Lee again went against the Recruiters' advice and told him, "No thanks, I only want to do three years and get out, by then I can join the Humberside Police Force. I want to join that RCT lot and get me driving licenses, saves me paying for it and anyway, it'll help me to get into the Police."

This time the Recruiter bowed to Lee's wishes and sent him off to Sutton Coldfield to go through the final selection process. On Lee's 1 ½ mile run, he finished in an exceptional 7 minutes 20 seconds and the Selection Staff urged him to apply for a placement in the Parachute Regiment. Unsurprisingly, Lee wasn't having anything to do with what other people thought was best for him. On being pressed to join the Paras on his final interview at Sutton Coldfield, he put his foot down with a firm hand and said, "No! I want to join them Royal Corps of Transport lot and get me licenses, I don't want to jump out of any airplanes." The staff at Sutton Coldfield gave up and agreed to his wishes. "When I got back to Scunthorpe I received a letter from the ACIO (Army Careers Information Office) asking me to come in and take my Oath of Allegiance, which I did. Afterwards they paid me the grand total of, I think it were £10 or £12, and they then welcomed me into the British Army.

When Lee arrived at Aldershot Railway Station he was met by a skinny RCT Cpl 'Full Screw' called Pete O'Brien and another Cpl called 'Dez' Ackerman. Lee had very long hair at the time and he looked like a blond permed version of Kevin Keegan. The new recruits were billeted in a block that was directly opposite the Guardroom and overlooked the main road which ran the full length of the front of Buller Barracks. Lee was accommodated in a four-man room and Cpl Pete O'Brien told them all, "Right, listen in you lot. Tomorrow morning you will all get your arses outside on the Main Square by 0755 hours at the latest. You will all parade in three ranks, that's one behind the other twice, where I will size you all off and you will retain that position every-time you form up for a parade over the next 12 weeks." Lee thought, 'Shit, things are getting a bit serious.'

Lee had never shaved in his entire life, "I only had a bit of bum-fluff on my face and in the morning one of the DS (Directing Staff) had to show me how to shave, and I wouldn't mind, but the bloody Army expected me to do it every morning thereafter! After my very first shave I nearly bled to death, I went back to my bed-space with half a bog roll holding my face together". The recruits paraded outside the accommodation block and could hear their Instructors approaching before they clapped eyes on them, "Keep the noise down! Stop talking that man! Stand still in the ranks!" The squad was hurried over to the NAAFI building which was where Reggie's Barber Shop was located. Reggie, who had been cutting hair at Buller barracks for many years, didn't have a qualification to his name, but he did own a pair of clippers. Whilst Reggie was shearing the recruit's hair, his wife would sit in the corner of the room staring menacingly at the recruits, whilst smoking and barking out orders to poor old Reggie. Lee rather unkindly describes Reggie's wife as, "The ugliest fucking monster I've ever seen in my entire life, she would sit in the corner looking like 'Jabba the Hutt' with her tits hanging over the top of her knees." When the squad left the NAAFI building, they all looked like the French convict, Henri Charriere, from the prison film 'Papillon'.

The BFT (Basic Fitness Test) wasn't a problem for Lee. He could do a three-mile run in his sleep and probably faster than anyone else in his squad. One area of Lee's fitness where he did come up short though was his upper body strength. He was put on remedial PT in the hope that the PTI's could build up his upper body muscle tone. The PTI Staff pulled out the wooden beams in the gymnasium and made him do a lot of pull-ups and push-ups, they didn't 'beast' him but did put him through his paces. Lee couldn't climb a rope to save his life before doing the remedial PT, "But afterwards I could shoot up and down a rope quicker than a trained monkey. The PTI's at Buller Barracks were very good at what they did."

One item of equipment that all the recruits soon misplaced was an issued white china mug. On room inspections the lads had to lay out their military equipment on their beds ready for the Cpl's to inspect and insult. Any dust, dirt or badly ironed bits of uniform, were frequently thrown out of the window by a disgruntled Training NCO. Bed blocks, boots, uniforms, cutlery and the inevitable white china mugs were often hurled out of the nearest window. The one place in each locker that NCO's weren't allowed to intrude and violate was the sacrosanct internal small cabinet. By military law this small and personal bit of space couldn't be meddled with by anyone other than the soldier himself, but only if it was safeguarded with a padlock. If the cabinet wasn't secured during an inspection though, then everything inside it was fair game. After seeing many a deemed to be filthy, white china mug smashed on the road outside their block, Lee diligently took to locking his mug up in his small padlocked cabinet. During kit inspections the Training NCO's obviously assumed that they had previously destroyed Lee's mug because it was never presented for inspection. The 'mug smashing' routine was a form of amusement that the Training Staff liked to play and after smashing every recruit's china mug, they thought they'd won the game.

During the last inspection before going to Leconfield, East Yorkshire, for Driver Training, Lee had rather smugly placed the only white mug left in the troop on his bed with the rest of his kit. The Cpl looked at Lee and said, "How the fuck have we missed that." Lee smiled and said, "I knew what you were all doing Corporal, so I made sure I locked it up in my personal cabinet." The NCO smirked at Lee and then threw the mug into the air, but instead of breaking, the mug simply bounced on the floor. He then said to Lee, "Right, come with me and bring that fucking mug with you." They went to the nearest window and the Cpl said, "Right, because you've been such a clever twat, you will now have the privilege of throwing your own mug out of the window." Finally, the last remaining white china mug in the Troop was smashed on the road outside.

Lee and his fellow trainees then went up to the ASMT (Army School of Mechanical Transport) at Normandy Barracks, Leconfield in Yorkshire to do their Driver Training, where it turned out that Lee's Driving Instructor was the famous RCT Boxer, Colin Booth. Colin had boxed for England, the British Army, the RCT, and just about every unit to which he'd ever been posted. Lee describes Colin, "He were a great instructor and I passed me HGV in a Bedford TK in about 24 hours." Years later,

Lee again bumped into Colin at Leconfield and told him that he had instructed him on his HGV Driver Training. Colin couldn't remember Lee and told him, "I might well have done, but you must realise that over the years, I've taught thousands of soldiers how to drive."

When the squad returned to Buller Barracks in Aldershot, they were placed in Holding Troop where they were accommodated in carpeted rooms and could sleep under their own duvets - bed-blocks were now a thing of the past. Lee reported to the Squadron Office one day and was told that his Posting Order had arrived. The Cpl in the office was a 63 (Para) Sqn RCT NCO, who was biding his time before being discharged from the Corps. When Lee told him that he'd been posted to 1 ADTR (1 Armoured Division Transport Regiment) in Bünde, West Germany, the Cpl laughed and said, "Fucking hell, you'll enjoy it there, it's a shit-hole."

Authors note: Even if a soldier explains that he's been posted to the best free whore-house in the world, condoms supplied, with no SSM's in a 20- mile radius, and it's also got an' Open All Hour's' complimentary bar next door, the listening troops will still say, "Fucking hell mate, you don't want to go there, it's a fucking shit-hole!"

The majority of Lee's squad were sent to either 8 Regt RCT or 10 Regt RCT and only two were on their way to Bünde. Lee was about to find out that the Para Cpl had got it somewhat right about Bünde and 1 ADTR, they were both shit-holes.

Lee and all the other Nig's (New in Germany) were picked up from RAF Gütersloh in a drab olive-green 49-seater Army bus. The transport had made several stops at a few Army barracks, leaving only Lee and his mate from Buller Barracks on the vehicle. After the 'coach' had driven out of Roberts Barracks in Osnabrück, Lee shouted at the German MSO civilian driver, "Oy mate, what about us? We're supposed to be going to Bünde." Their Teutonic chauffeur laughed out loud and spoke probably the only English words he knew, "Ha ha, you Bünde yes, ha ha." After driving through the town of Bünde, the MSO driver continued out into the sticks of Germany before parking outside the front gates of Birdwood Barracks. "Once we were off his shitty little bus, the MSO fucked off pretty quick." The RP Cpl came out of the guardroom and pounced on the two new arrivals. He made them double all the way up to the transit accommodation whilst carrying their heavy Army baggage. Lee thought to himself, 'Fucking hell, what's going on here, we're trained soldiers now, not recruits.'

1 ADTR consisted of four Sqn's, 1 Sqn, 3 Sqn, 4 Sqn, and 34 Sqn. The morning after their arrival, Lee was posted into Golf Troop in 4 Sqn where he and his fellow Nig were allocated bed-space's in a 4-man room in a single-story accommodation block. The other two beds wouldn't be allocated until more Drivers were posted into the unit. On their first night in the accommodation, the door to their room suddenly burst open and some 'old sweat' Cpl's came storming into the room. "Right you two, get your arses outside now!" Lee and his mate were frogmarched up to the NAAFI Bar where large glasses of lager beer were placed in front of them. They were instructed, "Right, get them down your necks." Lee protested the fact that he didn't drink alcohol but was commanded, "Well, you will now, get them down your neck, Nig!" The black NCO who co-ordinated this ceremony was a Corps boxer who went on to bully Lee's room-mate for weeks, he allegedly forced beer into young, inexperienced lads until they became so inebriated that he could sexually assault them.

One-night Lee and his room-mate were both given a severe beating by the two Cpl's. He clearly remembers having his shoulders pinned down whilst being punched in the face. The two victims were marched in front of Golf Troops' Staff Sergeant in the morning and upon inspecting their bruises, their Staffie enquired, "Right, who did this to the pair of you? Was it Cpl's ******** and *********?" The regime of brutality meted out by those two NCO's resulted in a code of silence passing amongst the bullied. It was an unwritten law in 4 Sqn that you didn't grass up the persecuting NCO's, that is, if you knew what was good for you. After their evening meal, Lee and his mate were again cornered in their accommodation and the black Corporal demanded to know, "What did you tell them in the Troop Office?" When Lee said, "We told them we fell over, we didn't mention either of you." Corporal ******** snarled, "Good, and you'll keep your fucking mouths shut if you know what's good for you." Before the Cpl's left the room, Lee and his mate both received another intimidating punch in the face. Lee believes that the bullying was co-ordinated by one of the key members in 1 ADTR, a principal Serviceman who gave instructions to his 'Rottweiler's' about who he wanted sorting out, after which the beatings would happen that very same night.

During a morning working parade, Lee's room-mate was noted as being absent and when asked where he was, Lee replied, "I dunno, he left the room before me, I thought he'd already be here." Un-noticed, the tormented and abused Driver had committed suicide and he was ultimately found hanging from the rafters in 4 Sqn's Dutch Barn. Within days the Chinese whispers had started, and Lee was told by another NCO to report onto the roof of the NAAFI building with his sleeping bag and some personal supplies. The unit were going to hold a 'demonstration' (protest) about certain members of the Regiment.

Authors note: Demonstrations/Protests within the ranks of the British Army are contrary to the rules in QR's (Queens Regulations) and the MML (Manual of Military Law). Anyone contravening these strict rules and laws is liable to have the full weight of military discipline fall upon them.

After 24 hours the protest came to an end and some of the Regiments' soldiers quickly disappeared from the camp, including the two vindictive Cpl's.

On Regimental Part 1 Orders, Lee spotted a notice asking for volunteers who would like a posting to the MT Section of 1 Armoured Division Signal Regiment (1 ADSR) in Verden. Lee approached his Staffie and requested the deployment but was turned down because he'd only been in 1 ADTR for about 12 months. Lee, however, was a persistent sort of young man and he kept on badgering those in command until he was granted the posting out of Bünde. A lack of interest in the posting by other Drivers obviously aided Lee's chances of being confirmed for the move.

On arrival at 1 ADSR, Lee noticed a striking difference in the attitude of the Royal Signals RP's (Regimental Policemen) in comparison to the RCT RP's back in Bunde. The RP Sgt addressed him in a friendly manner when he told Lee where the RCT Section was located on the camp. In the RCT building, Lee met Sgt's Chris Davis and Mick Jezamine *(Note: Sgt Jezamine eventually passed the All Arms Commando Course and P Company before becoming the Corps RSM).* Chris Davis and Mick Jezamine both worked in the Details Office. WO 2 Downey, the MTWO, (Motor Transport Warrant Officer) was away from his desk at the time and so Lee was wheeled straight into the MTO's Office. Captain D J (Dave) Winkle RCT (later Lieutenant Colonel), was a very fit and powerfully built ex-ranker who had served in 63 (Parachute) Sqn RCT, and although approachable and welcoming, he was not a gentleman to be taken lightly. Lee describes Captain Winkle, "He was a fucking big unit." After shaking Lee's hand, Captain Winkle gave him a rundown on what was what within the unit, he also explained what duties Lee would be responsible for within the RCT Detachment.

Lee looked a bit nervous as he stood to attention in front of Captain Winkle's desk. The MTO asked, "What's up with you? You look like a rabbit that's been caught in the headlights of a car." When Lee explained about his recent experiences at Bünde, Dave Winkle told him, "There's a lot of good guys at Bünde, but for every 10 good ones, you will always get another couple of arseholes. That happens in all units in any Army. There's only one person you need to worry about here though, and that's me. I'm the Daddy in this unit." Lee told the author, "Captain Dave Winkle RCT was absolutely fucking brilliant and my time at 1 ADSR turned out to be one of my best postings in the RCT. The Boss put me on a TTF (Truck Transporter Fuel) and UBRE (Unit Bulk Re-Fuelling Equipment) Course which was run on an in-house Training Programme."

When the RCT Detachment deployed on Lee's first Field Exercise with 1 ADSR, he drove a Bedford MK 4-tonner that was loaded up with 90 Jerrycans of diesel, 90 Jerrycans of petrol and a row of Kerosene Jerrycans down the middle. The RCT 22,500 litre TTF's would park up outside the wooded location and fill up the Royal Signals 432's before they went into the hide, they then had a full tank of fuel before Start-Ex (Start of Exercise). The TTF's performed poorly on soft ground and cross-country routes, so they stayed on the hardstanding throughout the exercise and the 432's were re-fuelled using Lee's Bedford MK and Jerrycans. He'd simply wait for a 'Bleep' (Royal Signal soldier) to knock on his cab door asking to be supplied with however many litres of either petrol, diesel, or kerosene. When the aforementioned 'Bleep' returned the empty Jerrycans to Lee, he would put them back on his truck but in a reversed position so, at a glance, Lee knew which Jerrycans were empty and which were full. The Bedford's, UBRE's, and TTF's worked as a team to ensure that all the 432's were supplied with enough fuel to keep their engines running and their radio batteries fully charged.

During a night on the town, Lee met a young German girl and eventually they decided to get married. Lee's Troop Staff Sergeant tried to warn him, "Don't do it! You're only 19 years old for Christ's sake, trust me, you are too young to get married. What do you know about anything?" Dave Winkle had been posted away from 1 ADSR by that time and the RCT detachment had been taken over by an ex ranker. Captain Pat O'Hara RCT (later Lieutenant Colonel) was a tall slim and Dashing Officer, of the first water. The new MTO agreed with Lee's Staffie, "It's up to you Driver Hunt, but if I was in your situation, I wouldn't get married this young." As it turned out, getting married to a German girl was a complex process and the paperwork had to be filled in neatly, legibly, and accurately. On several occasions mistakes had been made when filling out the relevant forms and consequently several wedding dates had to be cancelled. Lee is now philosophical about those delays, "That should have been an omen to me because the marriage was later doomed to failure." Someone, somewhere, was trying to do Lee a favour.

The civilian Unit Families Officer came up with a solution to these administrative problems, "If you both go to Løgumkloster in Denmark you can get married without going through all that British and German red-tape, but if anyone asks you, I didn't tell you that." Løgumkloster was a continental version of Gretna Green and anyone wishing to get married there, only had to be in Denmark for 24 hours to register for a wedding. The Danish processing was an expensive business though, and under advisement, Lee took a few bottles of top quality Duty-Free NAAFI whiskey to grease some Danish palms and help alleviate the administration costs. Lee was promoted to Lance Corporal within a year of getting married and was eventually posted into A Tp at 38 Sqn RCT at Wrexham Barracks, in Mülheim. A Tp was the BAOR Freight Tp of 38 Sqn and its Drivers spent a week at a time on the road collecting and delivering stores all over Germany. Lee initially loved the job but after spending a lot of time away from home, he became bored with it and so transferred into the QM's Department where he ran the Clothing Store.

Things were about to change for Lee and the other soldiers in 38 Sqn RCT in 1989 when Saddam Hussein's Army's invaded Kuwait and annexed Kuwait's oilfields, which they later destroyed. The soldiers in 38 Sqn RCT were initially told they wouldn't be going out to the Gulf because the freight system in BAOR wouldn't be able to operate without them. The Sqn also only had Foden wagons (which were notoriously bad at cross-country driving) meaning that they couldn't operate over the rough desert and sandy terrain. The MOD stated, '38 Sqn RCT is definitely not deploying out to the Gulf.' Within weeks the MOD stated, '38 Sqn RCT will definitely be deploying out to the Gulf.' The MSO (Mixed Service Organisation) was detailed to take over 38 Sqn's freight duties, leaving 38 Sqn free to deploy to Saudi Arabia.

There was plenty to do before 38 Sqn flew out to Saudi though. The Drivers had to travel to FOD (Forward Ordnance Depot) at Dülmen where huge reserves of military vehicles were stored in massive hangars. These trucks were being held in readiness for a war to pop around the corner. During the Cold War, these vehicles were permanently warehoused at Dülmen just in case the Russians invaded West Germany. UK based TA and Regular Army units would be deployed out to West Germany from the UK, they would then pick up their allocated unit transport as they went up towards the FEBA (Forward Edge of the Battle Area). But in this particular scenario, the Iraqi's were standing in for the Russians and they popped their heads above the parapet instead. The Drivers of 38 Sqn RCT picked up a fleet of Bedford TM's and Drops (Demountable Rack Offload and Pickup System) trucks. Not all of the vehicles were modern though because Lee was assigned a Mark 2 Short-Wheel based AP (Air-Portable) Land Rover. Although some of the vehicles were past their 'sell-by' date, they had all been regularly maintained and were perfectly serviceable.

The vehicles were driven up to the North German Port of Bremerhaven and loaded onto a massive civilian cargo ship that had been chartered by the MOD to get them out to the Middle East. While the trucks were sailing down to the Port in Al Jubayl, the Sqn drafted in DROPS Instructors to run 2-day courses on the new style vehicle. The Drivers and Section Commanders had to be brought up to speed on the truck before deploying out to Saudi Arabia.

Captain Batley was the Sqn QM; an ex-Para with a stack of medals on his chest already, he called everyone by their first name even in front of more senior Officers, but out of respect, everyone called him, "Sir!" The QM called Lee into his office one day and said, "Our department is going on Advance Party out to Saudi and we'll be deploying in December. The rest of the Sqn won't be joining us until January 1991. We have no desert kit, no rations, and no allocated accommodation for when we arrive. We have to prepare everything in readiness for the rest of the Sqn's arrival in our Area of Operations." The QM took eight members of his Department on the Advance Party with him, Cpl 'Cal' Sims, LCpl Ian Cameron, Dvr Mick Coleman and Lee were just part of the team that would try and scrounge the stores needed to, set-up and run the ammunition, ration, and clothing accounts. They also had to find an accommodation block large enough to billet the whole Sqn. The small advance party left Mülheim and headed for a nearby RAF Station in BAOR. They travelled in Lee's assigned Mark 2 Short-Wheel based AP Land Rover which was towing a mini water bowser, and a Bedford MK 4 Tonner that was towing a much larger water bowser. Lee had recently been sent on a 'Water Duties' Course at Sennelager and he would be responsible for testing the water every time the bowsers were filled up.

It took 36 hours for the team to fly out to Saudi Arabia in an RAF C130 Hercules Transport Aircraft, bearing in mind they did have a minor stop-over at RAF Akrotiri in Cyprus. There was nothing to do on the journey except read a book or get their heads down for a few hours, as with most soldiers, they got out their sleeping bags and did the latter. The QM's staff were all wearing temperate combat clothing when they landed in Saudi and when the rear ramp was opened to offload the vehicles, Lee told the others, "Fucking hell it's hot", just in case they hadn't noticed the 140-degree temperature. The two-vehicle convoy then headed off to Al Jubayl to fill up with fuel, water, ammunition and rations. They then had to do a recce to find some suitable accommodation. Captain Batley found a vacant motel complex not far from the port which could at least be used as a staging post to get the Sqn's boots on the ground. The Advance Party moved in and Lee noted, "It was infested with cockroaches, but hey, it had a kitchen and at least the showers worked."

After testing the motels' tap water, Lee designated the local water supply as 'undrinkable' and the complete system had to be purged by the Royal Engineers. In the meantime, Lee 'borrowed' an ancient 22,500-litre water tanker and filled it up at the port. After pumping the fresh water into the ground tank at the motel, everyone got to enjoy a shower in the morning. The QM had his shower slightly later than everyone else and when he eventually did get lathered up Lee heard him shouting plaintively, "There's no fucking water! Why the fuck isn't there any water?" The reason was, the ground tank had a crack in it and the water was simply draining away. Lee did another run down to the port to refill the tanker and the Royal Engineer's set up a water-pump system so that the building could be directly supplied from the tanker itself.

Lee had tried to purloin some Desert Combat clothing for the Sqn from units that were already out on the ground, but none of them were forthcoming because everything was in short supply. He'd taken the Sqn's AF H 1157's (Clothing and Equipment Records) for every soldier in the unit that was deploying out to the Gulf, and after noting the sizes needed, he submitted clothing demands through the military supply system. The demands were eventually fulfilled and the kit arrived in cardboard boxes. Lee loaded the Desert Combat Clothing, Boots, Scarves, Sunglasses, T-Shirts, and 'Hat's - Floppy', into the QM's 4 tonner and drove around the various locations delivering the necessary kit.

One morning, before the Ground War had started, the QM's Staff were scoffing their breakfast whilst reading the private mail that had just been delivered and distributed. As Lee headed towards the QM tent he was collared by Captain Batley. The QM said, "Lee! I need you to drive me down to Al Jubayl this afternoon in Betsy." *Note: The QM had christened his Mark 2 Short-Wheel based AP (Air-Portable) Land Rover, 'Betsy.'* They would be in convoy with another RCT soldier who would be driving one of the Sqn's JCB MHE vehicles (these had superseded the Army's old Eager-Beaver Fork-Lift trucks). Lee would drive 'Betsy' and the QM would do the navigating using a 'Trimble' sat-nav. Because the JCB couldn't travel any faster than 25 mph, the round trip would take at least 3 days to complete. They set off just after lunch and before it became too dark, Captain Batley told Lee, "Right, we'll stop here and camp for the night." They pitched a tent, cooked themselves a meal and got their heads down so they would be up before dawn ready to head into the Port at Al Jubayl.

On arrival at the Port, Captain Batley had an informal chat with the news reporters Kate Adie and Martin Bell, who he knew very well. Lee thought that Kate Adie was a great laugh and he enjoyed the brief encounter with these two news moguls. After dropping off the JCB, the three RCT soldiers then stayed overnight in the relative luxury of the BBC hotel. In the morning the QM took Lee over to one of the available satellite phones so that he could have a brief chat with his wife back in Germany. Lee hadn't spoken to his German wife in over 6 weeks and after hanging up the handpiece, the QM asked Lee if everything was ok at home. Lee assured his boss that everything was fine, and they then headed back up to 38 Sqns' desert Location. Bizarrely, before they began the return journey, the QM made Lee empty his six 9mm SMG (Sub Machine Gun) magazines and ordered him to hand over the 180 rounds of ammunition. Lee was concerned about what would happen if they were ambushed out in the desert, but Captain Batley reassured him, "Don't worry, we'll be sorted. I need your ammo, so hand it over."

The QM followed the Trimble directions and about halfway back he told Lee to pull up in the middle of the desert. Captain Batley turned to Lee and told him, "I've got you out of the way, so we can have a quiet chat. The Families Officer back in Mülheim has informed the OC that your wife is throwing some wild parties back in Mülheim. To add to the problem, one of the Rear Party Clerks has been bragging about how he is shagging several of the wives whilst our Sqn Main is deployed out here. He has also written letters about this to some of the lads in the Sqn out here in Saudi Arabia. Some of the boasting letters have been handed into the SSM."

The QM handed over a sample of the letter's so that Lee could read them. Lee could feel the anger welling up inside him and even though he was fit to burst, he remained calm and said, "Ok sir, fair do's." The QM continued, "It's even worse Lee, that clerk has been posted out here as a BCR (Battle Casualty Replacement) and is at this very moment, in our Sqn location in the desert. Lee was quite succinct, "I'm going to kill the c**t!" (Or as a British Army Officer would say, "I'm going to kill the lady's front bottom!") The QM replied that this was why he'd taken Lee's ammunition off him, "You're not going to do anything stupid Lee, you'll leave it all up to me, do you understand?" Although still angry, Lee replied, "Ok Boss, I'll not do anything stupid, I'll leave everything up to you." They then continued with their journey back to the Sqn location.

When they got back to the Sqn location, Lee went for his evening meal in the tented cookhouse. He noticed that before going in to get their meals, the RCT lads were now taking their webbing off and placing it on a palleted area outside the tent. *Note: The reasons for this were two-fold. Firstly, a soldier's Fighting Order webbing is cumbersome in a crowded area and there simply wasn't space inside the tent for the diners and their webbing. Secondly, in the event of a chemical attack each soldier had to get to their respirators within seconds.* They took their personal weapons in with them though and kept them at arm's length.

Lee's clerical 'Nemesis' was sitting at one of the trestle tables and was stuffing a meal into his mouth. Lee filled up his metal tray with food and sat on the opposite side of the table where the nefarious clerk was eating. The conversation was brief to say the least.

Lee: "Hiya"

Clerk: "Hi"

Lee: "How are you?"

Clerk: "Yeah, pretty good."

They continued their meal in silence and Lee was the first of them to leave the tent. As he passed the palleted webbing outside, Lee stooped down and took a loaded SMG magazine out of a Drivers ammunition pouch. he then furtively put a small coin in the top of the magazine.

Note: The Sterling 9mm SMG works on a blowback system. After the weapon is cocked and the trigger pulled, the working parts spring forward and they automatically pick up a round from the magazine which is spontaneously forced it into the barrel and fired. At the same time as the ammunition is fired, the working parts are blown back and return to the cocked position. By keeping the trigger pulled the weapon will continue to fire repeatedly and will only stop when pressure is released on the trigger, or the magazine eventually runs out of ammunition. If a small coin is placed in the magazine and on top of the ammunition, then the working parts will spring forward without picking up a round and the weapon won't fire.

As Lee's Antagonist came out of the cookhouse tent, Lee shouted at him, "I want a fucking word with you!" Lee then showed him that the magazine was loaded but he kept his thumb over the small coin holding the rounds down.

Without further ado, Lee loaded the magazine onto his SMG and heard the reassuring click as it was locked into position, after cocking the SMG he threateningly shouted, "So, you've been fucking my wife, have you? Get on your fucking knees." Along with the QM and several other soldiers, the SSM stepped forward to try and stop Lee from firing what they thought was a fully loaded and cocked firearm. The SSM shouted, "Lee! For fucks sake, put the weapon down, he ain't worth it!" Lee told them all to back off before shoving the submachine-gun in the clerks' face and said, "Right, now tell me to my face that you've been shagging my wife." Whilst kneeling at Lee's feet the clerk started pleading for his life, "I haven't Lee. I swear to you mate, for Christ sake you've got to believe me mate, I haven't been shagging your wife, honestly."

Lee told the suspected lothario, "You're dead" and he then squeezed the trigger. The working parts slammed forward, and the weapon jumped but didn't fire, just as Lee knew it wouldn't. The questionable Romeo's bladder suddenly let forth with a stream of urine. The watching audience sprang into action, someone took the SMG off Lee whilst others bundled him to the floor and held him down. Lee was dragged off to the Ops wagon where he can clearly remember the QM shouting at him, "For fuck's sake Lee, I told you to leave things to me." Meanwhile, the SSM was outside the box-bodied truck and through the open door, Lee could clearly see him snarling and shouting at the clerk and pointing an accusing finger in his face. The SSM suddenly exploded with anger and chinned the Clerk who fell crying onto the desert floor; the clerk really wasn't having a good day. The OC told Lee to crack on with his duties before saying to the QM and SSM, "I'd like a word in private please." Lee obviously wasn't privy to that committee meeting, but it transpired that the Corporal clerk was immediately sent back to Mülheim where he packed his kit and was posted off to another unit. Lee was re-issued with his ammunition only after the clerk had boarded the plane back to Germany.

When the Ground War started, Lee and the rest of the Sqn drove up to Logistic Base Echo at Hafar al Batin, they then headed North and passed the Wadi al Batin, driving into the wilderness of the Iraqi desert. The Sqn had been warned this part of the desert was where Saddam Hussein had reputedly based his elite Republican Guard Army. Whilst laagered up in the desert, Lee spotted a crowd of Iraqi soldiers approaching their location, "I nearly shit my pants and thought to myself, 'what the fuck is happening now?' The Iraqi soldiers just seemed to magically appear out of the haze with their weapons held over their heads. They'd suffered from the coalition air-bombardment and simply wanted to surrender without firing a shot."

Lee was ordered to man a GPMG on a Louch Pole, mounted on the back of a Long-Wheeled Based Land Rover where he provided cover for the soldiers searching the surrendering prisoners. In the event of the prisoners running away, Lee was given the following instructions, "If any of them make a break for it, then shoot the fuckers." Lee thought, 'Hmm, right, ok then.' He then silently prayed that none of the Iraqi prisoner would make a sudden break for freedom. After the very hungry and dirty Iraqi's prisoners had been disarmed and searched, the RCT lads prepared some rations for them. The Iraqi's told the RCT Drivers that they were grateful the British Army had come to save them. The Iraqi forces had been ordered to stand and fight to the last man by their General, or their families would be executed. Some confirmed that their families had already been murdered by the Saddam Regime.

After only 100 hours of ground-war fighting, the war in Iraq was over and Lee returned to Mülheim and moved into the single men's accommodation. He eventually patched things up with his wife before 38 Sqn RCT in Mülheim was shut down, Lee was then posted to 14 Support Battalion RLC ARRC (Allied Rapid Reaction Corps) in Rheindahlen. After being promoted to full Corporal, Lee took over his own Section and deployed out to Bosnia with 14 ARRC. Whilst on the tour Lee received a telephone call from a soldier who had broken his leg during pre-deployment training. He told Lee, "She's shagging around again mate." Lee was sent back to Rheindahlen for compassionate reason's so that he could try and save his marriage, again. On arrival in the Rheindahlen Garrison he found that his Married Quarter was empty and it had been completely stripped of all furniture. All that was left in the flat was an old Army kit bag with some of Lee's spare uniforms. After handing back the accommodation, Lee returned to Bosnia and spent his R&R (Rest and Recuperation) leave on his own in Split.

On completion of the Bosnian Tour, Lee was posted from 14 ARRC to DST (Defence School of Transport) in Leconfield, East Yorkshire where he worked in the gymnasium as an AKAI (Assistant Physical Training Instructor). The QMSI (Quartermaster Staff Instructor) was WO2 Jeff Wade APTC. Lee thought that Jeff was a great bloke and he was very disappointed when re-assigned as a Block NCO rather than working in the gymnasium. Lee eventually got re-married to a female soldier who was a Signalman in 2 Signal Regiment at York. *Authors Note: To be politically correct I suppose she should have been called a Signal-person*). Lee's wife soon became pregnant and after being discharged from the Royal Signals, they were eventually allocated a MQ in Shipton Crescent at Leconfield.

SSgt Kev Miller RCT was Lee's Troop Staffie when he was at 14 ARRC in Bosnia and Rheindahlen. Kev had subsequently been posted to the RCT MT support unit at 22 SAS Regiment in Hereford and they bumped into each other whilst Kev was on a course at Leconfield. Kev was wearing the beige beret that all SAS attached personnel wore and he said to Lee, "Why don't you apply to come and serve in Hereford, it's a great posting. I'm due to leave the Army soon and I could train you up to do my job after I'm discharged." Lee was waiting for the Sergeant's Board to be posted and was told he wouldn't be allocated another post at Leconfield, so he applied for the MT Support job at Hereford. The job involved being responsible for a substantial number of fleet vehicles, the acquisition and renting of hired cars, and he'd also have direct links to DVLA (Driver and Vehicle Licencing Agency).

When the promotion board was published, and Lee gained his Sergeant stripes, he was posted to 9 Supply Regiment RLC in Chippenham for a six-month posting. He was told to set up an MT unit for the Gurkha's, after which, he would be granted a preference of posting. Lee quickly set the unit up and in the mean time, 84 Medical Supply Regiment also moved into the same barracks. The Medical unit CO was Major Nigel Hartley RAMC, a Cornishman who was an ex-Regimental Sergeant Major of the Coldstream Guards. 84 Med Supply's RQMS was an enthusiastic Liverpudlian Warrant Officer called Tony Penman, Lee bumped into him one day whilst walking around the camp. Lee asked Tony if there were any jobs going in his unit because at that time, he was bored shitless. Tony dragged Lee over to his Headquarters and introduced him to Major Hartley, "Boss, this bloke is an MT Sergeant and he is looking for a job, I think he could be the new MT Sergeant we've been asking for." Major Hartley said to Lee in his rich West Country accent, "Oi think yew'd bedder sit yersell down Sarge so we can 'ave a chat." Major Hartley picked up his phone and did some ringing around which resulted in Lee leaving 9 Supply Regiment RLC on the Friday, and on the following Monday, he started work in the same barracks as the MT Sgt of

84 Medical Supply Regiment RLC. It was a fateful move that Lee may have good reasons to regret.

84 F Med after deploying in the 2nd Gulf War. SSgt Lee Hunt on the left and WO2 Tony Penman RAMC is on the far right.

In January of 2002, 84 Medical Supply Squadron RAMC deployed out to Saudi Arabia to help give Saddam Hussein yet another slapping. Lee was tasked to deploy with them, but before Lee got onto the RAF C130 that would fly him out to Saudi Arabia, he had a lot of work to do. He only had four RLC Drivers in his MT Section (*In 1993 the Royal Corps of Transport had been replaced by the Royal Logistic Corps*) and working with those few lads, Lee had to load a mass of refrigeration units and containers onto DROPS (Demountable Rack Offload and Pickup System) vehicles. Lee had to hire in a civilian Crane Operator to get the loading done - at the exorbitant price of £300 a day. After the containers were loaded, Lee and his drivers drove the kit down to 17 Port and Maritime Regiment RLC at Marchwood near Southampton. They were then transferred onto an LSL (Landing Ship Logistic) and the equipment sailed out to Al Jubayl.

When 84 Medical Supply Squadron finally arrived 'In Theatre,' and had collected their vehicles, containers and refrigeration units, the OC discovered that a lot of other basic equipment was needed for his unit to live on a day to day basis. The OC informed his RQMS, WO2 Tony Penman RAMC, and his MT Sgt, Lee Hunt RLC, of exactly what he needed, "Because of where we're located and the lack of facilities here, we are going to need some shower and toilet block units. Go and see what you can scrounge, Number 1 and Number 2." The OC had taken to calling Tony Penman Number 1, and Lee his Number 2. They both took a convoy of three trucks up to 27 Logistic Regiment RLC which was located at Shaibah Logistic Base. On entering the camp, they spotted a row of pristine toilet and shower blocks that were awaiting collection from some other unit. Lee told the disinterested guard on the gate, "We're here to collect those toilet and shower blocks over there." The guard paid no attention to the 84 Med Supply soldiers as they loaded the units on the back of their trucks, and then scooted back out of the camp.

The OC noticed the new ablution blocks after they had been set up and said to his RQMS:

OC: "Where the fuck did they come from Number 1?"

Tony Penman: "Erm... well there's a bit of a story behind these units' sir. I .. er.. well.. it's a bit difficult to explain really sir ... Number 2, can you tell the OC, exactly how these toilet and shower units came into our possession?"

Lee Hunt: "Well Number 1. It's like this ... I can neither confirm nor deny exactly how these units came into our possession".

OC: "I don't want to know".

Lee Hunt: "That's probably best, sir".

Two days later Lee found a US Army Hummer vehicle parked in the middle of nowhere. Nobody else was near the vehicle and after searching around it, Lee discovered it was neither booby-trapped or mined. He immediately thought, 'Fuck it, we'll have this.' The Hummer started first time and after getting it back to their location, the lads hand-painted it in a more British Army colour before adding an inverted V on the sides and top. This would identify the truck as Friendly Forces whilst being driven out in the Ulu. Lee gave the same treatment to three GMC Chevy Pick-ups he had also 'acquired' from Al Jubayl docks. The Chevy's had double axles on the rear of each truck and they gave a good account of themselves both on and off-road. When the OC had to attend an 'O Group' at his Brigade Headquarters, Lee offered to take him in one of the 84 Medical Supply vehicles. Lee climbed into the Hummer and the OC said, "What the fuck is this?" Lee casually replied, "Don't you recognise it sir, it's 84 Medical Supply Squadrons' Armoured Hummer Truck. Other than that sir, I can't give you any further information". The OC didn't want, or need, to know anything else.

On another occasion Lee had several jobs to do on a circuit of the medical units that 84 Medical Supply supported. With Private 'Scouse' Norman as his Driver, Lee set off in a unit Land Rover Defender and headed off to collect a 40-kW generator alternator from another Medical unit. Lee intended to take it to a local civilian engineer to have its internal copper wiring rewound. *Note: This was cheaper, and more expedient, than trying to get a replacement alternator through the Army supply chain. The total cost of doing the job locally was only $10 US Dollars.*

Another one of 84 Medicals' outposts was sited at Umm Qasr on the outskirts of the Al-Faw Peninsula, they medics would need extra blood supplies for the expected Royal Marine casualties on an impending Military Operation. Lee and 'Scouse' dropped off the blood and had lunch with Captain Diane Carolana RAMC

(Later Lieutenant Colonel) and some of the other RLC drivers within her unit.

Ssgt Lee Hunt's wrecked Land Rover after being hit by an attempted suicide bomber.

On the return journey they were driving along the MSR (Main Supply Route) codenamed 'Broadsword' when Lee spotted a white Civilian SLK Mercedes driving towards them on their side of the road; the driver seemed to be deliberately heading straight for them. Lee said, "Scouse, pull off the road a bit, will you?" As they drove on the very edge of the tarmac road, the SLK turned towards them and again steered straight at them. Whichever direction 'Scouse' turned, the SLK simply veered towards their Land Rover Defender. Lee states, "It seemed like he was playing a game of chicken." Today, the following few moments of this horrific incident remain hazy for Lee, but in his memory, he can still remember a massive bang as the two vehicles collided in a head-on crash, which happened at a combined speed that approached 120 mph. Lee can recall not being able to move as he drifted in and out of consciousness, but during one semi-conscious spell he moved his right arm and shouted at 'Scouse' to determine whether he was dead or alive. He then sank back into oblivion.

A passing RLC Corporal called Simon opened Lee's passenger side door and spotted the rank slide on the front of Lee's combat jacket, he shouted, "Sarge! Are you alright, can you hear me Sarge?" Blood was coming out of Lee's groin area and it was spilling onto his seat. Simon, somewhat un-reassuringly told Lee, "The back of your head is all fucked up Sarge, it's all smashed to fuck." Lee told Simon to get a First Aid Pack from the rear of the Land Rover, the Corporal then placed a First Field Dressing on the back of Lee's head and pressure was applied to the wound by Lee leaning back on the passenger head-rest. Lee told the author at the time of his interview, "Fuck me that was painful." 'Scouse' and the two other soldiers travelling in the rear of Lee's Land Rover were all unconscious and Lee later learned that his Liverpudlian driver had broken several of his ribs as well as both of his arms and legs. The steering wheel of the Land Rover Defender had been bent forwards by the inertia of the collision, and 'Scouse's' vice-like grip on the wheel.

During the Land Rover and SLK's collision, the Army vehicle had somersaulted through the air and rolled down the side of the road before, miraculously, landing on its wheels. In the ensuing acrobatics, Lee had suffered a broken leg, a fractured ankle, skull, and sternum. The rifle racks behind the seats in the Land Rover didn't have any rubber covers on them and the bare metal had pierced Lee's head. Simon had sent an urgent radio message from his own vehicle asking for medical assistance and it wasn't long before an RAMC One Ton Land Rover Ambulance tipped up from 202 Field Hospital RAMC. Lee can remember being strapped onto a spinal board before the Medics finally loaded him into their ambulance.

In 202 Field Hospitals' tented reception area, Lee's condition and injuries were expertly diagnosed and assessed before he was given a blood transfusion. A back- slab cast was put on his leg and ankle and the wounds on his skull were cleaned and repaired using super-glue. The Medics also put him on a morphine drip which made Lee feel like, "I couldn't have given a flying fuck about anyone or anything." Lee was later interviewed by the Royal Military Police about the crash and he filled in an FMT 3 Military Road Accident Report Form. He was told by the RMP's that they had discovered the boot of the SLK was packed with explosives and it should have exploded when the car had collided with his Land Rover. The Iraqi soldier driving the SLK was instantly killed in the ensuing collision.

Within a week Lee was evacuated from Iraq on an RAF hospital aircraft and after a brief stop-over in Cyprus, was taken to the Military Wing of the Good Hope Training Hospital in Birmingham. A 12-year-old Iraqi boy by the name of Ali Abbas was on the same flight as Lee, and they were transferred to the Good Hope hospital with other casualties. Ali had been severely burned when a missile had hit his family home, which resulted in his entire family being killed. The tabloid media were desperate to get an interview with Ali because he'd had his arms and legs amputated and there was a suspicion that the Coalition Forces were to blame for the air-strike on his house. For three weeks, Lee had to sit in an upright position in his hospital bed with his leg in traction, he had to remain like that whilst waiting for an operation to put some strengthening rods and pins into his leg. One of the male contracted cleaners on the ward started chatting to Lee whilst he mopped the floor, asking questions like, "How did you get your injuries?" "What are they going to do about your injuries?" "Will the British Army just get rid of you now"?

Lee became suspicious of the overly inquisitive cleaner when he started asking if any of the soldiers on the military ward knew on which ward Ali Abbas was being treated. It turned out that the 'cleaner' was in fact a scumbag tabloid journalist looking to get a scoop on the young Iraqi lad. It all got a bit ugly when a normally quiet Scottish Infantryman patient became quite distressed. He got out of his bed and grabbed the Reporter by the throat and threatened to kill him if he persisted with his questions. Security was summoned by a staff member and the Reporter was thrown out of the hospital.

After six weeks in hospital, Lee got in contact with Major Hartley who was still out in Saudi Arabia with the rest of 84 Medical Supply Regiment, "Boss! I've got pins in my leg and I'm medically downgraded to P7 HO NNI (This grading meant Lee could only serve at Home Only, but Not Northern Ireland, and he was excused all duties except sitting down and watching Porn on his laptop). I'm on crutches now and feel the need to get back to the unit. I'm bored to fuck." The OC told Lee that there wasn't anyone at Chippenham because everyone was still deployed out in Saudi Arabia, adding, "Go home on sick leave Number 2, and stay there until I get back to the UK. I'll be in touch." Lee stayed on sick leave for three months and when 84 Med returned from the Middle East he immediately went back into the unit; his leg was still in a full leg plaster cast and he was using crutches at that stage though. There was some good news waiting for him when he spoke to Major Hartley. Lee had been promoted to Staff Sergeant and was posted back up to the Quartermaster Department of DST (Defence School of Transport) at Leconfield.

When he reported to the QM of DST, (Lt Col P J Shields MBE, QGM, F Inst LM) at Leconfield, Colonel Shields told Lee that he'd would be taking charge of all the Block NCO's and would be responsible for running the units' Accommodation System. Lee reported to Staff Sergeant John Wilson who he'd be taking over from, John Wilson was a colossus of a Scottish soldier who was being promoted to WO 2 on posting to the Scottish Transport Regiment in Glasgow. His gear was already packed up and car loaded ready to head off to his next posting. The Accommodation side of things at Leconfield was a massive account which included responsibility for nearly 2,000 bed-spaces spread over twelve massive accommodation blocks, these figures included the Officers' and Sergeant's Messes. Because of the sheer size of the camp and the number of stores involved, John and Lee's Handover/Takeover was going to take quite some time to complete.

Lee: "Hiya John, great to see you again."

John: "Aye, and you my friend."

Lee: "What do we have to do for the Handover/Takeover mate?"

John: "See that big folder on my desk."

Lee: "Yes."

John: "Well, everything you need to know is in that file mate."

Lee opened the accommodation account dossier and discovered there wasn't a scrap of information inside.

Lee: "There's fuck all in here John."

John: "Yeah I know."

Lee: "You're a twat John."

John: "Yeah I know, good luck with this fucking boring job Lee, see you around pal."

And with those few choice words the Handover/Takeover was completed. John then jumped into his car and headed off to Glasgow, caring not a jot.

Lee trod water as an Accommodation Stores Staff Sergeant for the last two years of his Army career. After being offered a Medical Discharge from the Army he chose to be a Locksmith and did a Pre-Release course on the subject. Whilst he was working in London, Lee's wife left him and stripped the house of everything before moving in with her parents in Manchester.

Lee started his own business as a Locksmith and named the firm, 'Defender Locksmiths Ltd,' after the name of the Army vehicle he was travelling in when he was injured in Iraq. His business is going from strength to strength. Lee got married to his fourth wife Sarah on Friday the 13th of August 2010 (Lee obviously isn't afraid of tempting fate) and they are happily living in Scunthorpe.

24836475 Sergeant Richie (Shirley) Temple
RCT and RLC 1988 – 2002

Richie Temple is probably the politest Trog/Trogg to have ever served in the Royal Corps of Transport", that is according to Ted Fost who is probably one of the roughest and toughest Trog's/Trogg's to have ever served in the RCT (Royal Corps of Transport).

Richie and his older sister grew up in Gorleston, Great Yarmouth. Their dad had been a Lance Sergeant in the Grenadier Guards and had served in Cyprus, and in Northern Ireland during the early days of the troubles. In those days the 2nd Battalion Grenadier Guards slept on the streets of Belfast and patrolled in thin skinned vehicles whilst wearing only army HD (Heavy Duty) woollen jumpers for personal protection. It was the stories about his dads' Army career that influenced Ritchie into joining the British Army and his dad gave him some great advice, "When you sign up son, get a trade and career that you can use after leaving the Army - don't join the Infantry!"

On entering his local Army Recruiting Office, Richie kept an open mind about which Corps or Regiment he wanted to join. Having said that, he was tempted to go for a vocation in the RE's (Royal Engineers) so that he could at least learn how to be a 'Brickie.' Unfortunately, at that time there weren't any RE vacancies and Richie was steered towards driving Army trucks for a living. He was literally coerced by the recruiting staff into joining the RCT. Richie was 17 years and 4 months old when he got onto the train bound for Buller Barracks in Aldershot. The RCT NCO that met the recruits at Aldershot station was a stern and grim looking Corporal who immediately set out his stall. He made one of the wide-eyed and unshaven recruits have a shave on the station platform and then told the rest of them, unbelievably, "There's going to be a 'Paki' in your squad, you'd all better make sure he doesn't get through Basic Training." *Authors note: Instances of discrimination within our Corps were few and far between. The men I served with in the RCT didn't tolerate such bigotry. However, Richie explained that the young Indian recruit did fail the Course, but not because of added pressure from his fellow recruits.*

All Army recruits suffer from varying levels of home-sickness and Richie was no different, let's face it, he was the youngest recruit on the Course and had come from a genuinely warm and loving family home-life. He was now in an environment where he was 'Beasted' by snarling NCO's, from early morning until late at night, and when he went to the cookhouse he had to throw his food down his neck to make sure he acquired enough sustenance to get him through the next 'Beasting.' It wasn't all bad news though, everything he did was different from his old life style at home and although their tasks were genuinely very hard, he made friends easily and loved the team-work amongst his fellow recruits. He enjoyed the weapon training and looked forward to his first visit to the rifle ranges. When Richie fired a 7.62mm SLR (Self Loading Rifle) in the Standing Position for the first time, he was nearly blown off his feet.

A lot of very proud relatives attended Richie's Passing Out Parade when the squad returned to Aldershot, but most proud was Mr Victor Joseph Temple, ex Lance Sergeant of the Grenadier Guards. Victor turned up at Buller Barracks, Aldershot, wearing an immaculate blazer that had a Grenadier Guards Badge embroidered onto its breast pocket, he looked incredibly smart. Richie's dad admitted to him that he had always regretted leaving the British Army in 1970 after completing only 7 years' service. Richie was now a fully trained soldier and Army Driver just setting out on his military career, surely, he wouldn't make the same mistake as his dad?

After their Passing Out Parade, the recruits were sent to Driffield, East Yorkshire to complete their Driver Training. Although in accommodation at Driffield, Richie clearly remembers being bussed just a few miles down the road to Leconfield every day to do Driver Training. "I never had any problem passing my dual test in an MK 4 Tonner, but then going onto driving a small car with a much lighter clutch took some getting used to. I bounced that Army car around the Leconfield airfield like I was driving a kangaroo, I did pass all of my driving tests first time though."

After passing the Driver Training phase, Richie and his 'new boy' comrades were put into Holding Troop to await notification of their new posting. Richie hadn't a clue which unit did what and so wasn't particularly bothered where the Corps sent him. After being warned off for a posting to 10 Regiment RCT with 11 other Drivers, a fellow recruit warned him that 10 Regt was a famous RCT boxing unit and was one of the toughest units in the Corps. Richie was posted into A Tp, 9 Sqn RCT (A Troop 9 Squadron RCT) along with another young lad who'd accompanied him from Buller Barracks, "10 Regt turned out to be my best posting ever in the RCT. My time, and the soldiers I met in 10 Regt, made me the man I am today."

Within days of arriving in 9 Sqn, Staff Sergeant Phil Stonier asked Richie if he wanted to do some Adventure Training for a week, he could go sailing round the Hook of Holland if he volunteered. The trip was up for grabs because no-one in the Sqn seemed to be very interested in the jaunt, Richie grabbed the opportunity with both hands. After having a fantastic week-long excursion in

Holland, he returned to Bielefeld and seized yet another fantastic opportunity, he agreed to go on 'Exercise Snow Queen.' Again, no-one in the Sqn seemed interested in taking part, maybe it was the word Exercise that was putting them off. 'Exercise Snow Queen' wasn't an Exercise in the true military definition, though. There weren't any miserable stags on guard duty, you didn't sleep in stinking and manky sleeping bag, no camouflaging of 10-ton trucks, you wouldn't be constantly shouted and screamed at by Senior NCO's, and your sleep routines would last longer than just 2 hours a night.

'Exercise Snow Queen' was held in the beautiful snowy mountains of Bavaria in the RCT's Ski Chalet. The fortnight exercise included, being taught how to ski, drinking lots of Bavarian lager, eating lots of Currywurst and Pommes frites, and sleeping in a warm, comfortable bed. Whilst Richie was having the time of his life in Sonthofen and Oberstdorf, the British Army were paying him good money to suffer the experience. The experience was such a great adventure for Richie that he went on to do another three 'Exercise Snow Queens,' all at the tax payers' expense.

The Corporals in A Tp, 9 Sqn were all like Cpl 'Gringo' Green. They were a hard-bitten lot and Richie's Section Commander, Cpl Ted Fost, was probably the hardest of them all. There was a genuine 'work hard, play hard' ethic within the Sqn's NCO's and Richie describes them all as being, "very firm but fair." Ted Fost scared the crap out of Richie because he had the appearance and demeanour of a cold-hearted East London gangster. For a laugh, Ted sent Richie up to the unit's Battery Shop with two very heavy 10-ton truck batteries and an AF B 252 form (The AF B 252 was a form that was filled in before placing a soldier on a military charge, you can see where this is going). Richie spoke to the LCpl running the battery shop, "Good morning, Corporal Fost says he wants these two batteries charging," he then handed over the AF B 252. The old RCT joke was running a bit thin on the Battery shop JNCO, who'd already had another hundred or so new Driver's report to him with the same inane request. On seeing the AF B 252 Charge Report he shouted, "Oh just fuck off will you!"

As time went on, the childish practical jokes started wearing thin on the new lads as well, so when Richie's close friend Driver Stu Wade (Stu had arrived in 10 Regt at the same time as Richie) was tasked to go down to the stores and get a 'Slave Lead', he laughed it off and said, "Yeah, yeah, a fucking 'Slave Lead', very funny, I know they don't exist, what do you take me for, a fucking idiot." In the RCT world, a 'Slave Lead' was the nickname for a 9-foot, NATO, Heavy Duty, Vehicle Jumper Cable, used to jump start a truck with flat batteries. Stew kept laughing the order off and nearly ended up getting a slap for not doing as his Section Commander had instructed. Tragically, in the late 1990's, Stu died after being hit by a taxi and 27 Regt RLC named the NAAFI Bar 'The Wade Inn' in his memory.

Richie did a short stint in the Guardroom on the Regimental Police (RP) Staff where the chicanery and tomfoolery didn't stop. During a night shift, the Duty RP's slept in the back restroom on an Army metal bed complete with waterproof mattress. During his rest periods Richie had to remain fully clothed and always kept his boots on so that he could react immediately to any orders given by the Guard Commander, but he could cat-nap and doze off when not needed. The lights in the rest room were switched off at night for the benefit of the resting guards not on stag, but there was constant background noise from soldiers moving about, going on and off stag, making themselves a brew, or heading to the toilets. The other Regimental Policemen sometimes had peculiar ways to wake up the relieving RP's for their shift on duty.

Driver Richie Temple RCT 9 Sqn 10 Regt RCT.
Richie was laid on his back one night and was on the very edge of falling asleep when his nostrils were filled with the smell of

human faeces. The smell was so repugnant that he immediately woke up and saw a shadow standing next to his bed, it was Corporal John Bedford. John had stuck his fingers up between the buttocks of his arse before creeping up on Richie and placing his fingers under his nose. For the average civilian this behaviour will seem disgusting and more than a little strange, but to the soldier who owns the smelly fingers, it's simply the funniest thing you can do to wake up, and annoy, another soldier.

After 4 months Richie returned to the warm embrace of A Tp and passed his HGV 2 licence in a Bedford TM before proceeding onto his TTF (Truck, Transporter, Fuel) and UBRE (Unit Bulk Refuelling Equipment) Course. Once qualified, Richie deployed on 'Exercise Pack Saddle' and was attached to several AAC (Army Air Corps) units to meet their Aviation Fuel needs. The TTF's had to remain on hardstanding throughout the Exercise because of their weight, otherwise the Tankers would have sunk into the soft earth and they didn't have any extra drive to their other wheels to get them out again. TTF and UBRE Drivers also couldn't camouflage their trucks because of the extreme fire risk, "It was a piece of piss on Exercise," said Richie, "It was just like being a civilian fuel driver on a contract with the MOD."

On yet another big Exercise, Richie and the other TTF and UBRE Drivers were told to report back to camp and prepare their vehicles for deployment out to the Gulf. Richie and the rest of 10 Regt spent the next 10 days prepping their wagons for war, there was no time available for pre-deployment leave. When everything was made ready, the trucks were driven in convoy up to the North German Port of Bremerhaven, where they were loaded onto a massive ship for transportation out to the Middle East. Embarrassingly, at least half of the tankers in Richie's Section broke down on route and had to be patched up by the accompanying REME Vehicle Mechanics. On arrival at the docks, Richie noticed hundreds of military vehicles lined up and waiting their turn to be loaded onto the ships. Within days of being bussed back to Bielefeld the whole unit was flown out to Cyprus on civilian airliners, they then flew onto Riyadh in Saudi Arabia, courtesy of RAF C130 Hercules cargo planes.

Units were accommodated in a 2,000-bed camp which was initially, and unimaginatively, called 'Tented City' by the British 'hierarchy.' The name was subsequently changed to 'Baldrick Lines' because that's what the British 'Lowerarchy' sarcastically called the place. (Baldrick Lines referred to the scruffy, disgusting, and unpalatable Private Baldrick in 'Blackadder goes Forth'). In the two to three weeks wait for their wagons to arrive at Al Jubayl port, the unit went through a rigorous training schedule that consisted of practicing their individual Nuclear, Biological and Chemical (NBC) Drills, First Aid Training, volleyball competitions and the mandatory sunbathing. There wasn't any desert kit available to the soldiers who had initially deployed out to Saudi Arabia. They even had to buy their own Desert Boots.

Most British Army soldiers were still sleeping in the old fashioned 1958 pattern, feather filled, sleeping bags that had lost most of their stuffing many years previously. What the British Army did have in plentiful supply, and was made readily available, were Nerve Agent Pre-treatment Set (NAPS) tablets. Taken before being subjected to a chemical attack, the pills were supposed to build up a soldier's resistance to Nerve Agent poisoning and as far as Richie knew, no-one in 10 Regt took even one tablet. They'd heard that the pills were likely to cause impotence in men, and every Trog/Trogg would rather choke on his own vomit than suffer from a floppy penis.

Driver Richie Temple with his friend Pepsi during the Gulf war.

By Christmas day the wagons had arrived in port and were spray-painted in desert colours. Before the lads celebrated their festive dinner, they opened the Christmas presents that had been sent from home. Richie opened a present from his dad and took out a blow-up rubber doll, complete with its sexy nylon underwear. He christened the doll Pepsi after the pop duo, Pepsi and Sherlie. Richie was often called Shirley because of his surname Temple, and so, hence forth, they were known as 'Pepsi and Shirley.' Richie went for breakfast on Christmas morning, carrying Pepsi under his arm. As he entered the cookhouse tent, everyone at breakfast gave him and Shirley a standing ovation as he queued up for his scoff, even the CO (Lt Col P Chaganis) and the RSM roared with laughter.

Later that day Richie and his co-driver, Jim Eppy, were tasked with delivering some fuel to the American Forces. As Jim slowly drove the TTF past some parading US Marines, Richie stood out the top of the cab through the cupola hatch and he held Pepsi in his arms. He waggled her arm during the drive past and made her wave to the US Marines whilst singing "We wish you a merry Christmas." The Yanks nearly pissed themselves laughing. When the war kicked off, Pepsi proved to be very useful because she manned the General-Purpose Machine Gun (GPMG) on top cover when Richie and Jim travelled on the Main Supply Route (MSR).

10 Regt RCT was instrumental in the setting up of Baldrick Lines as well as the in-load, delivery, and stockpiling of tons of ammunition, rations, fuel and medical supplies needed for the up and coming conflict. President George H W Bush, his wife (and First Lady) Barbara Bush, and General 'Stormin' Norman Schwarzkopf, came to visit the coalition forces, and a handful of 10 Regt's soldiers were invited to attend their visit. Richie and his mate Gilbert, (Driver Anthony Davies), were just two of the select

few. (*Gilbert was christened with this nickname by Cpl Ted Fost because he believed Driver Davies bore an incredible resemblance to the ugly green puppet on the children's programme, 'Gilberts Fridge)'.* The 10 Regt two-some were at the back of the reception party, but they predicted which direction the VIP's were taking and did a flanking move. Richie got to speak to the American Commander-in-Chief who deigned to sign his desert sun hat for him. Many years later, Richie is still in possession of that hat. Kate Adie was also flapping around in the background and she briefly interviewed Richie on camera:

Kate Adie: "What do you think about Margaret Thatcher resigning?"

Driver Richie Temple: "I didn't know she had."

This intense and dynamic interview hit the cutting room floor and wasn't used on the Nine O'clock News.

For three weeks, 9 Sqn's TTF's drove up and down the MSR from the Riyadh Fuel Depot, delivering their loads up into the desert near the border with Iraq. The coalition army had to stockpile enough fuel for every tank and truck used when the coalition forces eventually went to move forward. The fuel was off-loaded and stored in massive rubber Bulk Fuel Installations (BFI's) that were set up in the middle of the desert and run by the RE's. During the build-up phase, the TTF drivers that weren't driving were usually sleeping in the passenger seat whilst their co-driver did a stint. The 10 Regt Drivers became so tired at times that they were issued with plastic water sprays to use on their faces to stop them from falling asleep at the wheel. Whilst dumping their fuel at a BFI one night, Richie saw that Driver Graham Robertson, (known as Jock or 'Robbo'), was doing the same at another installation when suddenly a massive flame shot out the top of an open hatch on Robbo's TTF.

Driver Richie Temple RCT, TTF Operator during the Gulf War.
Richie grabbed his green vehicle fire extinguisher and ran over to Robbo's TTF and passed the pathetic fire-fighting equipment up

to him. He thought to himself, 'Fucking hell, we're all going to die.' The small transport extinguishers were issued to every vehicle in the British Army and they had to be banged upside down on a solid surface to start them working. The RE's, based at the Field Fuel Depot, came running towards Robbo's TTF carrying a shedful of much bigger and better fire extinguishers. The extinguishers weren't needed in the end though, one RE soldier quickly resolved the problem by kicking the vehicle's top hatch shut and the flame was immediately extinguished. Robbo insisted that the fire had started because of static electricity and the fact he hadn't planted his TTF's earthing spike into the ground. To this day Richie still believes Robbo was checking his fuel cell dipsticks using a cigarette lighter. Robbo is now an oil rig manager in the North Sea. You have been warned!

The Tankers were right hand drive vehicles and so whilst Richie was knocking out the Z's on another night run, he was directly in line with any traffic that was encroaching on their side of the road. One of these encroaching vehicles was towing a trailer with an overhanging tank on it. Richie woke up to see a tank track heading straight towards his face at a combined speed of 80 mph. With lightning reactions, Driver Jim Eppy swerved to the right and away from the oncoming trailer. He probably saved Richie from suffering a face like Gilbert's.

When the air war started, the British Forces Broadcasting Service (BFBS), constantly played the Phil Collins record, 'In the air tonight' over the airwaves, they also gave warnings about when Scud Missiles were heading towards the coalition Forces. Whilst filling up at Riyadh fuel depot, Richie and Jim were again listening to Phil Collins and the record was interrupted as the broadcaster announced, "We have just been given a report that a Scud Missile has been launched in Iraq and it is heading towards Riyadh."

Richie and Jim were in the cab of their TTF at the time. They looked at each other and fell silent for a couple of seconds whilst this bit of information sunk in. "FUCK!" They then scrambled around the truck looking for their NBC suits and respirators. After getting 'suited and booted,' they spotted the Scud approaching and witnessed a US Patriot Missile intercept and destroy the incoming warhead. Richie explained, "We'd all been doing NBC training for years and complaining how boring it was, but when push came to shove, those drills just kicked in and we simply got on with the business wearing full Individual Protective Equipment (IPE)."

On 16th January 1991, 'OPERATION DESERT STORM' began and the Coalition Forces crossed the border into Iraq to start ejecting the invading Iraqi Forces out of Kuwait. The day before the ground war started for real, Richie and Jim parked their fully loaded 22,500 litre TTF near the sand embankment that denoted the Iraq/Saudi Arabia border. They were told to laager up ready to move forward after the tanks and infantry had already crossed the border. It was still night time when they eventually crossed the border and drove through an RE cleared path through the mine-fields. "People don't understand how fucking hairy it was driving into Iraq. We had to negotiate a marked track through a minefield, we had 22,500 litres of fuel behind us, and for tactical reasons we couldn't use our headlights, we simply followed a small light that was shining on the rear axle of the truck ahead of us."

To top all this off, the RAF had kindly scattered thousands of cluster bombs over the entire area." *Authors note: 10% of these bomblets remained unexploded by the time the Coalition Forces had crossed into Iraq and today these brightly coloured explosive devices can attract children more easily than a packet of smarties. They have now been banned under international law.* Once in Iraq, the lads were ordered to dig a shell-scrape defensive position next to their truck and were told to sleep in the mini-trench to ensure their own protection from Scud's. Richie and Jim dug the shell scrape but ignored the Standard Operating Procedure (SOP) and slept in the cab of their wagon instead. It turned out to be an excellent idea. The following morning, they noticed that their shell-scrape had been decimated by a convoy of Coalition Armoured Vehicles that had passed their TTF during the night.

The Iraqi Ground Forces had been absolutely hammered by the Coalition Air Forces and by the time Richie had moved up the line there was clear evidence of the Iraqi annihilation. Trench emplacements had been abandoned and helmets, webbing, and weapons of all types and calibre had simply been cast aside. The retreating Iraqi soldiers also left their dead comrades behind. Even further up the line, some filthy and disheartened Iraqi soldiers approached Richie's TTF with their hands held above their heads. They were hoping he'd take them prisoner but all that he could do was offer them some food from their compo rations and point the Iraqi's in the direction of the rear echelons. Rumour control filtered some information down to Richie and he was told the Coalition Forces were heading all the way up to Baghdad. That was proved unfounded when the convoy turned south and drove down Highway's 8 and 80, heading towards Kuwait.

Highway 80 headed north from Kuwait City and went straight to the Iraqi city of Basra. Since 1991, the motorway has been re-named 'The Road to Basra' or 'The Highway of Death.' The death and destruction reaped on the Iraqi's fleeing from Kuwait City was horrendous to say the least. General Schwarzkopf gave the following statement: *"Firstly, we bombed the highway coming north out of Kuwait because there was a great deal of military equipment on that highway, and I had given orders to all my Commanders that I wanted every possible piece of that Iraqi equipment destroyed. Secondly, this was not just a bunch of innocent people trying to make their way back across the border to Iraq. This was a bunch of rapists, murderers and thugs who had raped and pillaged downtown Kuwait City and now were trying to get out of the country before they were caught."*

Nevertheless, the sight and smells that greeted Richie as he did top cover on that journey to Kuwait turned his stomach. The sight of the cadavers that had died from the most appalling burns and injuries was like something out of a horror movie and the cloying sickly smell of burnt flesh reminded Richie of the odour from a roast pork joint. "We knew they were the enemy and that we were there to defeat them, but I kind of felt really sorry for them. No-one should die the way they did. It was terrible."

When 10 Regt arrived back in Baldrick Lines they spent the time squaring things away in readiness to fly back to BAOR. Everyone headed for the NAAFI Bar when they got off the coaches in Catterick Barracks with the sole intention of downing an ice-cold beer. It didn't take many beers to get everyone pissed out of their tiny minds because they hadn't consumed any alcohol in the last 6 months. Richie woke up in the accommodation corridor surrounded by empty beer bottles and cans. Cpl Eddie Craigie woke him up by shouting, "Right, who wants to go on an attachment to Canada for 6 months?" Being unmarried and not having any other pressing engagements, Richie volunteered, Eddie went on, "Right, you need to get your arse up and report to the Adjutant, come on, fucking move yourself!" Half-pissed, unshaven, and still wearing his Desert Combats, Richie headed off in the direction of RHQ and reported to Captain Cameron Macnish. Cameron was an Australian Officer who had transferred into the RCT from the Royal Australian Corps of Transport (RACT).

Richie bimbled straight into Captain Macnish's office, which was on the top floor of RHQ. He sat down in the visitor's chair without paying any due compliments like saluting or calling the Captain Sir. Cameron sarcastically said, "Yeah, that's alright Richie, don't bother marching into my office and saluting or anything like that will you, you just sit your bloody arse down in my office won't you." Richie sprang back out of the chair and immediately apologised. Captain Macnish said, "No worry mate." The Adjutant then closed the door and they had a brief chat about the previous night's piss-up before sorting out Richie's travel arrangements. Because of time constraints, Richie only managed to have 7 days leave at home before reporting back to 10 Regt in time to fly over to Canada. "I felt sorry for my parents really because they'd been constantly worried and stressed about me being away in Iraq. They didn't know what was happening to me day to day, but because we were actually there we just cracked on without thinking about it. I went home for about a week after we got back and then simply buggered off to Canada for 6 months."

Cpl Richie Tassle was Richie's Section Commander for the detachment out in the British Army Training Unit Suffield (BATUS) and the RCT lads all partied their way through Canada. The beer was cold, and the girls were very 'appreciative', Richie stated, "Let me put it this way, I was 'appreciated' on many occasions by many 'appreciative' Canadian women." After two weeks the Section deployed on the first of two 3-week 'Med Man Exercises' where Richie spent his time delivering fuel to the Armoured units out on the prairie. He was constantly aware of the howling Coyote's and the need to keep an eye open for poisonous rattle-snakes. Post-Exercise the lads were given 7 days Rest and Recuperation (R & R) and some of them decided to use that time to visit the United States. To save wasting their beer money on hiring a car for the trip, Richie asked an older woman (who was often very 'appreciative' of him) if they could borrow her car for just a day or two. Richie told the woman that in exchange for lending them her car they would buy her four badly needed brand-new tyres. He also told her they were only popping just over the border into the United States. Once they were in the States one of the lads said, "Why don't we visit Seattle?" They all agreed to the idea and set off on the trip that involved driving over the Rocky Mountains and the round trip ended up being 1334 miles.

They then drove north to Vancouver, which put another couple of hundred miles on the clock. They didn't buy the badly needed balding tyres and even managed to crack the cars windscreen whilst, (to their credit), putting some oil into the engine. In Vancouver the lads dropped their kit off at a cheap hotel before grabbing a taxi and telling the driver, "Take us to where the action is in this town." The Cabbie narrated as he drove them downtown, "Right guys, you see this road here, this place is just full of strip joints and prostitutes, you don't want to be here..." The lads in the back shouted in unison, "STOP, drop us here, this'll do nicely."

When they got back to BATUS, Richie dropped the car keys through the ladies' letter box and did a runner. He left the car with no fuel in the tank, a cracked windscreen and still in dire need of those promised four new tyres. He then joined the others in the local bowling alley which was the only place you could buy a beer on a Sunday. The car owner came hobbling into the bowling alley on crutches and was clearly wearing a full leg plaster cast. She had a face like thunder. Richie received a dressing down that could only have been mimicked by a Regimental Sergeant Major (RSM). Because the lads hadn't returned within the agreed 2 days (they stayed in the United States for 7 days) she was going to call the Canadian Police and report her car as stolen but gave Richie the benefit of the doubt and got her old bicycle out of the garage and used it to get around. The bike hadn't been used for years and the brakes failed as she zoomed down a hill before crashing into a brick wall and breaking her leg. The lads all pissed themselves laughing at her tale of woe and Richie was lucky not to get crowned with a hospital crutch and being reported to the OC of BATUS. *Authors note: It's lucky you're such a pretty boy Ritchie!*

When he'd finished another 'Med Man Exercise,' Richie started working for the RCT Detachment doing Airport runs and other admin details. Whilst in the Headquarters corridor, the RCT SSM shouted, "Temple, get your arse in my office, now." Thinking he was in trouble for another misdemeanour, Richie was surprised when the Warrant Officer suddenly smiled and handed him a Lance Corporal's stripe, "Just joking Temple, you're promoted to Lance Corporal." He then explained that the 'Lance-Jack' tape was the hardest to win, and the easiest to lose, and advised Richie to work hard and stay out of trouble. A couple of other soldiers were promoted on the same day and that night they all went down to the 'Sin Bin' club in Calgary to celebrate. Richie woke up the next morning in a civilian police cell and hadn't got a clue how he got there. After checking his knuckles and teeth he knew he hadn't been fighting. The SSM's warning from the previous day was still fresh in his mind.

The Custody Officer told Richie that he'd been found by a police officer the previous night sleeping in a bush and he was being held in the drunk tank for his own safety. On being released from the Police Station, Richie thought he'd got away with his indiscretion but on Monday morning he was called into the SSM's office where he was punched in the stomach. The SSM berated him, "Two fucking days Temple, you were promoted only two fucking days ago - and you've already been locked up in a police station for being drunk. If the OC had been here, you would have been busted this morning. You're on R & R to California soon and when you report back here you'd better have two huge sticks of rock in your possession, one for each of my children. Now get out of my fucking office!" Richie came back to BATUS with two of the largest sticks of candy that he could find in the US. At his leaving party, the SSM presented Richie with a framed copy of the police 'Drunk Tank' report as a leaving present.

In October 1991 Richie went back to A Tp, 9 Sqn for about 6 months. On his first week back in the Sqn, 10 Regt held a mandatory Cross-Country race through the Teutoburg Forrest. Richie honestly admits, "For the whole race I was at the back with all the fat knackers, after pissing it up in Canada for 6-months I was blowing out my arse. It was really embarrassing and so afterwards, I went for a run every day until I got back to a good level of fitness." By the time Richie had completed another 'Exercise Snow Queen,' his 3-year posting to 10 Regt was coming to an end. He put in a preference of posting request and the cheeky twat ← (*Authors suggestion*) submitted a dream sheet posting list to be sent to either, Belize, Canada, or Cyprus. It was in 1991 that the dynamics of 10 Regt changed entirely because female soldiers were now able to serve alongside male Drivers in the field. Relationships started developing within the Regt and that male dominated, hard-drinking, macho environment was gone forever. Richie rather undiplomatically said, "The girls were sometimes given a nice easy ride (pardon the pun) and so maybe it was a good time for me to be posted to 24 Sqn RCT in Belize.

The first night Richie arrived at Airport Camp, Belize he met other RCT looney tune lads who were also based in 24 Sqn RCT. He met the likes of Lance Corporal Eddie Ward and Driver Paul 'Midnight' Darwood. Eddie came to the RCT after quitting the Royal Marines Training Programme when he was within 2 weeks of winning the Green Beret. Paul picked up his nickname 'Midnight' when he was posted into Bunde. There were three black guys in his Sqn and depending on the colour of their skin they were called 'Ten to Midnight, 'Midnight' or 'Ten past Midnight'. In today's Politically Correct world that might be deemed to be racist and unacceptable, but back then it was just a nickname.

After downing some beers in the Sqn bar, Eddie suggested that they all nip down to Raul's Rose Garden which was a seedy whore-house with a licenced bar attached. Richie turned down the offer because after his tour in Canada he was now back to full fitness and had taken a personal oath to quit drinking. He wasn't going to go down that road to alcoholic unfitness ever again. Fast forward a couple of hours and Richie's resolve had been broken easier than a wet Kit Kat chocolate bar. Richie described Raul's Rose Garden, "You wouldn't want to be there if you were sober because it was a disgusting hole. You started the night in a drunken haze and went to bed with Miss World, but you woke up in the morning with Miss Piggy." When asked if he wanted to go on the Jungle Survival Course that was run by the British Infantry and Special Forces, he told them, "No I fucking don't, I'm RCT. If I do have to sleep in the jungle at night, then I'll doss down in the cab of my truck, thank you." Richie did go on a 2-week Field Exercise in the jungle with the resident Infantry Battalion and was amazed at the local Indian tribes living in grass huts, they wore nothing but grass skirts. On hearing the monkeys and other creatures screeching at night, he kept his resolve to safely sleep in his wagon at night.

The troops who were due to return to their parent units sometimes put up a 'Chuff Chart' by their beds and counted down the days to get home. Richie was astonished by this, "Why would you want to leave this place, we got to go on the quay's and rest under a palm tree whilst drinking rum and eating a Bar-B-Cue. We'd often fly up to Cancun in Mexico to party the weekend away, so why would anyone in their right mind want to leave this paradise?" After a while it became monotonous and Richie started to realise it was like eating cake and cake, it became boring and he couldn't stomach the thought of eating yet another Bar-B-Cue. He was living in a 24-man room with a locker and bedside cabinet, there wasn't any televisual entertainment, there were 7 bars on camp and if anyone rang the bell and bought drinks for everyone, "Because the booze was so cheap, the bill would be less than £4. We did nothing but drink during our time out there and got proper drunk every time, towards the end of my tour in Belize my kidneys were killing me, and I couldn't wait to get home."

The OC of 24 Sqn received a Posting Order for Richie, posting him to 1 Infantry HQ and Signal Squadron, based in Tidworth Hampshire. Richie thought, 'That sounds shit' and his mates cheered him up by telling him, "Don't go there, mate, that's a shit-hole of a posting." Every attempt at changing his Posting Order failed and so Richie resigned himself to the inevitable. Two weeks before heading off to Tidworth, Richie and 'Midnight' were both summoned to the Sqn HQ and informed that they were both now being posted to 26 Sqn in Northern Ireland.

Ritchie and 'Midnight' danced with joy around the Sqn corridor. Apart from a 6-month tour to Cyprus, Richie would spend the next 9 years serving with 26 Sqn RCT.

A Tp, 26 Sqn dealt with Staff Cars and its Drivers were referred to as 'Hand-baggers' by the other Drivers in the Sqn. B Tp covered details and drove the units' articulated and Pantechnicon lorries. Richie was assigned to C Tp in 26 Sqn which was the Bus Tp of the Sqn. He did a lot of airport runs, transporting Army Cadets, and dealing with the Wives' Club trips. According to Richie, Army wives can be a pain in the arse after they've drunk several bottles of wine, "I'd rather be in the middle of a riot in Belfast than drive a 52-seater bus full of pissed up army wives. They were all either arguing with each other or trying to touch me up." *Authors note: It's unfortunate that you're such a pretty boy Ritchie.*

After 4 months in Lisburn, Richie went on a detachment to the Courts and Witnesses Section at RAF Aldergrove near Belfast. The Courts and Witnesses unit was an RMP Section with a small transport attachment, consisting of just five RCT soldiers. Any military personal involved in court cases within the Province would be picked up by Richie and safely delivered to the court, and afterwards they'd be taken back to the airport or to their transit accommodation. The team worked all over the Province, from Londonderry to South Armagh and it was fascinating work for Richie. On one occasion at West Belfast Crumlin Court House, Richie was told, "See him in the dock over there, he's the Quartermaster of the IRA." Richie also transported Private Lee Clegg and 7 other Paras to and from the court in a 26 Sqn minibus when they faced a murder charge. On 30th September 1990 a stolen Vauxhall Astra with 3 teenagers inside, sped through the Para's Vehicle Check Point (VCP) without stopping. 17 shots were fired, and a forensic team proved that one of four shots fired by Private Lee Clegg was the one that killed Karen Reilly.

The case went on for three weeks and Richie was briefed that there was a high risk that his minibus could be ambushed. He had to drive the Paras from Aldergrove to Crumlin Court House every day and there were only a few different routes that he could take. Richie felt very vulnerable whilst on route because he and the RMP escort were the only 'tooled up' soldiers (they were carrying 9mm Browning HP Pistols) on the transport and there didn't appear to be any extra security for them. At the end of the case, Private Clegg was sentenced to life imprisonment for murder. The silence in that minibus on the way back to Aldergrove was palpable. Years later the conviction was quashed, and Clegg was finally released from prison. He went back to serving in the Parachute Regiment and heroically served in Afghanistan as a Regimental Medical Assistant (RMA).

After 6 months at Aldergrove, Richie went back to C Tp in Lisburn and on Christmas Eve he and several other guys from the Sqn decided to go to an out of bounds disco in the middle of Belfast. Their ridiculous cover story for a night on the piss was that they were all dancers from Belfast's Christmas pantomime. Whilst Richie was on the dance floor, a very attractive blonde-haired woman called Hazel approached him, and because of the loud music, they had a rather shouted conversation. Her first words were the ones no soldier ever wanted to hear from someone with a strong Irish accent, particularly whilst out of uniform, in Belfast, and not tooled up.

Hazel: "I know you."

Richie: "No you don't."

Hazel: "Yes I do."

Richie: "No you don't."

Hazel: "Yes I do, you're a squaddie."

Richie: "No I'm not."

Hazel: "Yes you are."

Richie: "No I'm not."

Hazel: "Don't be a twat, you work on camp and so do I."

Hazel worked in the Forces flights and ferry bookings office on camp and thereafter they started bumping into each other on a regular basis. They often met up in 26 Sqn's Bar and occasionally bumped into each other because of mutual friends and eventually a relationship developed. One of the perks for working with the airlines had a knock-on effect for Hazel. She was privy to cheap air flights and the two of them often flew to the UK to watch Richie's beloved Norwich City FC. Sgt Jimmy Langdon was Richie's Tp Sgt and he often told him to submit a leave application and leave it on his desk, if anything went wrong then he was covered by army regulations. When Richie returned from his trip Jimmy would simply rip up the application and the time off wouldn't be taken off Richie's leave entitlement. After paying only £10 for their air-tickets, Richie and Hazel flew to London to watch the Tottenham Hotspur v Norwich City game. They arrived early and so went to a British Legion Club for a few drinks, after telling the old boys in the club that he was currently serving in Northern Ireland, they bought him numerous pints of beer.

Sgt Richie Temple RCT at A Troop 24 Sqn RCT in Lisburn

The next morning Richie woke up in a hotel room with Hazel and hadn't got a clue as to where he was. He nudged her and said, "Shit, where are we?" Hazel definitely wasn't happy, she shouted, "Where are we! You were a fucking nightmare last night! We we're on the underground after the match and I got lost! I didn't have a fucking clue where we were going, we also missed the last flight back to Belfast you idiot!" Richie didn't contribute much to the conversation but did add, "Shit, where the fuck are we?" After being told they were still in Heathrow Airport, Richie suddenly twigged he was technically AWOL and helpfully said to Hazel, "Oh Fuck." When they got another cheap flight back to Belfast (thanks to Hazel's contacts) Richie reported to Sgt Jimmy Langdon with a crate of beer, and the existence of the universe was righted again when Hazel forgave Richie. *Authors note: It's fortunate that you're such a pretty boy Ritchie.*

On another football occasion Cpl John Wilson RCT decided to watch a Rangers F.C. football match in Glasgow with other members of the Sqn. He took a military bus and they all headed for the Belfast docks, boarding a ferry to Stranraer. On arrival in Glasgow, John took the lads to his local pub and they started throwing beers down their necks. When it got close to Kick Off time they went to the Ibrox Stadium but weren't allowed into the ground because they were so pissed. John and Richie went back to the pub and continued where they'd left off. By 0200 hours the lads were scattered all over Glasgow and Richie finally lost contact with big John Wilson who was, more than likely, pissing it up somewhere else in the centre of Glasgow. Richie was drunk as a skunk by now and because he'd missed the bus back, he took a taxi from Glasgow to Stranraer and paid for another ferry ticket to Belfast. John Wilson and some of the other lads had to catch a flight back to Belfast and they'd all paid about £300 for the overnight trip to not see Rangers Football Club play a game of football.

Halfway through his time at 26 Sqn RCT, Richie and Hazel flew to Australia for a 2-week holiday (the flights cost them an astronomical price of £100) and whilst there they did the famous walk/climb over Sydney Harbour Bridge. Once they reached the top of the bridge the view of the harbour was fantastic, the sun was shining and there was a beautiful blue sky above them. Richie thought that it would be an amazing place to propose to Hazel, but he lost his courage and bottled it. When he did eventually propose it was for practical and mundane reasons rather than romantic.

Captain John Storey informed Richie that he was being posted to Abingdon and Richie explained to his boss, "Look boss, Hazel and I have been together for the last few years and our hand is being forced by the Army. We'll have to get married if we want to stay together and that sort of pressure could be disastrous for a newly married couple, or we could try and maintain a long-distance relationship and we may drift apart, can you help us out? John Storey fixed it for Richie to do a 6-month UN Tour of Cyprus before getting another 3-year posting back to 26 Sqn. In 1995 Richie was sent to Nicosia where he worked in the G1098 Store before taking over the mail runs. He is quite candid about his UN tour, "The British Army gave me a medal for getting pissed, delivering the mail, and holidaying with Hazel." Whilst in a casino on the Turkish side of the island, Richie again got drunk and he woke up the following morning wondering if he'd asked Hazel a question the night before. When he asked her, Hazel had a beaming smile on her face and said, "Yes, and I said yes." To his eternal shame, Richie was so drunk he can't remember proposing to Hazel.

After finishing his UN tour, Richie went straight back to 26 Sqn in Lisburn, on the 7th of October 1996 he was ironing his uniform in the accommodation block when a sudden and massive explosion from the main car park violently shook his Portacabin. Hazel's office window and desk was facing where an IRA planted car bomb exploded. The force of the blast blew her office window into her face and the building. Richie immediately ran over towards the Sqn office block to make sure Hazel was all right. He initially thought that the POL Point was on fire or that the barracks was being mortared. On his way he noticed a huge crater on the car park tarmac where the car bomb had detonated. HQ 26 Sqn's building was virtually destroyed. He saw Hazel's office window was missing but he couldn't see her anywhere. He was directed away from the POL Point because it was presumed that another bomb might be planted there for maximum effect.

WO 2 James Bradwell of the RE's was booking out of the 26 Sqn Ops Room and was severely injured from the blast, alongside thirty other casualties. The injured were taken to the camp Medical Centre for first aid treatment. Malevolently, the IRA had also planted another bomb by the Medical Centre because they knew that's where the casualties would be taken. When it exploded within minutes of the first bomb, James Bradwell was caught in the second blast and died of his injuries four days later. Richie eventually found Hazel and apart from a few cuts and bruises she was unharmed. Her office window was coated in an anti-bomb plastic sheet and when the device detonated, the window wrapped around Hazel's head and face like a Clingfilm wrap. The mental effects of that day were to play an important factor in their future life together.

Richie did a Senior Military Qualification Course (SMQC) back in England, which he needed to gain promotion to Sgt. Cpl Davey Cairnes RCT was on the same Course and the night before the final SMQC Exercise, Davey suggested they go and visit some friends of his at Sandhurst and have a couple of beers. They both got completely hammered and, "We were hanging out our arses on that Exercise, my problem is I'm too easily lead." said Richie, "but luckily we both passed the Course." Richie and Hazel also got married in Richie's home town of Gorleston near Great Yarmouth and they honeymooned in Turkey.

For the next 2 years Richie worked at Force Intelligence Unit Northern Ireland FIU NI)) until the unit shut down and he went back to 26 Sqn (which had by now been re-designated 54 Sqn RLC) as Details NCO. By this time, Richie had done 14 years in the RCT, he'd been in the Province for nearly 9 years of those years. He played football for his local civilian team, he'd bought a house local to his unit and the RUC were trying to recruit him because they thought he'd make a great copper. Within months of being posted to 54 Sqn RLC, Richie was promoted to Sgt and Hazel had had their son Jack. They had to wait for notification of Richie's future posting before deciding what next step they were going take together.

They decided to see what it was like at A Tp, 20 Sqn RLC in Regents Park Barracks, London before making any firm decisions. Richie was sent on a Staff Car Driving Course and eventually became the 'Handbagger' he never wanted to be. Hazel got a job at Mill Hill Military Postal Unit but because of Child Care costs, she was spending all her wages on Jack's Child Care and so left the job. Their Married Quarter was in Whetstone and Richie had the stress of travelling into work on the tube. By Christmas 2001 Richie decided to apply for Premature Voluntary Release (PVR) from the Army and went on an assessment course with the Norfolk Police near where he was living. He was readily accepted, even though technically he was still serving in the ranks of the British Army. They asked him, "Can you start on a training course on Monday Morning?" Richie asked for permission from Major Stone RLC who was the OC of 20 Sqn and, fortunately, he sanctioned the proposal. When this Officer was a 2nd Lt at Buller Barracks in Aldershot, he was Richie's Troop Commander during his basic training.

Richie has now been a Policeman longer than he was a Soldier in the RCT, but he still considers himself to be a Trog/Trogg more than a Copper. Unlike his dad, he has no regrets about leaving the British Army early. Richie and Hazel had always wanted another child and after drinking a full bottle of Absolut between them, they decided to let fate take its chance. Lilly 'Absolut' Rose was born in February 2010.

The Temple family still lives in Gorleston, Great Yarmouth and Richie continues to serve in the Police Force.

24911149 Staff Sergeant Derek (Robbo) Robson
RCT and RLC 1990 – 2012

Derek William Robson was born in Wingate, County Durham on the 19th January 1971 and up to the point when he joined the British Army, he'd never been abroad. Unlike most of the other soldiers in this, and the authors other RCT biographical books, Derek doesn't have any military memoirs at all in his family history. Like most of the men that lived in the County Durham area, Derek's grandfather was a Miner.

Sarah Elizabeth Robson, Derek's mum, was a hard-working Psychiatric Nurse at Winterton 'Mental Asylum' in Sedgefield, County Durham and whilst she did night duties at the hospital, her husband, Derek William Robson, worked as a Labourer during the day. Derek's father only had two interests in his life, a small rented gardening allotment and his pigeon's. Because of their fathers' indifference to his wife and children, Derek and his three-year older sister Debbie didn't have a good relationship with him. Their dad's crops and birds always came first when it came to grabbing his attention, so much so that he never went on holiday with the family because the allotment and his pigeons always needed his undivided attention. Unsurprisingly, Sarah divorced her husband when Derek was about 15 years old because around the house, she did absolutely everything and her husband, sadly, did absolutely nothing.

Prior to getting to the meat of the divorce proceedings, Derek, his sister, and their mum, moved into another house whilst the divorce settlement was finalised. When the divorce dust had finally settled, Sarah eventually bought back their old house and the three of them moved back into the family home. Derek felt much happier living with just his mum and sister because they didn't have to hear any more arguments between his parents, and they also didn't have to suffer those awful long cold silences.

When given the choice of where they wanted to live, Debbie and Derek, unequivocally, chose to live with their mum.

Sgt Derek Robson in Afghanistan with 13 Air Assault Regt.

At school Derek didn't achieve anything of note; it had nothing to do with his parents' divorce either, he simply wasn't interested in anything on the curriculum apart from sport. He wasn't scared of hard work though because he worked on newspaper and milk rounds to earn some spending money. Towards the end of Derek's education, he failed to turn up for his final examinations which culminated with his mum getting a local education authority bill of £60 for the missed tests. At the time leading up to his final exams, Sarah didn't know that Derek wasn't attending school because whenever she came home from an exhausting night-shift at Winterton Hospital, Derek was just coming back in from his early newspaper or milk rounds. So, when Sarah headed off up to bed for some desperately needed sleep, Derek was surreptitiously staying at home whilst his mum was knocking out the Z's upstairs. Derek's mum was not best pleased when she came downstairs a bit earlier than expected one day; she caught Derek watching the television with the volume down low. Derek told his mum, "*I don't want to go to school,*" and although his mum knew that by the letter of the law Derek should be attending school, she left the final decision on what he was going to do about his last weeks in education entirely up to Derek himself.

When he'd officially left school, Derek was employed on a Youth Training Scheme (YTS) one day a week at a college course in Gateshead, the other four days were spent on work experience, for which Derek was paid the princely sum of only £27 a week. On quite a few occasions the firm he was working for neglected to pay him for various implausible reasons. After 18 months Derek had had enough of being used for cheap labour and he decided to look for work elsewhere. He moved to a paint-spraying job in Stockton-on-Tees near Middlesbrough where he earned about £120 a week, he only got the job though, because he lied through his teeth on the interview and told the boss he could do things he'd never actually done before in his life. The work was spasmodic but, "*I earned every penny of that bloody*

£120 though; whilst wearing a dust suit I had to mask up windscreens and rubbed down the bodywork of commercial vehicles with sandpaper. Although, one benefit of the job was that I got to drive the heavy goods vehicles into and out of the spray bay, even though I only had a car licence."

The job became monotonous in the end though and the wages weren't getting any bigger either, so Derek applied for a job with the Nissan Car Company in Sunderland. He was taking a lot of time off work from his Stockton-on-Tees job to attend the interviews at Nissan (Derek's mum used to phone in sick for him) and, incidentally dear reader, the Stockton-on-Tees employers didn't know that Derek was looking for another job. Derek was successful in the Nissan interviews and made it through to the final selection process which necessitated him buying a new suit for the final selection phase. So, Derek took even more time off from his Stockton-on-Tees work to purchase the right clothing ensemble for his final Nissan job interrogation. In the end Derek wasn't one of the Nissan chosen few and so the money spent on the new suit proved to be a fruitless exercise and to top it all off, his very patient Stockton-on-Tees employees eventually gave him the sack.

Whilst drowning his sorrows in the local pub a short while after his sacking, Derek bumped into one of two old school-friends who had joined the British Army after leaving school. One had joined the Junior Leaders Regiment RCT, whilst the other had enlisted into the Royal Engineers as an HGV Driver. The lad that had joined the RCT eventually jacked it in half way through his training, but the happy Sapper regaled Derek with tales about what a wonderful life it was serving in the British Army. Derek decided that a career in the Army was just the thing he needed; he'd get his HGV licences and then leave the Army after a few years and get a job earning some decent wages driving Heavy Goods Vehicles.

Fortunately for Derek, the Recruiter at Horden Armed Forces Careers Office near Peterlee was an RCT Sergeant. After doing the relevant interviews and written tests, Derek was offered the chance to join the RE's as a driver but was told that the waiting list was about 6 months or so, either that or he could join the best Corps in the British Army within the next couple of weeks. It was a no-brainer for Derek and at 19 years of age he headed off to Buller Barracks in Aldershot.

An RCT Cpl wearing his smart Number 2 Dress uniform, 'Twat Hat' and bulled boots, met Derek and the other recruits outside Aldershot Railway Station, he carried a Mill-board in his left hand and started shouting out names. The tough looking JNCO eventually shouted, *"Robson. D!"* and anyone with a modicum of wit would have shouted back, *"Here Corporal!"* Derek on the other hand meekly replied, *"Yeah."* It wasn't a good start to his Army career. The Cpl bristled with anger and shouted, *"Yeah, what the fuck do you mean yeah?"* Derek quickly wised up and said, "I mean, yes Corporal, I'm here." The Cpl sneered at Derek's long hair and menacingly spat the words, *"That fucking lot will be coming off tomorrow!"* It didn't get any better for Derek when the Cpl demanded to know if everyone had brought their passport photographs with them, as per the joining instructions that Buller Barracks had sent out to them weeks previously.

Derek had forgotten about that part of the information and he re-upset the tough looking RCT Cpl who seemed to have calmed down a bit from Derek's earlier casual attitude towards him. The very angry and pissed off JNCO stomped up and down the platform while the new arrivals went off to find a photo booth.

"It was all a bit fast and furious when we arrived at Buller Barracks, but none of it really fazed me," says Derek, *"it all seemed like a bit of an adventure. Some of the NCO's in Buller Barracks were really good and others were bloody awful"*. Derek remembers looking at the Cpl's creases in his Number 2 Dress

trousers and thought to himself, "*How the hell does he get his creases that sharp?*" It wasn't until Derek was called into one of the Permanent Staff Instructor's (PSI's) rooms that he saw how they managed to be so smart all day, and every day. The 'switched on' RCT NCO's had acquired about seven sets of Shirts, Denim Trousers, Heavy Duty Jersey's and all the extra kit they needed. With all that extra kit that had been ironed and was ready for use, they could do a quick change when necessary.

Within two weeks of starting his Basic Training, Derek had to go on sick leave because he was injured during a fitness session whilst playing football. He was slide tackled by Driver Leafley who took Derek's legs out from underneath him and in doing so, unfortunately brutally dislocated Derek's shoulder. As he landed on the grass after the heavy tackle, Derek knew some serious damage had been done to his shoulder and he thought, "*Oh shit, this isn't good*!" A Land Rover from the Guardroom took him up to the Cambridge Military Hospital (CMH) in Aldershot where an RAMC Doctor told him, "*The dislocation is so bad you'll need an operation to put it right, Driver Robson*". A couple of days after the operation, Derek went back to Buller Barracks and reported to his Troop Commander whilst wearing a sling and carrying a letter. The sick-note informed the Training Staff in Buller Barracks that Driver Robson wouldn't be able to continue with his Basic Training and that he should be placed on sick leave for the next two weeks to recuperate.

When Derek reported back to the RCT Depot a fortnight later, he was told that he was now too far behind in his Basic Training and he couldn't re-join his original Squad. There also wouldn't be another Course starting for another month or so and he was sent back on leave again. After 6 weeks of drinking with his pals and doing very little else, Derek decided he didn't want to go back to Aldershot and be submitted to all the crap that the British Army threw at him. By the time Derek's new squad was being assembled, his previous Squad were all on their Passing Out

Parade and would soon be doing their Driver Training Phase. Derek was very pissed off about his situation in life and so he put his negative head on and became a pain in the arse with his Instructors. He simply wasn't interested in continuing with a career in the British Army. He applied for a Troop Commanders interview and explained that he now wanted out of the Army; he was, though, constantly fobbed off by his Troop Commander and Troop Sergeant.

On yet another room inspection, Derek hadn't secured his foot locker with a padlock and the Cpl trashed his kit all over the room, which got a big laugh for the JNCO and the trashing resulted in Derek's padlock going missing. Derek was determined he wasn't going to be bullied into buying a new one from the PSI's, and so his foot locker was trashed on every inspection because it wasn't locked with a padlock. It was a battle of wills and after a while the PSI's gave up because the situation simply couldn't continue, it was starting to look like a case of victimisation. On Week 8 of Derek's training the PSI tried to bill Derek for a stained mattress. The stains were circled by a pen and signed by the NCO who did the inspection, in that way the mattress would be paid for by several soldiers over the years. The Cpl found a small mark that hadn't been circled and signed, but Derek refused to sign a damages bill because he was adamant he hadn't caused the stain. The JNCO waved his finger in Derek's face and threatened him, "*This won't be the last you'll hear of this Driver Robson.*" The Staff at the Depot eventually gave up in the end because Derek simply refused to sign the bill and so prophetically, it actually was the last Driver Derek Robson heard about it.

When Derek finally 'Passed Out' of the Depot his mum and two friends from school came down to Aldershot for the parade. The weather in January was so bad that his mate Craig Fulcher brought them all down in his 4x4 or they simply wouldn't have been able to see the parade. Derek's father couldn't make it down for the occasion. The snow was so thick on the Parade

Ground that the procession was held in one of the drill sheds. Derek then headed off up to Leconfield in East Yorkshire to do the Driver Training phase of their course. Derek took two attempts to pass his HGV II driving test because on the first attempt he overtook a cyclist on a railway crossing. *Authors note: That was a school boy error Derek, a school boy error that any decent Trog would never have made. Any decent Trog would have knocked him off the bike using his wing mirror.*

On completion of his Driver Training, Derek and the other trainees reported back to Buller Barracks to get their posting orders. He wanted to go on an adventure to the British Army on the Rhine (BAOR), but anywhere abroad would do for him. He hadn't travelled anywhere outside of England in his life and now that he was in the Army it would be his chance to finally get on a ship or aeroplane and explore other areas of the world. He checked the postings list on the notice board and saw that he was being posted to 27 Regiment RCT. He called out to his mates, who were in the main going to units based in Germany, *"Where's 27 Regt lads?"* When someone told Derek that 27 Regt RCT was based just over the road from Buller Barracks, he shouted, *"You've got to be fucking kidding me!"* He joined two other younger lads who were also posted to 27 Regt and noted that, *"We only needed our own two bloody feet to get to our very first posting."*

Driver Derek Robson RCT was posted into 7 Sqn as an 8 Tonne TM GT Driver; and he arrived in the unit just as the Sqn was returning from the first Gulf War in 1991. The lads in 27 Regt thought Derek was a seasoned soldier because he was by now 20 years old and looked a bit older than the other two newly arrived young Drivers. It was a blessing really because it meant he didn't have to go through any of the horrendous RCT alcohol fueled initiation ceremonies. Although pissed off at being sent *"Just over the road,"* Derek was given some good news a couple of months later. 7 Sqn was deploying to Nicosia on a six-month UN tour in

Cyprus from January to July 1992. He was assigned to work on the Sqn's trucks rather than the Mini-buses and Staff Cars. Each day involved Derek doing resupply details to Dhekelia Garrison where he'd pick up the necessary stores and then deliver them out to the observation posts spread along the Greek Cypriot/Turkish border points. The men stationed in the Sangers needed Water and Rations and depending on which contingent the supplies were destined for; the stores were labelled accordingly. DANCON was for the Danish Contingent or CANCON for the Canadian Contingent and so on.

Before taking over their duties entirely, the 7 Sqn Drivers did the rounds with the previous contingent's soldiers' and so they got to know, 'what was what' and where everything was located on the Island. Derek explained about his experiences in Cyprus, "*I had a brilliant time out there and it was probably the best thing I've ever done in all of my service in the RCT and RLC. I even did some details up to the top end of the pan handle taking some urgently needed supplies to the refugees on the Turkish side of the border. The Sqn took over from a Gurkha unit of the Queens Own Gurkha Transport Regiment (QOGTR) and at the end of the tour a medal parade was held at RAF Akrotiri, the local commander on the Island presented everyone in the Sqn with their UN medals just before 7 Sqn flew back to the UK.*" Once he was back in 'The Shot', Derek completed his BII Drivers Course and JCB Forklift Qualifications in Aldershot. After serving in Aldershot for two years Derek felt he'd had enough of Paratrooper gobshite's, and so when the Corps started looking for volunteers to serve in Northern Ireland in 1992, he jumped at the chance.

Once he'd established himself in B Troop, 26 Sqn RCT in Lisburn+, Derek passed his HGV Class I test driving a civilian type articulated lorry, he was also trained up on the Saxon Armoured Personnel Carrier (APC) which had by then replaced the notorious APC's of yesteryears, the iconic Humber 'Pig' and that wonderful six-wheeled APC, the Alvis Saracen. During a night out with the lads from 26 Sqn, Derek met, and infuriated a young woman called Becky. Becky's dad was an Army Major serving in an Intelligence Corps unit that was based at the Brigade HQ in Lisburn. Becky was standing up at a table in a noisy and bustling bar; she'd only just stood up and was loudly talking to her friends on the other side of the table because they simply couldn't hear what she was saying. Derek saw the empty chair that Becky had just vacated, and he moved it so he could sit down on it himself. When Becky sat back down on the seat that she thought was still behind her, she fell onto the floor and went 'base over apex' *(British Army translation - arse over tit)* and she lost the dignity and demeanor that was expected of a young, and very elegant, Officers daughter. Derek immediately helped a very embarrassed and incensed Becky up onto her feet and he apologised profusely, but his RCT mates didn't help matters when they told her he'd only done it for a laugh and that he was simply trying to get her attention.

Shortly after that night out, some of the Drivers in the Sqn travelled over to Scotland by ferry in a couple of minibuses and they collected thirty civilian style flat- bed trucks which they brought back to Lisburn. The wagons were going to be used on details to collect and dispose of all the building materials and equipment from border locations like Crossmaglen; ill-famed British Army and RUC location's like these were at last being vacated and disassembled. It was a quieter time during the 'Troubles' in Northern Ireland which would hopefully lead to an end of the hostilities. *(Authors note: On the 28th of February 2007 the last watch tower in Crossmaglen was finally knocked down.)*

Meanwhile back in Lisburn, Becky was feeling a bit vexed because Derek hadn't 'phoned her, she'd given him her telephone number after calming down from the 'chair-gate' incident, and yet he hadn't had the decency to give her a phone call. On their first date, Derek rather predictably took Becky to the pictures and they had a drink in a bar before he took her home to the Officers Married Quarter patch at a respectable 2200 hrs. As they walked in the front door, Derek hoped that Becky's parents had gone off to bed because he was very nervous about meeting them. Her parents were both in the living room waiting to see that their daughter was bought home safely. Derek thought to himself, "*Oh shit.*" After Becky had graciously introduced Derek to her mum and dad, the old folks made their excuses and discretely retired for the night. Derek said, "*From that first meeting, my in-laws have been absolutely brilliant.*"

Within 12 months Derek was sent on a 6-week APTIs (Assistant Physical Training Instructors) Course in Aldershot. There were 110 students on the course and they were split up into Sections of about 15 men. On their first day at the Army School of Physical Training *(Authors note: Since 2010 HM Queen Elizabeth II has graciously bestowed the PTI's with a Royal prefix to their Corps name, the APTC is now called the Royal Army Physical Training Corp)* and is based on the Queens Avenue in Aldershot, on the first day the candidates had to do a Basic Fitness Test (BFT). When a Quartermaster Sergeant Instructor (QMSI) blew his whistle, the course students all sprinted off at a great rate of knots which left Derek standing on the start line thinking "*Fucking hell, where did they all go?*" The first runners crossed the finish line in about 7 minutes, but the majority came in around the 9-minute mark, when the results of the 1 ½ mile BFT run were published, Derek's name was 90th out of the 110 candidates on the list. Derek was ok on rope climbing but he wasn't so good at the gymnastics phase of the course, "*But what went in my favour was how well and quickly I progressed and improved on a course that I hadn't had any time in which to prepare for. Many of the other students had obviously put in a lot of extra pre-course training.*"

Derek got fitter and stronger as the course progressed and on the last days' BFT, he was one of the top 20 runners. He always rested at weekends and was ready to go again on the following Monday. Derek honestly states, "*I didn't pass the course with flying colours and I was never going to get top student, but overall I think I did very well under the circumstances.*" He was presented with the crossed swords badge which AKAI's wear on the right sleeve of their uniforms.

On return to Lisburn Derek was promoted to LCpl and he boxed for his unit which was soon to be re-designated 26 Sqn RLC when the RCT metamorphosed into the RLC. For the boxing fixture, Derek fought at Light Middleweight (71kg) against a Royal Signals soldier. A month before the competition, the team went up to RAF Aldergrove to do some boxing training, one reason for the move up to Aldergrove was so the team members couldn't be dragged into work. On the morning of the weigh-in, Derek was a couple of ounces over his fighting weight and so he had to run around the athletics track to sweat off the excess weight.

Derek's opponent on the night was a massive Signalman who had the benefit of a longer reach; a concerned Derek thought to himself, "*Shit, this is going to hurt.*" The Royal Signals 'Bleep' won the first 2 rounds of their fight but Derek clinched the last 3-minute round. Although he lost his bout, Derek received a letter from the OC saying that he'd been awarded 'The Most Spirited Boxer' prize, which Derek believes was their way of saying he was the best 'loser' on the night. It was about that time that Derek heard about the up and coming RCT to RLC transformation. Some of older RCT lads in the Sqn categorically decreed they wouldn't wear the new RLC cap badge and stable belt. It wasn't long after Derek had passed his PTI Course that he was promoted to Lance Corporal and he picked up a posting to 76 Sqn, 2 Close Support Regiment RLC which was based in Gutersloh, it was a newly formed logistic unit and 2 CS Regiment RLC did an official parade to mark the change-over. Because the unit was just forming, the new soldiers who were going to make up its ranks slowly started to dribble into the unit.

Six months after Derek had gone to Gutersloh, Becky's dad was posted to the Falkland Islands and she was offered the choice of either going with him to the South Atlantic or live in the UK with family or friends. Derek and Becky decided that they should get married instead and they were wedded on the camp in Lisburn before her parents flew down to the Falkland Islands. Derek and Becky sent out the wedding invitations and the only person not to attend was Derek's Dad, who told the happy couple, "*If it was being held in Wingate I'd be prepared to go, but I'm not travelling all the way to Northern Ireland.*" The rest of Derek's family and friends all travelled over to Lisburn by minibus. Some of them were quite nervous about going to the Province because of its well-known history of violence. Driver Ed Hall RCT was Derek's best man at the ceremony; they served in the same troop and were even accommodated in the same room in 26 Sqn's accommodation block.

The newly married couple had to wait 6 weeks before they were allocated a Married Quarter in the Gutersloh area and so Becky went to stay with Derek's sister for a while. Derek eventually served for 4 years in 2 CS Regt and during that time 76 Sqn went to Canada during the summer months on Med Man 1 and 2 Exercises. During the deployment onto the Canadian prairies at British Army Training Unit Suffield (BATUS), Derek did his usual job and was a Demountable Rack Offload and Pickup System (DROPS) Section 2 i/c. The DROPS trucks and Equipment they signed for was all in good order, but their Sqn was worked so hard by the Battle Group they were exhausted all the time.

When the drivers weren't out supporting and supplying the Battle Group, they were back in camp having lectures on all the Army Training Directives (ATD's).
Several of the Sqn's drivers fell asleep at the wheel of their trucks and some had accidents and close calls purely because of a lack of sleep. To rectify this problem each driver was issued an eat and sleep card that had to be diligently filled in, it would then

indicate how much sleep they were, or were not getting. To make matters worse, it rained a lot in Canada at that time and the training area was turned into a quagmire. Tanks often had to pull the trucks out because the wagons had sunk down to their axles in the thick, cloying mud. *"The fact that our drivers were getting bogged down in the mud had nothing to do with bad driving skills,"* said Derek, *"It didn't matter where you drove on the prairie, our wagons became bogged in up to their axles even whilst driving on unused tracks and ground. We often had to be pulled out by the Tank units we were there to supply. It was exhausting work."*

Sgt Kev Preston RLC was Derek's Troop Sgt and they got on very well together, they'd often played football together and had often socialised with each other back in Gutersloh. On one detail, Derek and his Section had been out on the prairies until well past midnight and after returning to the Sqn Hide they were told, *"Breakfast is from 0700 till 0800 hours, make sure your lads all have a good breakfast in the morning and ensure they aren't late on parade."* In the morning, Derek checked his lads had all washed, shaved, cleaned their weapons and had prepped the hide area before they all headed off for breakfast. The Section turned up for breakfast at 0710 but their troop admin had all been completed. Other drivers from the Sqn were eating their scoff and cleaning their weapons at the same time. A very tired Sgt Preston kicked off because Derek and his lads weren't at the G1098 at 0700 hrs. Derek tried to explain that his lads had done all their admin and yet some of the others Sections' drivers in the Troop, were still cleaning their weapons whilst wearing the previous night's cam cream and most of them were also eating their breakfast with filthy hands and weapons.

Sgt Preston wasn't listening to any arguments from Derek and he ordered Derek and his lads to double round the G1098 whilst holding their weapons over their heads. The injustice of it all was too much, and Derek suddenly shouted, *"This is bullshit!"* A massive ding-dong between Lance Corporal Derek Robson and Sergeant Kev Preston kicked off in the G1098 area and he told his Troop Sgt, *"This is fucking crap"* before storming off back to his truck. Kev caught up with him a short while later and ripped into him, Derek felt he just had to take it on the chin because although he felt justified, he still shouldn't have shown such disrespect to his Troop Sergeant. Derek should never have lost his temper and shown disrespect like that to a SNCO because Derek was, after all, only a JNCO. In the end Sgt Preston was a man's man, and a day later the whole matter was forgotten about and they continued with the Exercise.

On another night, Derek came back into the Sqn hide with a three-vehicle convoy that had been out on the prairie all night long. He and his drivers got to the Sqn's G1098 tented cookhouse a few minutes before the chefs stopped serving breakfast. After parking up they got their breakfast and were about to start throwing it down their necks when their Troop SSgt came over, *"Right Corporal Robson, you need to get your three trucks back out of here and report to the Battle Group Headquarters immediately for a rush job."* The Section drivers all scraped their food into a bin and then went straight back out again. The Sqn Officers were so keen to keep a good image of the unit; they jumped every time the Battle Group gave them orders like, *"We're Live firing shortly and we need X amounts of this type of ammunition immediately."* The RLC Privates and JNCO's felt like they were being abused by the Battle Group and their own unit. Derek explained, *"Shit always rolls down hill in the army. The orders came from the Battle Group Headquarters, they were then passed down to our own Squadron Headquarters, Sqn Ops would then pass it onto the Troop SSgt's and Sgt's before the lads, who were at the bottom of the shit-pile, did all the donkey work. The shit never rolls up hill."*

When Endex (End of Exercise) was finally called, Derek was glad to be going back to BAOR. The RAF C130 aircraft on the return journey to Germany, had had half of its seats taken out so that the aircraft could be loaded up with more cargo. Derek got his sleeping bag and kip mat out of his Bergen, found a suitable area where he wouldn't be trampled on, and slept like a log nearly all the way back to Paderborn Airport. Within weeks of getting back to Gutersloh, 76 Sqn were given orders to deploy out to Bosnia. On hearing this Derek immediately applied for a Troop Commanders interview and told his boss that he was a newly married soldier, and that in the time since he and Becky had tied the knot, they'd spent 6 weeks apart whilst waiting to be allocated a Married Quarter. Derek had also been away from Becky for a month on the 'Med Man Exercise' in Canada and he'd also spent a month on his Junior Military Qualification Course (JMQC). Derek wanted to spend some quality time with his wife. The Troop Commander agreed and Derek was subsequently taken off the deployment list.

Derek went across to HQ Sqn for 2 years and he worked in the MT Office, but within 6 months of joining them, HQ Sqn was also sent to Bosnia. Their own Troop Sgt didn't deploy with them though, and so Derek and the other drivers in his troop were Commanded by Cpl Greenberry (*known to everyone as GB*). When the Troop arrived at Divulje Barracks, Split in Croatia, the MT lads were put under the command of the Radio Operators (Rad Ops) Sgt for admin purposes simply because they didn't have a Troop Sgt of their own. Both elements paraded together every morning and then went about their own duties. Derek ran the MT office and the troop drivers carried out the details. There wasn't any element of danger or excitement during this deployment because everything had calmed down from the early days, "*It was just like being in barracks in Germany,*" said Derek, "*Every Day we did various MT tasks including things like driving the payroll and pay clerk up into Bosnia using a Land Rover.*" One thing Derek liked about serving in the Army was the fact that there was always a cut-off date on whatever it was you were doing, and you'd then start on a new job in a different unit. The aforementioned Cpl Greenberry was also an RLC Corps Skier and during the tour he was needed on the team for a skiing competition and was summoned back to Germany. Derek remained in Divulje to do the handover/takeover of the units' vehicles and Complete Equipment Schedule (CES). The handover/takeover was a stressful time for Derek, but the nervous tension was partly of his own making because he was such a perfectionist about his work, the rest of the stress was made up by the incoming RLC unit. When Derek had a job to do, he always did it properly and efficiently. It was unfortunate that the incoming RLC MT lads weren't that well-organized or knowledgeable. When the incoming drivers went out onto the vehicle park to identify and check the vehicle CES's, they weren't familiar with some of the equipment and would come back into the MT Office complaining, "*It's not there.*" After a while a very angry LCpl Derek Robson started shouting, "*Yes it fucking is, I know it's there because I fucking put it there myself yesterday. Right, come with me.*" Derek had to take some of the incoming drivers by the hand and mollycoddle them through the handover of fifteen different vehicles and all the MT stores. Losing track of time, someone came into the MT Office and said, "*Come on Robbo, you've got to get to the airport for your flight.*" Derek reluctantly handed over the unfinished paperwork to the incoming RLC NCO and said, "*There you are mate, have fun.*" He then caught his plane and flew back to Germany.

Time was growing short for Derek's posting at HQ Sqn 2 CS Regt. He was told by his Chief Clerk that he only had 6 months left in the unit and advised him to put in a posting preference. Becky's parents were being posted back to Northern Ireland and so Derek applied to go back to B Troop 26 Regt RLC. 26 Regt RLC had by this time moved from Lisburn to Kinnegar and was now called Northern Ireland Close Service Support (NICSS) Regiment. Kinnegar is about 5 miles North East of Belfast City Centre. Never one to sit down for long, Derek was still playing football for the unit when Sgt Gaz Taylor collared him and 8 other RLC soldiers to take part in a 'Tough Guy' Competition in Birmingham. To get them all ready for the grueling struggle they were about to face, Sgt Gaz Taylor beasted the volunteers with some exhausting and backbreaking pre-training. On arrival in the Midlands all the competitors stayed in an ex-SSM's barn overnight. The ex-Infantry soldier woke everyone up in the morning by firing a shotgun and shouting, "*Come on you lazy fuckers, get out of your sleeping bags!*" On the plus side, he provided everyone with a large mug of tea and a wad of bacon sandwiches.

The day after the exhausting competition, the RLC soldiers unceremoniously got back in their minibus and travelled back to Northern Ireland. Derek and Becky were allocated a Married Quarter in Palace Barracks, just outside Belfast. Becky was 6 months pregnant with their first child, Elana, (*Ellie was eventually born in Dundonald Civilian Hospital a few miles east of Belfast*). During his last 6 months at Kinnegar, Derek was promoted to full Corporal and he picked up another posting in N.I.

In 2003 Derek was sent to Portadown in South Armagh for the next two years. He served with 3 Infantry Brigade and Signal Sqn (3 Inf Bde). The Motor Transport Section in 3 Inf Bde was made up of a mixture of RLC and Royal Signals soldiers. Cpl Mark Garrity RLC was Derek's closest friend at the time, they worked and played football together and even lived next door to each other on the Married Quarters patch. SSgt Lee Hopkins R Sigs (later WO2) oversaw a 48-hour Infantry Exercise which incorporated digging in, camming up, going without sleep for the full two days, and carrying full kit and weapon whilst participating in Infantry roles and tactics. Lee also planned that everyone taking part in the Exercise should do the 8 miler Combat Fitness Test (CFT) just before they all deployed into the field. On the run, each candidate would also be carrying their full kit which included Bergen's, webbing, weapons and sleeping bags. Derek had volunteered for the whole Exercise but during the CFT an old Achilles injury suddenly flared up because he was now wearing the new style Army Combat High boots. Although Derek completed the CFT in a reasonable time, he could barely walk at the end of it because he was in so much pain. Derek knew it would be impossible for him to take part in the 48-hour Field Exercise phase and so he approached Lee to put him in the picture.

Derek: *Staff I'm not going to be able to go out on the Field Exercise. My Achilles tendons are giving me some serious shit.*

An unsympathetic Lee was brutal in his reply (especially when you consider that Derek was already a qualified and exceptionally fit PTI, he was also a soldier who didn't quit physical challenges without good reason).

SSgt Lee Hopkins: *Right, Ok, fuck off then. Go and report to the guardroom, fuck off out of my sight, you're just a fucking waste of space.*

Staff Hopkins gave Derek plenty of verbal abuse believing Derek was simply wimping out of the Exercise, and since there wasn't a Medical Centre on the Training area, Derek had to hang about in the Guardroom for 2 days until everyone returned from the planned scheme. When they did come back into camp after the Exercise, the soldiers were all in complete shit state and looked like they'd been dragged through a hedge backwards. Derek was disappointed that he couldn't take part in the Exercise but was even more frustrated in SSgt Lee Hopkins attitude towards him, *"Thinking back, I don't actually believe Lee thought I was a waste of space. He was a much better man than that and was obviously under a lot of pressure to get enough men out on the Exercise. But because quite a few of the lads had already dropped out before the Exercise had even started, he was under a lot of pressure. I do think though that doing the CFT before the Exercise commenced was a very bad idea."*

Lee Hopkins was killed several years later whilst serving in Iraq when he was travelling aboard a Rigid Raider that hit an Improvised Explosive Device (IED). His death was reported in the National Press headlines thus:

Warrant Officer Class 2 Lee Hopkins, Staff Sergeant Sharron Elliott, Corporal Ben Nowak and Marine Jason Hylton killed in Iraq.

'It is with deep regret that the Ministry of Defence has confirmed the names of four UK Service personnel killed in an attack on a Multi-National Forces boat patrol on the Shatt Al-Arab waterway on Sunday 12 November 2006.'

Something was niggling in the back of Derek's brain at this time, he knew a lot of soldiers who were Para Trained, and SSgt Lee Hopkins was one of them. Derek wanted to have a go at P Company just to see if it was as tough as everyone had stated. Derek's' Achilles problems were treated at the Medical Centre when he returned to camp at Portadown. His initial medical treatment was followed up with physiotherapy sessions until the problem was manageable. Derek had some other good news during his posting at 3 Inf Bde. Becky became pregnant for a second time and they named their beautiful new born baby girl, Megan. Derek's Army career had so far seen him serve (*in chronological order*) in the UK for two years, Northern Ireland for two years, then four years at Gutersloh in Germany, followed by yet another four years back in Northern Ireland. He was due to put in another posting preference and believed that, "*They were never going to let me go back to Germany again so soon.*" Even though he had asked to be posted back to Germany he thought he would be posted back to England.

Derek's OC was the Quartermaster at 3 Inf Bde and was a Para Trained Officer, he went to see him for some advice. Derek asked if he would be allowed to put in for P Coy and if he passed the course his plan was to serve with the Airborne Forces (AB) on his posting back to the UK. His OC agreed, and he put in for the course which would be held at the Infantry Training Unit in Catterick (ITC), Catterick Garrison, North Yorkshire. Derek thought that Para Trained Soldiers always had a very high opinion of themselves and he wanted to see if the Selection Process was as tough and grim as they declared. Derek did his own pre-course training in preparation for P Coy at Mahon Bks, Portadown. Every morning he took the unit for a PT session after doing a 3-mile run on his own. He did some tabbing (*Tactical Advance to Battle – an Airborne way of running and speed marching towards a designated area and retaining enough energy to fight on arrival*) with a heavy Bergen and he slowly built up the training distance, so that he didn't knacker his Achilles tendons again. Derek was regularly doing 15 miles whilst carrying a Bergen that weighed around 25kg. Eventually he was happy enough with his own fitness and felt ready for P Coy.

Just over 100 'All Arms' soldiers had applied for a place on the Course, some of them had served with Derek in other RCT and RLC units. The candidates all had to be easily identifiable to the Directing Staff (DS) and so Officers wore white 'T' shirts, Senior NCO's wore red, and the JNCO's and Tom's wore green. (*Airborne ranks always refer to Private soldiers as Tom's.*) The first day of the Airborne selection process always started with a Basic Fitness Test and a Combat Fitness Test. By the end of the first week the 100 candidates had already been whittled down to around 60 'potential' paratroopers. The Course OC told the remaining candidates that because they had got through the first week they all had the ability to pass P Company. He added, "*We've now got rid of those who simply didn't come up to scratch. Everyone here in this room has at least the potential to pass P Coy*". From then on, the remaining candidates were thrashed every day for the next few weeks which included some very trying orienteering Exercises, Derek was amazed that their Course didn't incorporate any swimming training; he was relieved about it though because he wasn't a very good swimmer.

'Milling' is an integral and essential part of P Coy and the Course candidates are paired off with a soldier of equal size and weight, given a pair of boxing gloves, and using controlled aggression they had to batter each other for a full minute. On no account were those taking part permitted to turn their back during the fight, they had to remain face to face and keep moving forward aggressively, it was all about the Airborne ethos of facing up to an enemy and not backing down from the fight. Some of the candidates tried to fight using a boxing style when it was their turn, these fights were quickly halted and the participants told in no uncertain terms, "*You are not here to fucking mince about boxing, you are here to knock each other's fucking heads off - now fucking get on with it!*"   Derek had to fight against a P Coy candidate who was also an RAMC Doctor; they were 'billed' as the last fight of the course so that the 'Doc' could provide medical cover for the entire milling period. Derek and the 'Doc' had a full-blooded fight which Derek marginally lost.

On the undulating log race over rough terrain, eight candidates worked as a team carrying a 60kg log approximately two miles. Each team was scrutinised on every step of the race to make sure they were all putting in 100% effort, and if they weren't, the DS were on hand to 'encourage' them to try a little bit harder. The DS rotated the candidates into different positions whenever anyone dropped off the log. When Derek's team approached the finish line there were two soldiers carrying the front on the log with just him on the back. The others were either running behind or were already on the dreaded 'Jack Wagon'. On test week Derek was in danger of losing his big toe nails on each foot because of a build-up of blood under them. The medics enjoyed trepanning them for him with a needle, the pain relief was instantaneous. Derek eventually passed P Coy and was elated to have succeeded, but even on the very last day about eight candidates were binned. There wasn't a big ceremony or fanfare to signify their achievement, on parade each candidate's number was called out and in front of the others they were rather callously told, *"Number 23...Failed."* Derek admitted to the author that P Coy is as tough as everyone says it is, it was the hardest physical challenge he has ever done in his life.

He now had to go back to his unit and wait to find out where he would be posted... England or Germany? Within weeks of returning to Northern Ireland, however, Derek was posted back to Gutersloh, this time he went to 2 Sqn, 1 Logistic Support Regiment (LSR) RLC. But before Derek left 3 Inf Bde, the Quartermaster (OC) told him that he was very disappointed Derek hadn't been given an immediate posting to 13 Air Assault Support Regiment (AASR) RLC in Colchester. The OC spoke to Derek before he and his family headed off to Gutersloh, *"Robbo, promise me that you'll do your jumps before you leave the Army, otherwise, it's all been for nothing."* Derek solemnly promised his boss that he would complete his military parachute jumps before he left the Corps. Derek admitted that P Coy was even harder than he thought it would be, he felt that he only achieved it because as an PTI, he knew how to train and what nutrition he needed to eat. He said some soldiers who did 'beat up' training at their units were carrying injuries before the course even started and didn't really stand a chance of passing.

In 2 Sqn Derek was initially appointed as a Section Commander on DROPS vehicles, but after serving two years in 2 Sqn, he hadn't been promoted and so requested a move into Regimental (Regtl) Ops in RHQ. This would be a higher profile job where his hard work would be noticed by the CO, Adjutant, and RSM. In camp the job necessitated him co-ordinating the Green Fleet vehicles around the Regiment, i.e. which vehicles went where and when. Each Sqn had to report their vehicle availability to Derek in Regtl Ops and those vehicles that didn't attend for their designated servicing, would be reported to Derek using a Failure to Report Form (FTR) from the Servicing Bay. Derek would then inform the Sqn Ops SNCO on the next monthly meeting and he would then bollock his own people if there wasn't a genuine reason for the vehicle not turning up. This procedure ensured that each OC would keep pushing his men to keep each truck fully serviced and properly maintained.

On Exercises with RHQ Derek and Cpl Paul Ward would set up 3 Ops Boxes (Offices on the back of vehicles). "We would also be responsible for setting up 12 x 12 tents which RHQ would use as a briefing room. And all this had to go under one big fuck off scrim net, the whole thing was massive and was a fucking nightmare to put up and take down." Having now done 12 - 14 years in the Corps, Derek started to get fed up with the RLC and Army life. He'd been at 1 LSR for three and a half years and still hadn't been promoted, even after doing the high-profile Regtl Ops job. Because regimental life in Barracks was starting to bore Derek, he decided to take part in the 'Gore Trophy Military Skills' competition which was held in Pirbright Barracks, Deepcut near Aldershot. The very physically demanding contest was only open to RLC units who could put in a team of eight male, female, or mixed sex teams which included an Officer, a SNCO, JNCO's and Toms. Each team was tested on their military knowledge, assault course skills, a timed 1.5 mile run as a squad, a falling plate shooting competition as well as their map reading, first aid, observation and a timed 10-mile race. Teams of soldiers from 63 Para Sqn usually made a habit of winning the competition.

The distraction was only a temporary fix for Derek though and after returning to Gutersloh he decided to try a selection course to transfer into the Military Provost Staff Corps (MPSC) *(the MPSC was made up of experienced soldiers from all Corps, Regiments and Military Arms who wanted to become Military Prison Officers at the Military Correction Training Centre)* at Colchester Garrison. It was around this time that Derek learned that his unit was deploying out to Iraq and so he decided to leave the course immediately and return to Gutersloh. Once back at 2 Sqn, Derek deployed out to Iraq as a DROPS Section Commander and on arrival in theatre he was involved in the handover/takeover of the vehicles, equipment, accommodation and offices from the unit that they were relieving. Within weeks of arriving, Derek was drafted into a Training Team of 6 – 8 British Military Instructors who were going to train up soldiers of the Iraqi Army, this would enable them to take over the responsibility of the internal security of Iraq. 2 Sqn knew Derek was going to be on the next promotion board list and so they'd given him acting rank of Sergeant before he'd joined the training team because all of the instructors had to be SNCO's.

The Training Team Derek had been assigned equipment and vehicles to transport themselves, and their personal equipment, up North to their base near Mittica. On arrival they were allocated a single office from which they could run their courses, and possibly the worst accommodation you could ever imagine. Derek was just getting into the swing of things when he was told that the RLC Pioneer Cpl who had been attached to his Sqn had been wrongly employed in the Bde HQ in Basra. The Cpl had complained bitterly about this appointment to his own CO and after his Lt Col spoke to 2 Sqn's OC, the Pioneer Cpl and was given Derek's job on the Training Team to shut him up. On arrival at the "dreaded" Headquarters, Derek was told he would be working as part of a large multi-national organisation which consisted of Danish, American, and British units. At the head of his small unit was a British Army Captain who simply wasn't interested in doing his job, he was coming to the end of his tour and was 'Home Happy'. When the disinterested Captain flew back to the UK he was replaced by a female RLC Major who not only took over his job, but she also continued doing her previous job at the same time.

From her first day behind the desk, Derek and the newly appointed Major clashed heads on many occasions. The unit was using an Expensive MOD Computer system that, when properly set up in the base area, would hopefully let the Ops Team know where all their vehicles were when they deployed out on the ground. Unfortunately, the system simply didn't work because there were no GPS Systems installed in any of the vehicles. The newly appointed Major wasn't much help to Derek because all she could come up with was, *"Well make it work then Sergeant Robson"* Derek wasn't much help either because he got annoyed with his inept boss and told her, *"What do you want me to do? I didn't build the bloody thing Mam, I was only brought in to work with it, and to be quite honest, I can't do anything until we get some GPS equipment installed in the vehicles."*

The RLC Major and Derek had worked in different offices from the moment she'd arrived in her new Post. One day she abruptly ordered Derek to move out of his small office into the main larger Operations room where most of the other contingents had a desk space rather than an office. Derek was pissed off by this stage of his tour because he'd been, *"Fucked about from Breakfast to Supper time. Let's face it, I'd started the Tour in Iraq as a DROPS Section Commander before moving onto a British Army Training Team (BATT), before finally ending up working in Bde Headquarters."*

When ordered to move, Derek sarcastically said to his female boss, *"Whatever Ma'am."* where would you like me to move to? There were two Polish Lt Col's that Derek was supposed to evict from their office space and one of them spoke just like the Croatian football manager Slaven Billic.

Derek: *Sir, I'm taking over your work space in here.*

Polish Lt Col: *Oh, and where are we moving to Sergeant Robson?*

Derek: *I dunno Sir, I've just been told to take over this area from you.*

Polish Lt Col: *I re-iterate to you Sergeant Robson, where are we supposed to work from, if you take over our office space?*

Derek: *I dunno Sir, I've just been told to take over this area from you.*

Polish Lt Col: *But where are we supposed to work from if you take over our office space.... Sergeant?*

And so it went on until Derek told the Polish Officer:

Derek: *Hang on a minute Sir, I'll go and have another talk with my boss.*

Derek went to speak to the OC and attempted to resolve the problem with his incalcitrant and yet timorous officer.

Derek: *Look Ma'am, the Poles won't move because they say they haven't got anywhere else to go to, you'll have to go and speak to them.*

RLC Major: *I told you to do it!*

Derek: *Well they're not going to move because they haven't been given any official orders to move and they also haven't been given any notification of where to go to, if you want them to move, then go and do it yourself.... Ma'am!*

Just over a month later Derek's Regiment would be heading back to Germany. The Polish Detachment was still working in the same office at that time because Derek's OC seemed to have forgotten about the move. One day whilst out for a run on the airfield, Derek's Commanding Officer drove pass him with his force protection team. The Commanding Officer noticed Derek and stopped to ask him how he was getting on?

CO: *How's it going Sgt Robson?*

Derek: *Yeah, things are going ok Sir.*

CO: *No, things aren't going ok Sgt Robson, let's have a chat. How is Major .... getting along?*

The CO had obviously been made privy to what was happening to Derek and the problems he was having. When the CO had driven off Derek felt a lot happier about the position he was being put in by Major .... RLC because he now had some confirmed verbal back up from his very experience and knowledgeable RLC Commanding officer. Derek was very disappointed about his experiences in Iraq and he was eventually replaced by a Liverpudlian RAF Warrant Officer. It seemed strange to Derek that for months he'd been doing the job as an Acting Sgt and was now being replaced by a senior Warrant Officer from the RAF. Incidentally, by the time Derek had completed his tour in Iraq, the computer system that was supposed to track the unit's vehicles, still wasn't working.

Substantive Sgt rank was granted to Derek when he returned to Gutersloh and he asked for an extension to his tour in Germany, which was granted. He moved from 2 Sqn to 23 Sqn in 1 LSR where he worked as a Troop Sgt for twelve months, before being posted to Preston in Lancashire as a medical units' MT Sergeant. Derek had by then completed 17 years in the Army and was thinking of signing off and going back into civilian life. He spoke to his old SSM who now worked in Regimental Headquarters (RHQ) about signing off. He asked Derek if he'd thought about the money he'd lose if he left the Army at that time of his military career. *"Sgt Robson, you do know that if you finish before completing your full 22 years' Service, you will lose a projected £200,000 in wages, pension, and final gratuity, just by walking out of those camp gates now. You need to complete your 22 years in the Army for your family's sake if nothing else."* It all made sense to Derek and so he didn't sign off and picked up a posting to 5 GS Medical Regiment instead.

Derek, Becky, and their two girls arrived at 5 GS Medical Regt RAMC, Fulwood Bks, Preston in 2008. They were very happy at 5 GS for about a year because they believed that their posting to Preston was going to be for at least three years. But when unit members were instructed that 5 GS Regt was soon to be disbanded, and its soldiers were going to be posted to other detachments, they were both very pissed off. Becky's dad had by now finished his time in the Army and he'd bought a house in Bridlington on the East Coast of Yorkshire where they still live today. Derek and Becky eventually wanted to live in Bridlington so they could be close to Becky's parents. Derek was offered a posting to the MT Section of 1 Battalion REME Workshops (1 Bn REME Wksp) in Catterick and he decided to take it. Ultimately, Derek decided the family needed to put down some roots in the UK which resulted in them also buying a house in Bridlington, Derek lived in the Sgt's Mess during the week and commuted home to Bridlington each weekend. Fortunately, because it would be Derek's last move out of Army accommodation, the MOD paid for the final removals from Preston to his house in Bridlington. It wasn't a perfect solution though and Becky was unhappy because she thought her husband and their two children should be living under the same roof together. Derek pointed out that he would be leaving the Army in four years anyway and it was better for them if they got on the property ladder sooner rather than later. In the event of further promotions or postings, Becky and the girls would always have her parents near-by for help and support.

On the work front at 1 Bn REME, the MTWO WO2 Joe Cocker RLC was being posted to the Falklands Islands for 6 months and so Derek was left to run the whole of the MT Section on his own as a Sergeant. Most of the soldiers in 1 Bn were REME Craftsmen and Derek felt somewhat isolated from his own Corps people. "*It wasn't bullets and bombs though, so I simply had to get on with it and just dealt with all of the everyday shit that came through my office door or in the post."* It was during this time that Derek was informed that his dad was suffering with dementia, and even though Mr. Derek William Robson had never had a great relationship with his children, it was very sad nonetheless.

An envelope was delivered directly onto his desk which contained a hand-written letter addressed to SSgt Derek Robson RLC from WO1 Jason Lowe RLC the Corps RSM. WO1 Jason Lowe RLC had previously been Derek's SSM in Gutersloh when he was at 2 Sqn in 1 LSR RLC. The letter congratulated Derek on his promotion to SSgt. Derek was confused because no-one had mentioned to him that he'd been promoted to Staff Sergeant and so he immediately went to see the RSM. The RSM also didn't know anything about Derek's promotion and so he packed him off to see the Regimental Careers Management Officer (RCMO) who was a REME Captain. It transpired that Derek had been promoted on the sweeper board where those who were recommended for promotion, but either didn't want the post or weren't specifically qualified for the job, were taken off and the next one down on the list was given a 'shot at the title'. Derek's was the next name on the list. However, by that time all the best postings had been taken and Derek was given three choices. One of those choices was 13 Air Assault Support Regiment (AASR) RLC in Colchester where WO1 Nick Hegarty RLC was the RSM at the time. Derek and Nick were old friends and he knew that Nick would look out for him while he was at his Regiment. Also, by going to 13 AASR he would be keeping his promise to his old OC at 3 Inf Bde by serving with the Airborne Forces and doing his parachute jumps course.

On his arrival in Colchester, Derek was placed into 15 Sqn as one of the Troop Staff Sergeants. After he'd signed into the Regiment, he was immediately sent down to Portsmouth where he joined up with his new Squadron who were all on Exercise. He caught up with them on a Landing Ship Logistics (LSL) that was just about to sail out of Marchwood Military Port, the home of 17 Port and Maritime Regiment RLC. Derek wandered up and down the ships' corridors shouting, *"15 Sqn! Hello, anyone from 15 Sqn on this fucking bucket of rust."* Staff Sergeant Derek Robson was still wearing his dark blue 'Crap Hat' beret *(a Crap Hat is a derogatory term used by all Airborne Forces to address anyone who isn't qualified to wear the coveted Airborne maroon beret).* When Derek finally found 15 Sqn he saw an old friend, Sgt Claire Batterbee RLC who he had served with whilst he was in Germany. She then introduced him to his new SSM and his Officer Commanding. The SSM casually asked Derek, *"How do you feel about attempting P Coy, SSgt Robson?"* With a cheeky smile on his face, Derek explained to his new SSM that he'd already *passed P Coy a couple of years previously (Once a soldier has passed P Coy he doesn't have to retake the selection before joining an Airborne unit).* The SSM confirmed with Derek, *"Great, I'll get you on a jumps course as soon as we all get back from this 3-week Exercise."*

It wasn't going to be as simple as his SSM had made it out to be though, it took Derek a long time to complete his parachuting course at Brize Norton. It would be quite a while before Derek could conclusively and legitimately call himself a qualified British Army Paratrooper. 13 Air Assault Support Regiment (AASR) was informed that they would be deploying to Afghanistan in about 12 months and there was a lot to be done before they got out there. Derek did some pre-jump parachute training in a hangar in Colchester to prepare for attending the Jumps Course at RAF Brize Norton. The first two military parachute jumps for Derek was out of the rear of a civilian style aircraft and not from the usual side door of an RAF C 130 Hercules aircraft. On his first jump he landed backwards and whacked his head on the ground because of the high wind speed. You can't steer a military parachute and so a Paratrooper must use his/her training to land as safely as possible, unfortunately, the Jump Course was cancelled because of the bad weather. It would take Derek at least another 12 months to get a place on another Parachute Jumping Course. Working around the weather, spare places on Jump Courses, Afghanistan training, and soldiers who had previously completed at least some of their jumps and took priority over others, all made it difficult for Derek to ultimately qualify and become a proper fully-fledged Paratrooper. Cpl Andy Wardle RLC was also waiting to do his jumps with Derek and they both spent a lot of time hanging around waiting for the right weather conditions. At one stage they were both pulled out of the waiting line-up to catch a flight out to Kenya where they had to take part in a 6-week Field Exercise with the rest of 13 Air Assault Support Regiment (AASR) in preparation for the Afghanistan deployment. Derek eventually deployed out to Afghanistan without completing his jumps course. He and Cpl Andy Wardle both wanted to go on tour wearing their Airborne Wings on the upper right sleeve of their uniforms, however this wasn't to be the case. They both completed their jumps course after they returned from Afghanistan.

The pre-deployment training was the most intense preparation Derek had done in his time in the Army, by comparison, the Iraq training schedule was a doddle when paralleled to what 13 Air Assault Support Regiment had to achieve for the Afghan tour. The equipment the soldiers were issued with was by far and away the best the British Army had ever been issued. Each individual soldier was supplied with new style Desert Boots, Gerber Multitool Pliers, Multi-Terrain Pattern (MTP) uniforms, T-shirts, new MTP Porous Under Body Armour Combat (UBAC) shirts that could be comfortably worn under the latest body armour, and the necessary webbing equipment, which included day sacks and Bergen's. Derek states, *"It was all excellent equipment."* Those deploying also received intensive training on the vehicles and weapon systems that would be available to them in-country. When the unit came back from their pre-Afghanistan training in Kenya, the troops were issued with a labelled individual pack containing their brand new personal clothing and equipment. The pre-deployment training taught everyone in 13 Air Assault Support Regiment about the types of IED's and mines the enemy were using and the mine detecting equipment that would be available for them to use in Afghanistan. They were also instructed about Electronic Countermeasure's (ECM) to protect patrol's from IED's. Bar armour was used on all sides of the military vehicles to prevent some of the missile damage from Rocket Propelled Grenades (RPG's). If any of that life protecting armour equipment was damaged on a patrol or operation, then even the small broken segments had to be replaced. To interchange or repair these damaged sections became a pain in the arse, even for just a small segment. Derek stated that, *"It was a massive time-line to organise everything for just one Combat Logistic Patrol in Afghanistan."*

Sgt Derek Robson RLC on the return journey of his Combat Logistic Patrol in Afghanistan.

On his pre-deployment leave in Bridlington, Derek and Becky found it difficult trying to explain to Elana and Megan about where Derek was going, why he was going, and what he'd be doing when he arrived on the other side of the world. It was nigh on impossible to explain to young children that their 'Daddy', or 'Mummy', is a soldier and that they were trying to make the world a better and safer place, for them and everyone else to live. How does any parent explain to their children about the inherent dangers that their father or mother are about to face, or explain to them that this goodbye could mean that they may never see their parent ever again?

13 AASR RLC flew to Afghanistan in a civilian chartered flight from RAF Brize Norton. The unit was to be based at Camp Bastion where their HQ and vehicles were already established. 13 AASR was relieving another RLC unit that was, post-tour, returning to their home base in Abingdon near Oxford. Not long after arriving in the Camp Bastion desert location, Derek's Squadron were detailed for their first Operational task. With their OC doing the navigation from the front seat of the lead vehicle, the RLC convoy headed out of Camp Bastion and into the unforgiving Afghan wilderness. The RLC drivers on that huge Combat Logistic Patrol (CLP) had to locate a Forward Operating Base (FOB) that was finally closing. The FOB's were nothing more than a secured, and often isolated, compound, used to support distant tactical operations far from the Main Operating Bases likes Camp Bastion. Depending on the size of the FOB, designated what facilities were available for the soldiers manning that position, things like a Mortar Pit, Field Surgical Team (FST), HMG's, Helicopter landing pad, Sangers, Bunkers, Entry and Exit Gates, accommodation, vehicle parks, etc. The convoy of trucks were tasked to collect every single piece of equipment and bring it all back to Camp Bastion, nothing that could be of any use to the Taliban was to be left behind. When the 15 Squadron drivers reached the FOB they would be collecting a mixture of

generators, vehicles, trailers, JCB's, tools, and anything else that could be of value, or use, to the Taliban.

Derek flew up to the FOB in a Chinook helicopter to do a Recce with an Officer from the Brigade HQ. Derek and his accompanying Brigade Officer both sketched out a scale map of the location, they then identified all the vehicles, equipment and ISO Containers that were being backloaded to Camp Bastion and then worked out how they were going to squeeze the CLP into a very small and crowded location. It wouldn't have been a good idea to simply park up outside the Hesco Bastions blast walls, allowing the Taliban to take pot-shots at the RLC drivers and their trucks. The American cookhouse was still functioning at that time and so the Yanks graciously fed their British cousins extremely well. On arrival at the FOB, the vehicles needed to be reversed into position in such a manner that they could be loaded up with the right equipment and then lined up in their correct convoy position for the return journey. The vehicles had to be organised correctly so that the CLP could depart the location in a quick and orderly fashion. Unbeknownst to Derek, the 15 Squadron CLP had encountered some problems of its own on the inbound journey (which included some truck's breaking-down and a few others becoming bogged in on unavoidable soft ground – looks like that training in Canada came in handy Derek). Those problems resulted in Derek and his accompanying Officer having to kill time waiting for the CPL to arrive at the FOB.

When the Delta Callsign's arrived at the FOB, each driver looked very dusty, dirty and extremely tired. With urgency, Derek collared each driver of the CLP in turn and personally pointed out to them all exactly where each driver had to park their trucks. Derek then told the driver's which piece of equipment needed to be loaded onto which truck and the time-line by which it was to be completed. That continued until each CLP vehicle had been methodically reversed into their correct positions and loaded. The vehicles being used to collect the equipment were 15 tonne

MAN trucks with Enhanced Palletised Load System (EPLS) fitted, aka Easy Peasy Lemon Squeezy by all RLC drivers. The EPLS was another version of the RLC's Foden DROPS trucks which could simply pull a palletised load onto the back of its own truck. Any equipment too big to go into an ISO container was secured onto a flat-bed truck using restraining chains or straps. When everything was finally loaded up, Derek went around every truck to make sure his drivers had everything they needed for the journey, and that each load was securely held in place before the CLP started on its return journey. This 50 vehicle RLC procession was comparatively small to others that had preceded it in previous RLC Operations. Other details had been known to reach over 150 trucks in total, but on this detail a small part of 13 Air Assault Support Regiment had to transport only 20 - 30 loads of the equipment that needed returning to Camp Bastion.

The CLP also had air cover for their return trip, which was provided by Apache Helicopters of the Army Air Corps (AAC) and a few of the RAF'S finest Fighter/Bombers who were also on hand just in case they were needed to deliver a heavy hand to the bad guys. The reader must bear in mind that the AAC and RAF couldn't give any sort of assistance to an RLC driver who was about to drive over an IED or if they were caught in the scope of a Taliban sniper. The Flash to Bang from Camp Bastion to the FOB *(Soldier speak for how long a journey will take – the metaphor refers to how long the effects of a Nuclear explosion will take from when the device explodes, to when its effects are felt at a determined distance.)* was supposed to be about 2 - 3 days journey for the CLP; but because of the breakdowns and some very soft terrain, it took considerably longer. The return trip ended up taking just as long because of similar difficulties experienced on the inbound journey, combine that with the fact that the trucks were now carrying a massive cargo weight, it took the CLP at least 36 hours to get back to Camp Bastion. Whenever the trucks laagered up in the desert at night, the accompanying Force Protection Troop surrounded the CLP vehicles about 50 metres from where they were parked to give protection against any Taliban night attacks. The Force Protection's vehicles were a mixture of Mastiff and Ridgeback Mine-Resistant Ambush Protected (MRAP) trucks.

Derek and some of the lads in 13 Air Assault Regt in Camp Bastion.

These armoured vehicles were equipped with Weapons Mounted Installation Kit (WMIK) and a variation of 7.62 mm GPMG's, .50 Cal Browning Heavy Machine Guns, Grenade Launchers, and an assortment of other personal weapons, Derek stated, *"Our CLP was protected by a mixture of formidable firepower, and some of the world's best soldiers"*. During the night the RLC drivers also mounted their own roving patrols to guard the inner sanctum of the CLP. The Troop Sergeant in the CLP had a sleeping plan of where every soldier in the patrol was resting and was responsible for rousing the next relieving sentry for his turn on sentry. Derek travelled back to Camp Bastion with the convoy in the cab of a MAN truck and on arrival at Camp Bastion, he personally witnessed that every driver in that detail had blood-shot eyes and was covered from head to foot in dust and dirt, they were all completely exhausted. Although Derek was involved in many other Operations during his tour in Afghanistan, that was the largest action in which he and his Troop were to be included during their tour.

At the end of his tour Derek was pleased to get back home to Bridlington because he was missing his family so much, Derek explained that whilst he was on his post-tour leave, "*I only did the normal 'blokey' stuff that everyone does every day of the year. Becky was at work and with Elana and Megan both at school, I had plenty of time on my hands.*" When Derek reported back to his Squadron in Colchester, he only had about 18 months to do to complete his full 22 years in the Army. This was by far the longest 18 months of his life. He did not enjoy this time and recalls it as being the unhappiest time of his life.

In August 2012 he left the British Army and looked for a driving job that wouldn't need any heavy responsibility resting on his shoulders. Like a lot of ex-soldiers, he'd had just about enough of that shit and simply wanted to drive for a living. And that is exactly what Derek has been doing ever since leaving the British Army. He currently works as a PCV driver for East Yorkshire Motor Services (EYMS) in Bridlington.

Epilogue

Like most Royal Corps of Transport (RCT) soldiers of the past, I playfully and light-heartedly denigrated those Royal Logistic Corps (RLC) soldiers' who shouldered the British Army's logistic responsibilities from the RCT. "They will never be as good as we were!" was my battle-cry as I safely swaggered about beneath the protection of my Royal Army Dental Corps (RADC) cap badge. I say safely, because I'd recently left the Regular British Army and was serving with 250 Field Ambulance (Volunteers) in Hull as a Territorial Army (TA) Soldier. At that time, many believed that the TA wouldn't be called upon to go to war, principally because they simply weren't perceived to be good enough. I draw the reader's attention to how that turned out for some members of the Royal Army Medical Corps (RAMC) - Cpl Mick Killeen RAMC, LCpl Matt Fairclough RAMC, Capt Sharon Antony QARANC, and Sgt Richie John RADC. (*Read 'Two Medics, One Nurse and a Gob Doctor' for their full story*).

In 1993 the RLC were handed the reins that had been held by the RCT since 1965, which was when the RCT took over from the Royal Army Service Corps (RASC), which itself had taken up those very same reins from soldiers of the Army Service Corps (ASC) in 1918. In 1918 the ASC soldiers were more than likely to have thought the same about the new RASC upstarts as did the Regular Army about the TA Medics before the 2nd Gulf War. Every soldier from time immemorial has always belittled the next ascending Corps or Regiments' soldiers with equal venom and disdain. Human nature seems to have always decreed that the 'next lot' will never be deemed as good as the ones handing the job over.

Even up to 2013, ex-RCT soldiers were still complaining about how much better they were than the new RLC 'lot.' Soldiers from other Corps and Regiments had by now taken up this mantra about the RLC being a **R**ight **L**oad of **C**rap and I have to admit that

I was one of those whingers who didn't know his 'A frame' from his 'Electronics.' Bearing in mind, ten years after the RLC had come along, there couldn't have been all that many RASC and RCT 'old salts' left in the Corps. A lot of them had probably been dispatched courtesy of the 1993 redundancy lists.

As a Corps, the RCT did an exceptional job bearing the brunt of the work supporting British Army Operations in Aden, BAOR, Belize, Bosnia, Canada, Cyprus, Hong Kong, Kuwait, Northern Ireland, Iraq, the Falkland Islands, and, as I've recently discovered, whilst researching and writing this book, we also did some of the Infantry work in the Dhofar War. *The following reports may help the reader to understand why our Corps' is so proud of its ability to immediately jump into a fighting role:*

Private Samuel Morley VC (sometimes spelt Morely) 19 years old, and Farrier Michael Murphy VC 21 years old, were both serving in the Military Train which was the fore-runner to the Army Service Corps. During the Indian Mutiny these young men charged forward on foot to assist an unhorsed Lt Hamilton and were injured themselves whilst defending the officer on 15th April 1858.

Assistant Commissary James Dalton VC who at 46 years of age was the first soldier to face the attacking Zulu Warriors at Rorkes Drift on 22nd/23rd January 1879 and was instrumental in saving the Garrison.

Temporary 2nd Lt Alfred Herring VC was solely in charge of holding back a German Advance at Montagne Bridge on 23rd/24th March 1918. This RASC officer immediately organised a counter-attack and captured 20 prisoners and 6 machine guns and held up the enemy advance for 11 hours. Throughout the night he went from position to position to give encouragement and advice to the men under his command.

The RASC soldiers were probably much the same as the RCT lads were before grabbing the reins in 1965, but during the First and Second World Wars the ASC and RASC did it all on a scale so massive, that even those who were on **OPERATION CORPORATE** (*Falklands War-1982*) or **Exercise Lionheart** (*BAOR- 1984*) can't possibly contemplate the commitment. The RLC has done a brilliant job since relieving the RCT of its duties, and they've added the awesome Afghanistan Battle Honour to '**our**' very own Corps Colours.

Final Note:
This book has taken me over a year to write and has been problematic at times. As a result of travelling, self-imposed stress, and working long hours, I have had rather too many Diabetic hypoglycaemic attacks which have resulted in the East Riding Ambulance Service receiving telephone calls from my beautiful wife **Nicky Clacy** in the early hours of the morning.

I realise how much pressure this puts on my Nicky (*and yet she never utters a word of complaint you know*) so I will now be taking some time off for a while. I will be taking Nicky on a few holidays and extended days out where we will both enjoy tea and sandwiches on a beach somewhere, my God **Nicky Clacy** bloody deserves it. I will be back though, and for my next book, I'd like to include the experiences of our RCT and RLC female soldiers. Please get in touch with me on Facebook you Trog's/ Trogg's/ Troggett's to organise your own personal interviews, but please leave it for about six months will you.

Brian (Harry) Clacy

Bibliography

In the Service of the Sultan: A first Hand Account of the Dhofar Insurgency by Ian Gardiner. Pen and Sword Books Ltd 2006.

The Secret War in Dhofar 1971 – 1972 by Mr David C Arkless. Pen and Sword Books Ltd 1988.

Other books by this author

Harry was a Crap Hat (2nd Edition)

Harry Always was a Crap Hat

Two Medics, One Nurse and a Gob Doctor

Rickshaws, Camels and Taxis (Rogues, Ruffians and Officers of the Royal Corps of Transport)

Tell it Like it Wasn't (The Art of Military Communication)

Tell it Like it Wasn't (Part 2)

Most Roads Led to 10 Regt

Franks War in a Thornycroft

All available from Amazon Books

Printed in Great Britain
by Amazon